Novels of Genocide
Remembering and Forgetting the Ethnic Other in Fictional Rwanda

Sidestone Press

NOVELS OF GENOCIDE
REMEMBERING AND FORGETTING THE ETHNIC OTHER IN FICTIONAL RWANDA

OLIVIER NYIRUBUGARA

MEMORY TRAPS
VOLUME II

© 2017 O. Nyirubugara

Published by Sidestone Press, Leiden
　www.sidestone.com

Lay-out & cover design: Sidestone Press
Photograph cover: Anna Omelchenko | Dreamstime.com

ISBN 978-90-8890-431-8 (softcover)
ISBN 978-90-8890-432-5 (hardcover)
ISBN 978-90-8890-433-2 (PDF e-book)

Contents

Acknowledgements	9
Introduction	11
1. Fiction and Reality	12
2. Novels of Memory	14
3. Who Remembers in the Novel?	15
4. Sampled Novels	17
5. Book Structure	22
PART ONE – ETHNICITY	23
1. Character Identities	25
1.1. Understanding Characters	26
1.2. Constructing Hutuness	29
1.3. Constructing Tutsiness	35
1.4. Implied Ethnicity	42
1.5. Identity Crisis	45
1.6. Summary and Discussion	51
2. Character Names	55
2.1. Beyond the Name	55
2.2. Hutu Character Names	57
2.3. Tutsi Character Names	64
2.4. Half-Hutu, Half-Tutsi Names	72
2.5. Summary and Discussion	78
PART TWO – STEREOTYPING	81
3. Beauty, Handsomeness, and Ugliness	83
3.1. Beauty	84
3.2. Handsomeness	92
3.3. Ugliness	96
3.4. Beauty and Ugliness in Fest'Africa Project Novels	100
3.5. Summary and Discussion	104
4. Smartness, Intelligence vs. Stupidity and Silliness	107
4.1. Smartness, Intelligence & Cleverness	107
4.2. The Smart and Clever Ones	112
4.3. The Stupid Ones	118
4.4. Mixture	126
4.5. Summary and Discussion	131

PART THREE - PROPAGANDA 135

5. Promoting a Certain Narrative 137
   5.1. Understanding Propaganda 138
   5.2. War and/or Genocide in Hutu-Authored Novels 143
   5.3. War and/or Genocide in Tutsi-Authored Novels 150
   5.4. War and/or Genocide in Fest'Africa Project Novels 159
   5.5. Summary and Discussion 164

6. Historical Contexts 169
   6.1. Historical Background in Tutsi-Authored Novels 169
   6.2. Historical Background in Hutu-Authored Novels 174
   6.3. Historical Background in Fest'Africa Project Novels ... 177
   6.4. Summary and Discussion 180

7. Conclusions 183
   7.1. Three Lines 183
   7.2. The Traps 184
   7.3. Missing Ethics? 185

References 187

To Grandma Cécile whose stories, tales, and songs from and about ancient Rwanda marked my childhood and kept coming back to my mind as I was writing this book. The tapes could not be rescued, but the essence has stayed.

Acknowledgements

This book has taken almost three years of intensive research but also of exchange both within academic and informal circles. I would like to thank Erin Mosely (based at Harvard University at the time) and Mark Baker (Monash University) who invited me to the 21th – 24th August 2014 'Rwanda Revisited: Monash University Aftermath Symposium' in Melbourne, Australia. I am also expressing my gratitude to Luisa Gandolfo (University of Aberdeen), who invited me to the 20th – 21st September 2016 symposium on 'Missing Memorials and Absent Bodies: Negotiating Post-conflict Trauma and Memorialisation' at the Institute for War, Holocaust and Genocide Studies in Amsterdam, the Netherlands. The former symposium allowed me to share the early draft and to test my approach, whereas the latter enabled me to discuss the almost finished draft with scholars from various relevant disciplines.

I would also like to thank all those who participated in the discussions I often initiated via Facebook about certain aspects of Rwandan culture and language. The threads of comments that resulted from those discussions contained invaluable insight that helped me clarify and nuance some of the points and arguments that are presented in this book. This is also true for some friends with whom I conversed on many occasions during family or social events. I would specifically like to thank Cyriaque Dukuzumuremyi and David Nyiligira.

To my friends who promptly sent me documents and other materials from Rwanda, I say: "*Mwarakoze cyane*". Though I can't name you here, I did appreciate your gesture and your contribution to this project.

I am also indebted to Richard Chetwynd, Emmanuel Bizumuremyi, and Jean-Valéry Turatsinze, for accepting to read and comment upon the manuscript, and to my proof reader Clare Martin-Bell for ensuring that all the *t*'s are crossed and all the *i*'s are dotted.

Finally, my thanks go to Sidestone Press editors Karsten Wentink and Corné van Woerdekom for their meticulous work to turn the entire project into the book that you are now holding in your hands.

Introduction

Can novels tell us anything about how memory processes take place in a given society? If so, what do they tell us and how? These are some of the questions I have set out to discuss in this book which focuses on post-genocide Rwanda. A popular and widespread belief about fiction in general and novels in particular, is that fiction should not be taken seriously as it does not, and cannot mirror, reality. The proponents of this belief argue that fiction is solely meant to entertain readers and to help them relax. For serious information, as the argument goes, people should *only* go for academic and professional publications that present research-driven and evidence-based information. In this book, I oppose that belief, as I strongly believe that fiction is another way of representing reality at a different level and in a more subtle way. My point is that the power of fiction resides in the freedom that novelists and other fiction authors have in order to select and elaborate upon aspects of their choices, including those that would appear controversial in non-fiction works. The assumption is that in societies with a contested past like Rwanda, laws and other unwritten rules intimidate and prevent people from expressing themselves freely through mass media and academic writings, about genocide, ethnicity, the war and the political system, amongst other subjects. For that reason, non-fiction authors, e.g., journalists, researchers, academics, etc., are often faced with a dilemma: They must choose between following the politically correct line [pro-government] and taking the dangerous and risky path by adopting the line that is critical to the dominant narrative.

Unlike non-fiction authors, fiction writers create their own world and its inhabitants, and, in principle, escape any law or unwritten rules in that fictional world. The past they create in their works is fictional and can resist the accusations of distorting any established historical event or fact. However, given the closeness between real situations and those created by authors, many fiction writers find it necessary to add a caveat telling the reader that any resemblance between characters and real world figures or between places in fiction and those in the real world are fortuitous. By adding that warning, they reinforce the belief that fiction and reality can be so close to one another that one can be taken for the other.

Moreover, being primarily a form of art, fiction always calls for multiple interpretations of what is going on in that fictional world. No one, including the author, can ever claim to have the best interpretation because each interpretation reflects, and emanates from the reader's background and prior knowledge, which all constitute what Landsberg (2004: 9) called 'archive of experience'. In the next few sections of this introduction I argue that the world which fiction authors create is not so different from the world which they observe or in which they live. One cannot fictionalise the world if one does not know the real world. In other terms, novelists and other fiction authors have a reference framework on which their work is based. That aspect makes the novel and other works of fiction a powerful way of looking at society, its past, its present, and its future, all from the author's creative perspective.

1. Fiction and Reality

Fiction seems relatively easy to define and scholars from various disciplines ranging from philosophy to semiotics and literary critique seem to agree upon what it means. The main aspect of fiction is the idea of *inventing* or *constructing* or *thinking up* a possible world and presenting it as if it were real (Schmid, 2010: 22 & 30; Eco, 2011: 70; Lamarque, 2009: 175-176). In this sense, fiction and reality are two different things. However, when one goes a step further to investigate and explore the subtle relationships between fiction and reality, things become more complex than they first appeared. It would be wrong to rush to the conclusion that fiction and the world it portrays are irrelevant to the reader, because the materials used to create the fictional world are borrowed from reality, and thus reflect a certain aspect of and a certain truth about that reality (Schmid, 2010: 30).

The literature on fiction abounds with theories that give insight into the relationship between fiction and reality. Scholars argue that the line that separates fiction and reality is blurry, as it is not always clear when fiction ends and when reality begins. Genette (1983: 11) held that one can never imagine the existence of 'pure fiction' and 'pure non-fiction', as each uses elements from the other. Eco (2011: 70), who authored several novels and theorised fiction at the same time, admitted inventing scenes and places in one of his novels and confessed that 'many of [their] details were inspired by the real sites'. In addition, the distinction between fiction and reality becomes even more blurry because language itself does not have a style or syntax peculiar to either (Lamarque, 2009: 176-177). In other words, the way in which things are described and situations presented in the real world is not so different from the way they are described and presented by novelists and other fiction writers.

The question that one would put is: do works of fiction tell any truths about the real world? A related question would be: how seriously should one take the social issues and conflicts presented in the fictional world? The answers reside in the aim of those works of fiction. In general terms, writing a novel is creating a possible world and inviting the reader to enter and explore that world. Eco (1990: 66) defined 'fictional possible world' as

> A series of linguistic descriptions that readers are supposed to interpret as referring to a possible state of affairs where if p is true then non-p is false…
>
> Possible worlds can be viewed either as "real" states of affairs … or cultural constructs, matter of stipulation or semiotic products.

The main idea here is that the author creates or invents a fictional possible world that does not challenge the reader's existing perception of the real world. The issues and conflicts in the fictional possible world should be possible and imaginable in the real world with some flexibility, otherwise the reader would feel cheated. In this sense, Eco (1990: 72) was right when he suggested that the knowledge of the actual world helps to understand the fictional world, because characters, scenes, conflicts, etc., in the fictional possible world, are evaluated against what the reader already knows about the real world. What the reader already knows about the real world includes people, their daily activities, their social relationships, their political systems, their cities and villages and their problems, etc. Authors use what Barthes (1968: 84-85 & 88) called *effet du réel*, i.e., the systematic effort to provide trivial, insignificant details of people and objects in the fictional possible world, in order to create a verisimilar world.

The aim of the novel in particular and fiction in general, could be said to be the creation of a verisimilar world that supposes a tacit deal between the author and the reader (Genette, 1991: 51). The former promises to create a world and present it as if it were real, whereas the latter agrees to trust the author and to display good will by pretending to accept what is going on in the fictional world (Eco, 1990: 81-82). Since the aim of this book is to map the ways in which memory processes take place within novels, it is worth wondering here why one should really care when one is talking about 'pretence' rather than genuine acceptance, and about 'verisimilitude' rather than 'truth'. Put differently, reading a novel is superficially and temporarily accepting it as truth regardless of what is happening in the fictional world. If that is the case, one could ask why it is worth spending time trying to understand how remembering and forgetting take place in a world that is not real. This question boils down to this: what is the relationship between 'truth' [the one believed to be attained in the real world] and 'verisimilitude' [the one the reader is invited to believe as truth in the fictional world]? Riffaterre (1990: xii – xiv) defined verisimilitude as

> A system of representations that seems to reflect a reality external to the text but only because it conforms to a grammar. Narrative truth is an idea of truth created in accordance with the rules of that grammar.

The main concept here seems to be that of 'grammar', which is to be understood as a set of rules that authors put in place to govern the fictional world they create. Anything happening in that world in accordance with those rules is verisimilar, and anything contradicting those rules creates distrust. One good example is Monénembo's (2000) *L'aîné des orphelins* [*The Oldest amongst the Orphans*], which is set up in post-genocide Rwanda. This novel's grammar tells the reader that the fictional world is called Rwanda and that the culture there is Rwandese. The reader agrees and embarks upon reading with that grammar in the back of their mind. However, at some point, one comes across Théoneste, a Hutu character, asking his wife to bring him a calabash of palm wine (Monénembo, 2000: 148; see also *Ibid*.: 149), a beverage that does not exist in Rwanda. One also encounters a woman named Karemera who was taught the *Intore* dance (*Ibid*.: 30). *Intore* dance is a cultural performance exclusively reserved for men, as it mimics a war situation. Associating it with women creates tension in the reader's mind.

Verisimilitude and truth are not so distant from each other and that is the point that Genette (1968: 6) made when he suggested that there is a tendency to equate verisimilitude [*vraisemblable*] and must-be [*devant-être*]. Rapin (as cited in Ginette, 1968: 6) distinguished 'truth' as referring to things as they are and verisimilitude as referring to them as they must be. The *devant-être* in the examples above is that palm wine is unthinkable as a popular beverage in Rwanda and that female *Intore* is not imaginable in Rwanda, all of which are cultural truths in the real world. One could also think of geographic truths [e.g., Rwanda is located in East Africa; etc.]; biological truths [e.g., a human being has one heart]; historical truths [e.g., Rwanda became independent on 1st July 1962]; etc. Ignoring or distorting these real world's truths in fiction makes the work of fiction less verisimilar and, as a consequence, less trustworthy. To be verisimilar, a work of fiction must respect the accepted norms and should integrate received maxims as true (Genette, 1968: 7-8). In my view, this acceptance and integration of accepted norms constitutes the meeting point between verisimilitude as we have it in the novels I have set out to analyse, and the truths about remembering and forgetting in Rwanda.

2. Novels of Memory

Memory is the process through which individuals, communities or societies represent and make sense of the past from the present vantage point (Nora, 1984: XXXVII; Lowenthal, 1985: 39; Halbwachs, 1992: 37; Irwin-Zarecka, 1994: 150; Brockmeier, 2002: 16). In this sense, the novels that attempt to make sense of the past are memory texts par excellence. Stowe's (1852) *Uncle Tom's Cabin*, Dickens' (1837) *Oliver Twist*, Achebe's (1966) *A Man of the People*, Ngugi Wa Thiong'o's (1965) *The River Between*, to name a few, reflect not only the authors' recollection of a given moment in the past, but also what respective societies and communities collectively remembered or still remember about that past. All the above-mentioned novels are 'fictions of memory', as they both reflect 'the workings of memory' and offer 'stories that individuals or cultures tell about their past to answer the question, "who am I?", or, collectively, "who are we?"' (Nünning as cited in Neumann, 2008: 334). I call the novels I analyse in this book 'novels of genocide' which means that they are novels of genocide memories. They are part of fiction of memory, as they all have genocide traumatic memories at the centre.

Literature in general, and novels in particular, is intimately related to cultural memory (Neumann, 2008: 335; Lowenthal, 1985: 224 & 228; Derrida, 2003: 68-69; Lachmann, 2008: 301; Erll & Regney, 2006). That intimate relationship can be approached from three perspectives: Firstly, 'literature as a medium of remembrance', i.e., literature as a medium through which authors and society at large recollect the past. (Erll & Regney, 2006: 112) Secondly, 'literature as an object of remembrance', i.e., as objects from the past that future generations inherit (*Ibid*.). And finally, 'literature as a medium for observing the production of cultural memory', i.e., literary works as concrete, palpable objects that make the memory production process observable (*Ibid*.: 113). For the purpose of this book I have selected 11 post-1994 novels of genocide authored by Rwandans and analysed them as objects that 'combine the real and the imaginary, the remembered and the forgotten' (Neumann, 2008: 334) aspects of the 1994 genocide.

3. Who Remembers in the Novel?

The novels I have set out to analyse obviously interpret certain events of the past in a certain way, and therefore, echo a certain reality about what ought to be remembered and what ought to be forgotten. The question that arises at this stage is: Who remembers and/or forgets in a novel? Literary theorists and narratologists have offered an insight into this question by distinguishing the real or concrete author on the one hand and the implied author on the other hand (Booth, [1961] 1983; Chatman, 1990; Schmid, 2010). The real author refers to the human being who is considered as the creator of the novel and of the world which it paints (Harvey, 1965: 34), whereas the implied author is much more abstract and complex. Unlike the biographical author, the implied author is not a human being, but rather the agency that guides the reading of any text, and without which the reader would not be able to make sense and interpret the works of fiction (Chatman, 1990: 74 & 87; Bal, [1985] 1997: 18).

This distinction takes one to a different question, namely one about the relationship between the real author and the implied author. In this book, I argue that the real author, the one who creates the possible world and thus defines its rules and its inhabitants' behaviour (Harvey, 1965: 34), also determines the intent of the novel and designs the pattern that serves the purpose of that intent. In this sense, the real author helps conceptualise the implied author. He or she also helps to interpret the novel itself on which he or she leaves his or her own marks (Chatman, 1990: 83-84). In the last analysis, the intent of the novel, i.e., its implied author, and the person who puts all elements together to create that intent, are intimately linked.

The above provides enough elements to answer the question about who remembers and forgets in novels of memory, including novels of genocide. The real author is obviously the one who revisits the past at the time of writing the novel; he or she is the one who selects characters, provides them with certain attributes, decides which events take place in specific places rather than others and ultimately designs situations that fit and serve the intent of the novel. Put differently, the biographical author of a novel of memory comes up with an idea to write a novel about a specific event of the past, because he or she wants the readers to conceptualise and remember that event in a certain way. That becomes the intent of the novel when it is completed and published. Chatman (1990: 75) suggested that the real author retires from his or her novel as soon as the latter is published, but the intent, born in the real world and interpreted by readers who live in the real world, remains. In the end, then, when the readers engage the novel, they start seeking that intent or authorial meaning as they are convinced that 'the characters are simply *porte-parole* of an author' (Docherty, 1983: xii – xiii; see also Booth, [1961] 1983: 75).

My point in this book is that the novels of genocide reflect in a more or less direct way the author's ethnic identity and related memories. The hypothesis is that ethnicity plays a prominent role and that the novels' intent follows the dual memory lines observed in post-genocide Rwanda (Nyirubugara, 2013). This claim is grounded in Booth's (1961: 70-71) theory that the implied author is the real author's second self. As the novelist writes, 'he creates not simply an ideal, impersonal "man in general" but an implied version of "himself"…'. If writing a novel is creating a *second* self, then it follows that the author's *first* self becomes central to the memory process that is underlying in the novels of memory, because the Self is, to a great extent, shaped by memory (Sorabji, 2006: 23-24; Freeman, 1992: 22-34). The Self can be briefly defined as that which makes an individual unique and distinguishable from others (Levy, 1972: 44). The Self itself is to a considerable extent the product of cultural memory, as no one is born with a ready-made Self that distinguishes one from other individuals. Instead, after its acquisition, the Self evolves and changes over time (*Ibid.*: 48-49) and, depending on prevailing conditions, e.g., wars, political conflicts, injustices, etc., leads to different ways of perceiving and pursuing the good (Taylor, 1989: 34; see also Nyirubugara, 2013: 141). It is, as Mead (1913: 375 & 377) was already arguing a century ago, a mixture of memory images that guide one's behaviour and responses to one's own acts or those of others. In this respect, as the argument goes, a 'child can think about his conduct as good or bad only as he reacts to his own acts in the remembered words of his parents'. At this point, one should be reminded of Landsberg's (2004: 19) observation that social structures are no longer the sole frameworks in which individuals acquire memories. In an era dominated by mass-mediated culture, private and group memories reach far more people outside of their traditional social frameworks. A logical consequence here is that these prosthetic memories acquired from films, novels and other mass media, play a significant role in shaping individuals' Selves.

This discussion around the author's Selves, the first and the second, guides my analysis of the novels of genocide in the sense that the second Self offers an interesting point of departure for an attempt to retrieve, or at least to have glimpses of, authors' first Selves. In *Complexities and Dangers of Remembering and Forgetting in Rwanda* (Nyirubugara, 2013) I analysed two autobiographical accounts, one by a Hutu and the other by a Tutsi, and concluded that the two authors organised their accounts around the same historical milestones, but offered contradictory interpretations of those milestones. Despite several similarities, e.g., same age, similar education, similar professional background, etc., the two authors' Selves were shaped by different past events that led them to a certain judgment about what they remembered and forgot, and how.

From a psychoanalytical perspective, works of art, including novels, are excellent media through which artists' unconscious fantasies transpire (Jackson, 2000: 4-5). Whether novelists want it or not, the possible world they create is a combination of their creativity, their experience, and received ideas, with their own fantasies. They see and represent the world through those unconscious fantasies, which influence what they select, love, hate, emphasise or highlight in their works (*Ibid.*: 3). In the last analysis then, authoring a novel of memory involves a great deal of introjection and, as a consequence, enables unconscious wishes in one way or another (*Ibid.*: 65-66).

The suggestion I made in *Complexities and Dangers* (Nyirubugara, 2013) and on which I build my analysis in this book, is that collective memory in Rwanda is characterised by what I called *dual interpretations*. I used dual interpretations to mean that each major historical event seems to have two different interpretations that follow ethnic lines. Another observation I take over from *Complexities and Dangers* is one that relates to *parallel remembrances*. By this, I suggested that in Rwanda's memory landscape there is the 'right' past to remember, and the 'wrong' past to forget. In his multiple publications on memories of extreme violence in transcultural settings, Rothberg (2006a; 2006b; 2009; 2011) theorised what he called the *multidirectionality* of memory. The starting point for his reflection is summarised in the following questions: 'What happens when different histories of extreme violence confront each other in the public sphere? Does the remembrance of one event erase others from view?' (Rothberg, 2011: 523). Rothberg (2006b: 161; 2006a: 304 & 307; 2011: 523) opposed the idea that various histories [memories] are in competition against one another in a zero-sum game. Such logic implies a winner and a loser (Rothberg, 2009: 3 & 5). Instead of this zero-sum approach, Rothberg (2006b: 162) proposed a model whereby collective memories of extreme events should be approached as *multidirectional*, i.e., as interfering and overlapping with one another. The multidirectional approach to memory means that memory is not only 'subject to ongoing negotiation, cross-referencing, and borrowing' but also 'productive and not privative' (Rothberg, 2009: 3).

The multidirectional memory theory is a helpful approach for the study of collective memories in transcultural settings such as the United States of America, where memories of slavery and those of the Holocaust are vividly present in the public sphere. The same is true for France where the memories of the World Wars, of the Occupation, of Vichy, of the Holocaust, of the Algerian War, etc., meet in the public sphere. Applied to a society and a culture where almost all violent and political events from the past systematically present two narratives constructed along ethnic lines, the multidirectional memory theory becomes less helpful. There is an obvious competition amongst the narratives of pre-colonial Rwanda, of the 1959 events, of the attacks of the early 1960s, of the 1990-1994 war, of the 1994 genocide and of the Hutu refugee massacres in eastern Democratic Republic of the Congo between 1996 and 1998, to mention a few episodes of Rwanda's past. On a political level, the zero-sum logic is obvious [and has always been obvious], as the regime in place allows and promotes one version, the dominant narrative, and criminalises the other. My effort in writing this book is not to advocate the competitive memory approach against the multidirectional memory approach, as the latter does not apply to the case at hand, but rather to map ways in which conflicting memories negotiate their place in that part of the public sphere known as novels.

4. Sampled Novels

The focus on Rwandan-authored novels of genocide is motivated by the fact that the memories of the 1990-1994 war, the 1994 genocide and the massacre of Hutu refugees in the Democratic Republic of the Congo between 1996 and 1998 divide the Rwandan society along ethnic lines and give rise to contestation. In post-genocide Rwanda, phenomena such as self-imposed amnesia, dual remembrance, memory-driven hide-and-seek language, amongst others, have become everyday realities (Nyirubugara, 2013). By focusing on these novels, I want to map memory mediation in *fictional* Rwanda, with the assumption that it parallels memory processes in *real* Rwanda. With the above in mind, it would make little sense to include novels authored by foreigners in the core of the analysis, because their memory mediation through fiction does not have any reference or point of comparison, given that they do not draw directly from the same cultural memory reservoir as the one from which Rwandans draw. However, a few sections (3.4; 5.4 & 6.3) that deal with the spreading of stereotypes and ideological truths, include novels authored by non-Rwandans for obvious reasons: They reinforce certain stereotypes and ideological truths evoked in Rwandan-authored novels. This approach will hopefully help fill the gap in scholarship on Rwandan fiction which has almost exclusively focused on the novels written by non-Rwandan authors (Hron, 2009: 164; also see Semujanga, 2008; Mazauric, 2007).

I should mention here that my initial intention was to include movies by Rwandan [co-]directors. I quickly decided to solely focus on the novels of genocide and leave the movies of genocide aside for two reasons: Firstly, having full access to as many movies as possible was an issue. Secondly, I was not sure that my comparative approach which consisted of simultaneously looking at productions by Hutu and Tutsi filmmakers would apply. Thus I limited my analysis to the novels of genocide, but most of the discussions and observations I make here do apply to the movies of genocide. My search efforts consisted in identifying a maximum amount of relevant novels of genocide via the Web [e.g., via Google Books, publishers' websites, online bookshops and library catalogues]. The main selection criteria were that the authors had to be Rwandan and that the subject was about the genocide and/or the war, the background of either the genocide or the war and the aftermath. The search resulted in six novels by Tutsi authors and five by Hutu authors. In the end, I had five Tutsi authors [one authored two novels] including one woman, namely Mukasonga (2012), and five Hutu authors including one woman, notably Bahufite (2016).

In what follows, I would like to offer *my* reading of the novels, which means that another reader might provide different summaries with a different perspective (Bal, [1985] 1997: 4). I believe that these short summaries are necessary at this stage, for most of these novels are not yet popular. I also believe that without the general ideas in the novels my discussions would make very little sense, as they would refer to unknown objects. For practical reasons, the summaries are provided in a chronological order, starting with the earliest novel, except when two novels have the same author.

Tutsi author Twagilimana's (1996) *Manifold Annihilation* is the earliest novel amongst the 11 I am analysing. The novel is a story of Victor Kalinda, a Tutsi man who went through both politically-motivated and marital hardships. Situated in 1992 Rwanda, the novel as a whole features a Tutsi man named Jean Mahoro, who had a revelation in the form of a nightmare. In that nightmare, he received the mission to write a book about the vision for tomorrow, by denouncing the suffering of people like Kalinda. The novel revolves around a family tragedy, with Kalinda's wife cheating and having four children outside of the marriage, and Kalinda himself sleeping with his daughter to have progeny. Besides these tragedies, the story includes cases of injustice and unfair cruel treatments inflicted upon the Tutsi and Hutu from the south following the outbreak of a Tutsi rebellion in October 1990.

In *By the Time She Returned: A Refugee's Tale*, Tutsi novelist Rusimbi (1999) tells the story of a Rwandan refugee family living in poverty in the Nakivale refugee settlement in Uganda. Kaitesi, the main character and Seba, her brother, lived in the capital Kampala, but had to face discrimination relating to them being Rwandans. Even though this novel is not situated in Rwanda, I label it as a novel of genocide because it describes the hardships the Tutsi refugees went through in Uganda and somehow justifies the reason why those refugees later waged a war and took power in Rwanda.

Unlike *By the Time She Returned*, the setting of which is mostly in Uganda, Rusimbi's (2007) other novel, *The Hyena's Wedding: The Untold Horrors of Genocide*, is about the immediate aftermath of the 1994 genocide. The novel features genocide survivor Kiroko Musonera, a high-school dropout who unknowingly married his cousin. As a young local leader, Kiroko actively participated in the rebuilding of his community in Nyamata, where only a few Tutsi had survived.

Hutu author Niwese's (2001) *Celui qui sut vaincre* [*The Ultimate Winner*] equally discusses the post-1994 period, but from the perspective of a former Hutu minister, Marc Ngendabanga, shortened to Ngenda, living in exile in The Empire [Belgium]. Through Ngenda's reflection and experience, the novel describes the victorious Rwandese Patriotic Front [RPF] regime as built on tyranny, lies, terror and war-driven thinking. At the same time, Ngenda is shown as a victim of injustice in The Empire. He committed suicide to draw public attention to the injustices victimising the Hutu.

Tutsi writer Sehene's (2005) *Le feu sous la soutane: Un prêtre au coeur du génocide rwandais* [*Fire under the Cassock*] is a first-person account of a Roman Catholic priest, Stanislas, who was caught up in the 1994 genocide in Kigali, Rwanda. Using a flash-back approach, the author starts with Stanislas' decision in a French jail to tell the whole truth about himself during the genocide. Stanislas, who is perceived as the real father Wenceslas Munyeshyaka, embraced the genocidal ideology, first facilitating the kidnapping of Tutsi refugees from his church, and then later taking the machete himself to kill of the majority of them. He also raped the Tutsi girls and women to whom he had offered shelter in the presbytery.

Rurangwa, a Tutsi, published *Au sortir de l' enfer* [*As the Hell Ends*] in 2006. The novel is an account of Jean-Léonard Benimana, a Tutsi law graduate who worked at the U.S. embassy in Kigali, while at the same time working as a journalist for *Kanguka*, a newspaper that published pro-RPF stories. The family of Jean-Léonard, a member of the rebel RPF, was slaughtered in April 1994 by fellow journalist Célestin Sembagare, who was writing for *Kangura*, an anti-Tutsi newspaper. Sembagare spared Jean-Léonard and sarcastically urged him to collect enough material for his editorials. After the genocide, Jean-Léonard went abroad to study and met his wife who had married another man.

In the same year, Hutu author Ndwaniye's (2006) *La promesse faite à ma soeur* [*The Promise Made to My Sister*] was published. In that novel, Ndwaniye tells the story of Jean Seneza, a lab-technician in a Brussels hospital who travelled back to Rwanda in 2003 after 17 years abroad. His twin brother was in jail for genocide, whereas his sister and her husband as well as their children had been killed during the genocide. Born from a Hutu father, dead before the genocide, and a Tutsi mother who survived the genocide, Jean's mission in Rwanda became one of hearing his brother's version of the story. The twin brother had been forced to guard a roadblock but had fled to Zaire when the rebels took power. Jean returned to Brussels with more questions than answers.

Mbabazi (2007), another Hutu author, wrote and self-published *Sheridan* to tell the story of two main characters before, during and slightly after the 1994 genocide. As he was attending a training in France, Hutu army commander Miko fell in love with a Tutsi girl called Kenya. Despite Kenya being an RPF militant who hated the Hutu regime that was in power at the time, Miko decided to take her to Rwanda with the promise of marrying her. The genocide broke whilst Kenya was in Rwanda and Miko back to France for another training. Kenya survived multiple attempts by Miko's sisters to have her murdered together with her stepsisters. Thanks to a Hutu woman previously unknown to her, she managed to flee the country to former Zaire. In the meantime, Kenya's stepbrother Mihigo was fighting alongside the RPF rebels. He witnessed RPF's organised, well-planned mass killings against Hutu civilians.

Writing in a totally different style, Hutu novelist Gatore (2008) published *Le passé devant soi* [*The Past Ahead*] to tell two seemingly separate accounts that end up in a story within another story. The novel is an account of the 1994 genocide in Rwanda, but neither the crime nor the country is mentioned in the novel. The novel stresses the issues of memory and identity in a highly subtle way and raises questions such as: What does it mean to be part of those who must be killed? Of those who must kill? Of those whose loyalty is in doubt? Of those who survived? The two parallel accounts have one thing in common, namely memory. In one story, Niko, who was an ugly and dumb man, was forced to kill his own father and lead a militia that killed thousands of barbarians. When there was no one left to kill, he ran away from everything and everyone who could bring back the horrible memories of the genocide. In the other parallel story, Isaro, whose family was killed during the genocide, refused the comfort of her adoptive family in France and set out to discover the traumatic memories of the same genocide. This is where the two stories meet, as Niko's story is the result of Isaro's search effort.

Tutsi author Mukasonga's (2012) *Notre Dame du Nil* [*Our Lady of the Nile*] is set in the late 1960s – early 1970s in Rwanda, i.e., in the last years of the First Republic that ended with the coup d'Etat of major general Juvénal Habyarimana in 1973. The Notre Dame du Nil School was meant to educate the women elite of Rwanda, composed primarily by the daughters of powerful Hutu leaders, businessmen and very few lucky Tutsi who managed to escape selection. At school, Hutu students occupied positions corresponding to the ranks of their fathers in the administration. The daughter of a minister was a minister, the daughter of an army colonel was a colonel, and the daughter of the Army Chief, was an Army Chief. The Hutu student leaders were relays of their parents in the capital, and kept threatening the few Tutsi students, whose place was meant to be occupied by 'true Rwandans' belonging to the mass populace. The novel ends with a massacre of Tutsi students by their Hutu schoolmates, which coincided with Habyarimana's coup d'Etat. Although this novel is located about 20 years before the genocide, it is still a novel of genocide because its primary aim seems to be to show the long suffering the Tutsi went through and the 'mini-genocides' that were committed in schools prior to the ultimate, general genocide. The reader is invited to look at the 1994 genocide as the last step in a long process, and to draw the conclusion that those who were students in the 1970s were the ones who grew up to lead the country in the 1990s.

Finally, as my manuscript was on its way to the publisher in December 2016, Liliane Bahufite (2016), a Hutu, published *Une vie qui n'est pas mienne* [*A Life that Is not Mine*] to tell the story of Nadine, a Hutu grandmother in her 70s who survived the war in Rwanda and the massacre of the Hutu refugees in eastern Zaire [now DR Congo]. As she was sitting in her home in Belgium, her granddaughter pressed her to tell her story of the 1990s. She and her family had lived in Goma camps in dire conditions. Nadine, who was 15 years old, had to drop out of school to work for a Zairean family in exchange for food. One day, her boss' son raped her after she had refused to marry him. Having no other choice and, following her father's advice, she agreed to marry him because, as a result of the rape, she had fallen pregnant. The young couple had to run away soon after because the Rwandan Tutsi-dominated army had invaded Zaire and was massacring Hutu refugees in camps. On their way through Zairean forests, Nadine's brother died and the family separated. A few weeks later, her husband died. Having managed to reach a temporary refugee camp, she wrote to family friends living in Europe asking for help. Those friends arranged for a flight to Brussels via Nairobi. In the meantime, she fell sick and ended up in a Brussels hospital in a coma in which she stayed in for months. When she woke up, she had lost all of her memory of the past. It was only when she was watching a film that she started to recover her memory, a process that was accelerated by a few sessions with a psychologist. She finally recovered her memory and could recognise her daughter, Aline. Despite her efforts, she never managed to find out what had happened to her father, mother and other members of her family. By the time Nadine was finishing her story, all her children and grandchildren had gathered around her, listening to the horrors through which she had gone. She had not realised that her story had captivated their attention.

I need to add a note here to explain why I did not include Gaël Faye's (2016) *Petit Pays* [*Small Country* or *Beloved Country*], even though it was authored by a Rwandan and partly discusses the genocide. The novel poses a methodological problem as the author does not fit into any of the two categories of authors, i.e., Hutu novelists and Tutsi novelists. His father is French and his mother, a Tutsi from Rwanda. The words of the novel's main character Gabriel, whose father is French and whose mother is a Tutsi from Rwanda, can easily be put into the author's mouth, though they are uttered in relation to the situation in neighbouring Burundi in 1994: 'I am neither Hutu nor Tutsi, I answered. Those [issues between the Hutu and the Tutsi] are not my cup of tea' (Faye, 2016: 183. Brackets added). A solution to this would have been to create another category of half-Rwandans, i.e., those born from foreign fathers and from Rwandan mothers. In that case, Faye (2016) would have been alone in this category, which would have made little sense as one needs quantity to be able to detect patterns. Moreover, *Petit Pays* is primarily about Burundi, though Rwanda, the 1990-1994 war, and the 1994 genocide appear as secondary subjects. The story of the genocide is told indirectly, as the main character does not witness it firsthand. Despite this exclusion from the sample, I do sporadically refer to Faye's (2016) novel where it helps to illustrate one point or another.

5. Book Structure

This book comprises three parts each containing two chapters. In the first part which is dedicated to *Ethnicity*, I focus on two important aspects that are likely to influence the perception of characters and their ethnicity. Chapter One discusses the construction of Hutuness, Tutsiness, half-Hutuness and half-Tutsiness. In this chapter I analyse and map the attributes that the novelists assigned to characters and draw out patterns that are associated with each category of characters. In Chapter Two I analyse the names given to the characters to find patterns in those names and how those patterns relate to the construction of ethnic identities. A suggestion is made in this chapter that names have powerful memory meanings that reflect characters' roles and behaviour in the novels.

The second part is dedicated to *Stereotypes* and aims to find out ways in which stereotypes in the real world interact with stereotypes in the novels. Chapter Three zooms in on stereotypes relating to beauty, handsomeness and ugliness and identifies patterns in their use and their association with ethnicity. Chapter Four focuses on stereotypes relating to smartness, intelligence and cleverness and their reverse. The idea in this chapter is to explore the ethnic dimensions of those stereotypes.

The third part places *Propaganda* at the centre of discussions, by identifying ways in which certain ideological truths are promoted in the novels. In Chapter Five I engage the novels to find out whether they advocate the idea of the war that made Hutu victims, or that of a war that broke out to stop the genocide against the Tutsi, or alternatively, that of a war that victimised the Hutu whilst a genocide against the Tutsi was taking place. In Chapter Six I investigate the novels to explore ways in which they build a historical context around their war-centred, or genocide-centred, or mixed narratives, by evoking actual historical events.

I should add a note here that all translations from French novels and other sources used in this book are mine. The same holds for all translations from Kinyarwanda.

Part One
Ethnicity

Chapter 1

Character Identities

Why does one read a novel? This is a fundamental question if one wants to understand characters and their role within the novel. People read novels, including allegorical ones, because they discuss human behaviour in a creative and entertaining way. Novels are about human past and present experience and attempts to warn us about the future. Of all elements of the novels, characters are the ones that give a human dimension to the experiences discussed in them. Similar to humans who already have identities and behave in accordance with them, characters are assigned identities and behave in ways that are in harmony with those identities. Simply defined, identity refers to what allows individuals to define what is important to them and what is not (Taylor, 1989: 30), or to ways in which they perceive and refer to themselves (Steveker, 2009: 9). It is intimately linked to cultural memory in the sense that the criteria that one takes into account in one's evaluation of what is important and what is not, are the result of accumulated experience over time (Rothberg, 2009: 4). Hofstede (2001: 2; 4 & 6) aptly called this identity-construction process 'mental programming', a lifelong process that takes place both at the individual and at the collective levels. In a similar vein, Gusdorf (1991: 246), referred to identity as 'a point of interconnection in a social fabric', which means that broad clusters can be made amongst the different individual ways of evaluating what is important and what is not.

This chapter builds on the observation that novels are about human experience and that characters play the role of humans, i.e., behaving like humans, in the fictional world. It follows on from this that characters acquire and develop identities that are comparable, if not quasi identical, to those of humans in the real world. If those identities were not comparable, then the novel would no longer qualify as a representation of human behaviour. Hutuness, Tutsiness, and Twaness played a decisive role in the last few decades in Rwanda and were epitomised before, during and after the 1994 genocide. Given the link between character behaviour in novels and human behaviour in real life, it goes without saying that those identities, especially Hutuness and Tutsiness, play a role in one way or another in the novels of genocide. The task of this chapter is first to theoretically discuss the 'character' as a concept to pave the way for further discussions on ethnic identities in the novels. After that theoretical part, I embark on the analysis of ways in which Hutuness and Tutsiness are constructed, both explicitly and implicitly, before closing with the identity crisis that tends to be associated with characters with mixed identity.

1.1. Understanding Characters

Any story, whether short like novellas or long like novels, needs characters who face complex situations, usually difficult ones, and who use the attributes given to them by the author to cope with those situations. However, describing characters like this would be simplistic, because one would be assuming that they are humans. Characters in a novel have many similarities with human beings but lack the most essential characteristic of humans, namely, *human* life. This section offers a short review of theoretical discussions about characters, especially their human-like nature and their construction. An interesting question in this respect is: What do characters tell us, if anything, about humans and, by extension, about the latter's recollection of the past?

There seems to be a consensus amongst theorists that the novel's ultimate aim is to represent human behaviour, character and the ways in which they think and perceive the world around them (Jackson, 2000: 72; Forster, [1927] 1974: 30-31). To achieve this, novelists create characters and assign attributes and tasks to them. In his classic book titled *Aspects of the Novel*, Forster ([1927] 1974: 16) distinguished seven aspects that any novel displays, namely the story, people, the plot, fantasy, prophecy, pattern, and rhythm. The most important aspects for this discussion are 'people' and 'plot', which could be interpreted as referring to the players and the rules by which they abide, all designed and controlled by the author. However, the term 'people' used in the context of a novel poses a theoretical problem because people are humans, whereas those called 'people' in a novel are not humans.

From the literature about character, it appears that characters have many things in common with humans. They speak the way humans speak, in a language humans speak; they seem to eat, walk, cry and have feelings the same way as humans do in the real world (Bal, [1985] 1997: 115; Eco, 2011: 75-76; Hochman, 1985: 7 & 59). Forster's ([1927] 1974: 31) use of 'people' should be understood as meaning that the resemblance between 'people' and 'characters' is so significant that characters look like people and vice-versa.

It is worth pointing out that characters should not be confused with other types of 'actors', as the latter concept encompasses all agents, not necessarily human-like ones, that accomplish one action or another (Bal, [1985] 1997: 5), whereas the former concept refers solely to 'the anthropomorphic figures the narrator tells us about' (*Ibid*.: 114). Those anthropomorphic actors are thoroughly described, given an identity and a name [in most cases] and all those efforts are aimed to create figures that the readers would perceive and imagine based on the standards and values of real people (Hochman, 1985: 8 & 48; Mead, 1990: 93).

The resemblance between characters in novels and people in a given society seems established amongst theorists, but the rationale behind that resemblance is far from obvious. In other words, why do novelists fabricate characters that are so close to humans despite the freedom they enjoy to explore other possibilities? The main reason is that 'literature is written by, for and about people' (Bal, [1985] 1997: 115; see also Eco, 2011: 29) and, for that reason, novelists cannot permit themselves to alienate the people for whom and about whom they write. Being humans themselves, they cannot escape from their own human nature, from their age or from their memory. Emerson's ([1906] 1942: 193-194) reflection about authors and the relationship between what they write and the society in which they live is worth quoting here. An author, he held, 'cannot wipe out of his work every trace of the thoughts amidst which it grew. The very avoidance betrays the usage he avoids'.

One important deduction that can be made from what precedes is that whatever fantasy world they create, novelists use cultural material from the real world to give shape to that world and to the characters who operate in it. This is where the authors' personal memories and society's collective memories come into play. The former offers a vantage point from which one enters the fictional world, whereas the latter provides a framework for a broader interpretation of that work of fiction. In other words, characters are inspired by the real people the authors have met or heard or read about at some point in their lives (Genette, 1991: 59-60; Docherty, 1983: xi). In her discussion of novels as sites of memory, Morrison (1995: 95-98) held that novel writing starts with an image from the past popping up in the novelist's mind. The author sees someone doing something, gives some meaning to that scene or image and creatively fills the blanks using text. In the case of novels of memory, the roles, tasks and ethnicity, amongst other attributes, that the authors assign to characters correspond to the authors' understanding and interpretation of certain behaviours, thus their individual memories, and link them to the wider collective memory of the time during which those behaviours were observed.

Despite the power the novelists seem to have in fabricating characters, the character-creating process does involve the readers and their own memories. Characters are created at two levels: The textual level at which the author portrays a character and creates a unique identity for him or her; and the constructed level at which the reader's experience and knowledge enter into play to generate their own image of a character, based on the cues in textual construction (Fishelov, 1990: 77-78). The power of the authors is therefore limited in the sense that they control the textual construction of the characters, but can in no way control what readers make of their characters. According to Hochman (1985: 56), 'As long as we have clear signification of traits and of patterns of behaviour, we are free to read them in terms of the gestalt we as readers get for the character'.

Characters and their behaviour in the novel closely involve cultural memory both at the individual [author's and reader's] level and at the collective level [memories shared by the author and the reader]. The relationship between the novelist and the reader looks like a contract that involves a memory dimension on both sides. In a novel of memory, like the 11 novels I am analysing in this book, the author makes a promise to the reader that the world portrayed in the novel is a fictional but possible world in which events of the past are represented in a verisimilar way. By purchasing a novel or borrowing it from a library or a friend, the reader tacitly agrees to the terms of the contract and agrees to behave as if he or she were one of the characters (Eco, 2011: 111-112). In other terms, the reader 'pretend[s] to live in the possible world of the narrative as if it were his or her real world' (*Ibid.*: 112). For this pretence to work, the author offers a possible world that is close to the intended reader's world, otherwise the reader withdraws from that world which he or she does not recognise. Also, if the readers agree to behave as if they were characters, it is because they expect characters who are close to what is imaginable in their own real life, i.e., characters with whom they can identify (Jackson, 2000: 66).

The questions that one could ask here are: What about the novels that start with a caveat that all characters, their names, and their actions in the novels were real in the real world? Can the reader still pretend to evolve in a thought-up, possible world? This is the case for Gil Courtemanche's ([2000] 2003) *Un dimanche à la piscine à Kigali* [*A Sunday at the Pool in Kigali*], which opens with the following warning:

> This novel is a novel. But it is also a chronicle and a reportage. The characters have all existed and in almost all cases I have used their real names. The novelist has designed a life and gestures for them and put in their mouth words all of which summarise or symbolise what the journalist [the novelist himself] observed whilst in their company… Some readers will consider some scenes of violence and cruelty to be the result of over-enthusiastic imagination. They will be mistaken. As proof, they just have to read the seven hundred pages of testimonies gathered by African Rights… (Courtemanche, [2000] 2003. Brackets added).

The reader is stuck here, because what one thought to be fiction becomes pure reality in the form of a journalistic report or chronicle. The novelist altered the terms of the tacit contract by inviting the readers to behave like newspaper or magazine readers and also by explicitly warning them against mistaking the world in the novel for a created, thought-up world. Moreover, the novel proceeds like non-fiction works do, for instance by quoting from academic sources (e.g. *Ibid*.: 39). In my view, if the work denies having any, or claims to have an insignificant, fictional dimension, it should not qualify as a novel. If one needs to seek documentary evidence outside of the novel, then one is rather dealing with non-fiction.

In short, constructing characters means producing memory, a process that includes careful selection of events of the past and characters that serve the novelist's intent without alienating the readers' recollection of the same past. To use the case of the 11 novels at the heart of this book, the past events revolve around the 1994 genocide, which has become part of Rwandans' and humanity's collective memory. Once the reader establishes that collective memory serves as the wider framework of the novel, he or she steps into the fictional world with his or her own memory of that event of the past,[1] much in the same way the author created it from the perspective of his or her own memory. In this sense, the novel becomes a meeting point of two individual memories both embedded in the collective memory of the genocide. Even though that collective memory of the genocide offers margins of selection and creative freedom to novelists, it also limits that freedom in considerable ways. The timeframe, places and events coincide in both fictional and real worlds and changing this would appear as a violation of the

---

1   Landsberg's (2004) notion of 'prosthetic memories' becomes interesting here, especially for readers who are not directly connected to Rwanda. Most probably, those readers engage the novels with prior knowledge about the topic, most of which comes from mass-mediated artifacts like movies, TV series, theatrical representations, etc. So, by the time the reader decides to read a novel of genocide, those already-acquired prosthetic memories of genocide provide the context as well as influencing the reading and interpretation processes.

tacit contract between the author and the reader. If that is the case, the characters are expected to behave in a certain way, to belong to a certain ethnic group or to a political party. In the next three sections I analyse the construction of characters' ethnic identities.

1.2. Constructing Hutuness

Ethnicity in Rwanda is a complex subject as it seems to be both denied and instrumentalised at the same time, especially at a political level. The dominant but wrong idea in public discourse and in a number of academic writings is that the current RPF regime has banned ethnicity in Rwanda. The claim is that Rwandans have a homogeneous Rwandan identity which has pushed ethnic identities to fade away. All that is still to be proven in a country where the Constitution still mentions the term 'Tutsi'.[2] My analysis here is not about how ethnic identities are negotiated in Rwanda's politics, but rather how they are negotiated in novels of genocide memories. As suggested in previous sections, novelists have a considerable advantage over non-fiction authors, as they are expected to *create* a possible world rather than report about the *real* world. The question then is: How are ethnic identities negotiated and represented in the 11 novels of genocide? In this section I attempt to map ways in which Hutuness is constructed, whereas in the next section, I focus on the construction of Tutsiness. Subsequent sections provide the analysis of cases of implied ethnicity and of identity crisis, respectively.

What are the cues that the novelists offer to suggest that a character is a Hutu? Once it is established that a character is a Hutu, what behaviour is assigned to him or her? These are the central questions that this section sets out to answer. In answering them, I only consider explicit indices that the authors provide, leaving no doubt about the Hutuness of the character. It is important to mention here that those cues make sense only when one considers them in the context that the novelist sets for the novel. For instance, Mukasonga's (2012) *Notre Dame du Nil* provides explicit signs that tell the reader that her novel is situated in the late years of the Hutu-dominated First Republic. These signs include the use of popular expressions in the political discourse such as the 'majority people' or 'people of the hoe' (Mukasonga, 2012: 33 – 34) or 'true Rwandans' (*Ibid.*: 207),

---

2   In a press conference on 28th January 2011, President Paul Kagame wondered where that idea [that ethnic identities have been banned] came from. A journalist had just criticised a charity that helped marginalised Batwa who were not happy about being called 'Those left behind by history' *[Abasigajwe inyuma n'amateka]*, rather than by their ethnicity. The President replied thus in English:
    … *There is nothing that targets any of the sections of our population to disadvantage them… And let me repeat this: If you want to call yourself Umuhutu, if you want to call yourself Umututsi, if you want to call yourself Umutwa, there is nothing that stops you doing that, that I know of. There is no law, nothing. But, what is in place, is to use what you are to the detriment of the Other who is different from you. This is the distinction, please! Why don't you understand this for all these years we've been here? We're not going to have an identity card like we used to have many years ago, with these bad governments, where you would carry an identity card saying you are a Muhutu, you are a Mututsi, you are a Mutwa, and therefore you would be treated according to that identity. Either given an advantage or denied the opportunity over others. This is what we have stopped! Period* (Podcast: 'President Kagame holds Press Conference 18 January 2011'; downloaded 28 May 2013 from http://www.paulkagame.tv/podcast/?p=episode&name=2011-01-18_President_Kagame_holds_Press_Conference-18_January_2011_.mp3 [site is now offline]).

the internal conflicts opposing politicians from the north to those from the south (*Ibid.*: 155-156), the coup d'Etat by a northerner after anti-Tutsi violence (*Ibid.*: 217-218). All these cues leave no doubt about the period in which the novel is situated and the ethnic tensions that marked that period.

The most recurrent cue that most Tutsi novelists use to suggest that a character is Hutu is the notion of power and its abuse. By portraying characters as identifying with, and cherishing, the anti-Tutsi policies of the regime in place in the late 1960s to the early 1970s, Mukasonga suggests that those characters are Hutu. In this respect, when Gloriosa Nyiramasuka, Defence Minister's daughter, told her schoolmates that she counted on their loyalty as 'true militants' and regretted that the Tutsi had exceeded the quota allocated to them in schools (Mukasonga, 2012: 31-32), she is automatically presented to the reader as Hutu. In the first place her father was a cabinet member and, in the second place, the daughter seemed to be militating for that government and its ideology. In a similar vein, Army Chief's daughter Goretti is portrayed with all attributes of power which she ostensibly displayed by coming to school in a military vehicle, escorted by soldiers (*Ibid.*: 29).

The same notions of power and its abuse are observed in Sehene's (2005) *Le feu sous la soutane*, though in a less refined fashion. Unlike Mukasonga who created Our Lady of the Nile Lyceum, certainly inspired by Our Lady of Cîteaux Lyceum, where she studied in the early 1970s (Mukasonga, 2006), Sehene keeps the real name of the church, Sainte Famille parish, where most of the novel is situated. The period of the novel is obviously set from April to July 1994, which is the 100 days of genocide. Whereas Mukasonga uses power and its abuse to show how Hutu characters gradually move from soft violence [verbal, gestural, psychological] to sheer physical violence, Sehene's novel equates power with violence, which both mark Hutu characters. For instance, the association of Damascène with the MRND[3] youths [these youths existed and were known as Interahamwe] and his worries about how to separate Tutsi and Hutu at the Sainte Famille church (Sehene, 2005: 11 & 65-66), make him a Hutu. *Le feu sous la soutane* is even more explicit in designating the characters' Hutu ethnicity and linking it to power. When Father Stanislas, a half-Hutu as I explain in Section 1.4, went to the mayor to request death certificates of the slaughtered Sainte Famille Tutsi refugees before burying them, the mayor sarcastically refused, arguing that one cannot bury people one does not know. This abuse of power and its psychological violence led Father Stanislas to conclude that the mayor, like Damascène, 'is Hutu before being a human being' (*Ibid.*: 83-84).

Rurangwa's (2006) *Au sortir de l'enfer* offers a slightly different approach to Hutu characters, though it keeps the notion of power and its abuse at the centre. Set in a period that ranges from a few months before the genocide to a few years after its end, *Au sortir de l'enfer* portrays most of its Hutu characters as having a certain idea of the power they held and, as always, were inclined to abuse that power to harm the Tutsi. One prominent character is Célestin Sembagare, a member of

---

3   The Mouvement Républicain National pour la Démocratie et le Développement, previously known as Mouvement Révolutionnaire National pour le Développement, was a state party between 1975 and 1991.

the CDR[4] party and journalist at *Kangura*, where he published anti-Tutsi articles, although those articles were signed by Hassan Ngeze. Sembagare openly said to Tutsi fellow journalist Jean-Léonard Beninama that he was waiting for the D-Day to kill the Tutsi (Rurangwa, 2006: 70-71). With these details alone, one knows that Sembagare is Hutu because he had the power to communicate through a mass medium, but he preferred to use that power to harm the Tutsi. During the genocide, Sembagare used his power to kill and rape Tutsi, including the family of Jean-Léonard Beninama, whose wrong-doing was writing pro-RPF [thus pro-Tutsi] articles in *Kanguka* newspaper (*Ibid.*: 82-83). It is worth noting the way in which Rurangwa uses real players [CDR, *Kangura*, *Kanguka*, Ngeze,[5] RPF, etc.] who already have a strong ethnic connotation in Rwanda's political history in the early to mid-1990s. The associations of Hutuness with CDR, *Kangura* and Ngeze and of Tutsiness with *Kanguka* and the RPF in real-life Rwanda, have been literally reproduced in fictional Rwanda.

Power and abuse of power and their association with Hutu characters comes back in Rusimbi's (2007) *The Hyena's Wedding*. Unlike the political contexts of *Notre Dame du Nil*, *Le feu sous la soutane*, and *Au sortir de l' enfer*, which are set in Hutu-dominated Rwanda, the context of *The Hyena's Wedding* is set in a Tutsi-dominated, post-genocide Rwanda. That difference of context results in a considerable decrease in the number of Hutu characters. In fact, the novel accounts for only one minor Hutu character and three insignificant actors who are only slightly mentioned once or twice. Despite this minor role, the notions of power and abuse of power persists as markers of Hutu characters and actors. The sole character, Rucagu, was in charge of solidarity camps that aimed to build houses for genocide survivors. Instead of ensuring that Tutsi survivors had a shelter, Rucagu rather evicted them from houses belonging to Hutu criminals returning from exile (Rusimbi, 2007: 30). Here again, Rusimbi gives a maximum of signs to induce the reader to consider fictional Rucagu as representing real Rucagu, who, like the fictional counterpart, is a Hutu in charge of the so-called *Intore* programme [patriotism training camps] and whom Rwandan media keep associating with genocide [an association that the novel also makes].

The three other Hutu actors – I would not call them characters as very little is known about them – are Mbarimombazi, a poor Hutu returnee begging to join the solidarity camp (*Ibid.*: 85-86); Karamira, a Hutu businessman and Interahamwe militia leader who, upon his return from exile, was sentenced to death and shot publicly by a firing squad (*Ibid.*: 67-68 & 107-108); and finally, unnamed Hutu police officers who belonged to the defeated army, and who admitted to being cowards in a commemoration event, because, they said, they had stood and watched when all the Hutu population was being taught to kill the Tutsi (*Ibid.*: 52-53). Even though the construction of Hutuness in *The Hyena's Wedding* stresses

---

4 The *Coalition pour la Défense de la République* was a Hutu-dominated party with an anti-Tutsi ideology.
5 *Kanguka* [Wake up], emerged in the late 1980s as one of the earliest independent newspapers in Rwanda. Owned by Valens Kajeguhakwa, a Tutsi businessman, this newspaper had Hassan Ngeze amongst its editorial staff. Ngeze broke away in early 1990s to start *Kangura* [Awaken]. This newspaper distinguished itself by writing hate articles against the Tutsi and all those associated with, or sympathetic to, them.

powerless Hutu submitted to a Tutsi-dominated regime, it nonetheless keeps the notion of abuse of power as an intrinsic trait of Hutu characters. All other forms of power that come from non-Hutu characters seem to be geared towards the good.

The approach to power and its abuse as a marker of Hutuness is also observed in Twagilimana's (1996) *Manifold Annihilation*. However, unlike other novels, this one creates two categories of Hutu: the pure and tough ones from the north – the sacred region – who dominated power (Twagilimana, 1996: 235), and those from the south who were collectively thought to belong to the opposition and to be sympathetic to the Tutsi rebels. In this context, power and its abuse is systematically attributed to the Hutu from the north with its victims being the Hutu from the south and the Tutsi. The most blatant abuse is the one that followed the staged, fake, attack during the night of the 4th to the 5th of October 1990, i.e., three days after the launch of the Tutsi rebel attack. During that night, heavy shootings were heard in the capital Kigali, but the next morning, no casualties were observed and nobody was killed (*Ibid.*: 98-99). The aim of the stratagem was twofold: providing a pretext to jail the Tutsi and Hutu opponents from the south and to pave the way for the intervention of foreign troops. As a consequence, thousands were jailed for months and, because of psychological and physical torture, were 'wrecks and misfits' when they were released (*Ibid.*: 34-35). In that same logic, the Hutu leaders from the north imprisoned journalists for denouncing abuses of power (*Ibid.*: 118-119), killed the Bagogwe Tutsi (*Ibid.*: 134-135) and the Tutsi in Bugesera region (*Ibid.*: 226-227), amongst other abuses of power.

A more revealing abuse of power is the one whereby Joseph Nduru, a rich and powerful Hutu from the north, diverted Kalinda's wife Celia. He used his power to transfer that family from Butare to Kigali. He used his money to buy a house for Celia, who forced her husband to move in. The result was that Celia and Nduru had four children who considered Kalinda to be their father. This particular case is interesting in the sense that it moves away from the collective and general observation that the Hutu leaders from the north targeted the Hutu from the south and the Tutsi, to focus on an individual case of a powerful Hutu from the north using his political and financial power to intentionally wreck a Tutsi family.

A different aspect of Hutuness is in Rurangwa's novel and resides in the way in which Juma is portrayed. Juma was an orphan who worked as a house boy at Benimana's, a rich and intellectual Tutsi family from which Jean-Léonard, the main character, was born. Despite the urge and calls of his Hutu friend Butihoro and other CDR fanatics, thus Hutu, Juma resisted and refused to betray the Benimanas, whom he considered his family (Rurangwa, 2006: 16-17). Juma is presented as using the little power he had or his powerlessness to resist evil during the genocide. He pretended to be amongst the killers by holding a machete and smearing blood on his hands (*Ibid.*: 86) whereas he actually wanted to divert the killers' attention away from the victims. After killing his new-born child and raping his wife, Sembagare took Jean-Léonard to the latter's parents, whom he had killed earlier. That is where he found Juma posing as a killer, and ordered him to kill Jean-Léonard who had fainted in the meantime. 'Juma… kill him when he recovers consciousness', Sembagare said. When Jean-Léonard woke up, he was surrounded by Hutu militiamen and it is at that moment that Allah-fearing Juma claimed his right, conferred to him by Sembagare, to kill Jean-Léonard. Despite the latter's urge to actually kill him rather than letting him suffer, Juma took him to safety in a different Moslem neighbourhood, where he stayed until the end of genocide (*Ibid.*: 88-91).

A similar Hutu character is Immaculée Mukagatare in Mukasonga's (2012) *Notre Dame du Nil*, as she, too, pretended to approve Gloriosa's anti Tutsi rhetoric and actions, whilst helping Tutsi classmates at the same time. She was so kind that she accompanied them to traditional healer Kagabo's and to sorcerer Nyiramongi's (Mukasonga, 2012: 57-58). When Gloriosa ordered the Tutsi schoolmates to eat after the Hutu had finished eating, Mukagatare played the game but kept part of her own food for Virginia and Veronica, her Tutsi classmates (*Ibid.*: 207-208). She later warned Virginia about the imminent killings, advised her to hide in her own [Mukagatare's] room, and arranged for her exfiltration to a safer place (*Ibid.*: 211-215). Mukagatare and Juma seem to be two rare exceptions of Hutu characters who did not misuse their power, however little, to harm the Tutsi. They rather used the minimal power they had to rescue the Tutsi in danger.

Mbabazi's (2007) *Sheridan* offers a drastically different image of Hutuness and its relationship with power and abuse of power. Unlike the Tutsi-authored novels discussed above which, as a rule, present Hutu characters as abusers of power, and the good Hutu as rare exceptions, *Sheridan* presents the good Hutu as a general rule, and the bad, power-abusing Hutu, as rare exceptions. Miko, the Hutu army commander, is the incarnation of a powerful but good Hutu. As a member of special forces, he would rather be expected to neutralise Kenya, a declared enemy of the Hutu regime. Instead, he turned her into a fiancée and protected her from his own malicious sisters Zuba and Masaro. Even when the war resumed after the death of President Habyarimana, he would go on his secret missions behind enemy's lines and would come back to look for his fiancée who had gone missing (Mbabazi, 2007: 181 & 215).

A similar case of a kind, good Samaritan Hutu soldier appears in Bahufite's (2016) novel, though that character was not explicitly named. He is simply presented as a former government soldier, which implies that he was a Hutu. That soldier emerged when Nadine's family had been separated in the Zairean forests and right after her husband had died. The remaining group of refugees counted eight adults and three children, including Nadine's daughter who was aged only a few months. It is at that moment that Nadine got a high fever and lost consciousness. When she recovered consciousness she was on the soldier's back, and her daughter was on the back of a young woman in the group (Bahufite: 2016: 186-187). For Nadine, it was humiliating for her to be carried by a man:

> I asked my friend to leave me there and to continue his march because I did not want to add to his burden. He ordered me to shut up and promised to carry me until the camp set up by early comers amongst the refugees, which was at a two-hour walk distance. That good news gave us energy to stand firm for the rest of the distance (*Ibid.*: 187-188).

Mukamana's assistance to Kenya when the latter was in danger is another case of a good Samaritan Hutu. Kenya had survived grenade blasts after being ordered to leave the ETO vocational school (Mbabazi, 2007: 167-168). She had also survived a heavy club blow to her head (*Ibid.*: 165). Together with Gatete, a Tutsi woman equally badly wounded, they decided to go to Mukamana's home, confident that that Hutu woman, who was not their acquaintance, would help them: 'Even if she is not especially my friend, she is going to rescue us, she is going to hide us. She is a righteous woman, we used to take the same bus every morning' (*Ibid.*: 177). Mukamana did rescue them together with another Hutu anaesthetist who helped heal their wounds. Unfortunately, Gatete was spotted and killed by Hutu militiamen (*Ibid.*: 184-185). Mukamana gave her deceased sister's Hutu identity card to Kenya, and both marched to the north, where they stayed in the house of Mukamana's parents.

The sole Hutu who are presented as abusing power to harm the Tutsi are Miko's sisters, Zuba and Masaro. Both opposed the relationship between their brother and a Tutsi woman. Masaro wanted the latter dead. When Kenya, who was still ignoring her in-law's hatred, called Masaro from Mukamana's to ask for help, instead Masaro sent the militiamen who found Gatete and killed her (*Ibid.*: 183-185). Later, when Kenya and Mukamana had reached Gisenyi, Masaro attempted to have her killed again. She sent in Matamata, a militia leader, to kill her. Matamata and his men invaded the home and brutally wounded Kenya with a sword on her arm. However, Matamata decided to let her live and even offered medical assistance after realising that she looked almost exactly like Kami-Kaze, her step-sister whom he had turned into a sex-slave (*Ibid.*: 256-259). Compared to other novels, *Sheridan* provides a more nuanced perspective on Hutuness by suggesting that people like Masaro and Matamata are rather exceptions, and those like Miko, Mukamana and others are the rule.

Another perspective on Hutuness emerges from Niwese's (2001) *Celui qui sut vaincre*, where the Hutu are presented as powerless all along the line. Former minister Ngenda is jobless and poor, and does not even have any legal status in The Empire [Belgium]. The intellectual power he still had was used to reflect on the Hutu-Tutsi conflict in Rwanda and to think about solutions. He was also praised for his psychological power, one that kept him confident and willing to live despite all the hardships of the present and the past. Lemaître, the owner of the farm where he used to harvest apples could not understand how Ngenda could still have a taste for life. In Europe, Lemaître reasoned, when one loses a job, one goes to a psychologist. Some even kill their families before killing themselves. If a catastrophe chased us away from our country, he wondered, would our ministers manage to live Ngenda's life? (Niwese, 2001: 10). Lemaître decided to do what Ngenda had refused to do, i.e., kill himself. Hutuness as it emerges from this description equals supermanship, that is, the power to resist unthinkable hardships.

A similar portrait of the Hutu emerges from Bahufite's (2016) *Une vie qui n'est pas mienne*, which, by the way, has no single Tutsi character, as it is primarily set in a Hutu refugee camp. Nadine, 15 years old, represents the Hutu girls who, because of the war waged by the RPF, were forced to live in inhumane conditions, to drop out of school, to integrate rape into their lives and to bury their loved ones killed by disease or by the new Rwandan army. The Hutu girl who stays in the reader's mind after reading the novel is one of a resilient superwoman victimised by war and injustice.

A few patterns of Hutuness have emerged so far from this analysis: One firstly sees Hutu characters in a Hutu-dominated system who systematically abuse their power to harm the Tutsi; secondly, one sees those few, in a Hutu-dominated system, who are presented as exceptions as they pretend to follow the powerful Hutu but end up protecting or rescuing the Tutsi; also , one sees those in a Tutsi-dominated system, who either keep misusing their power to harm the Tutsi or are powerless and forced to confess their past abuse of power. These three patterns emerged from Tutsi-authored novels. A fourth pattern is one of Hutu characters using their power to help and rescue the Tutsi, with a few exceptions of those abusing it to harm them. A fifth pattern portrays Hutu characters as possessing the power to manage and accommodate hardships, victimisation and injustice. The last two patterns emerged from three Hutu-authored novels, specifically from Niwese (2001), Mbabazi (2007) and Bahufite (2016).

As can easily be observed, some novels do not fit perfectly into these patterns and necessitate a different approach. Rusimbi's (1999) *By the Time She Returned* has no single Hutu character and, therefore, is not relevant for the analysis of the construction of Hutuness. Ndwaniye's (2006) *La promesse faite à ma soeur* presents a major challenge as it rarely mentions ethnicity. It tries to conceal all cues and signs that could betray the ethnicity assigned to the characters. However, a closer look at the few cues in the novel, permits making some interesting inferences as to how ethnicity is constructed. Gatore's (2008) *Le passé devant soi* is the most challenging of all, because the novel does everything it can to avoid any link to Rwanda and the genocide, whilst providing signs that make the reader think that it is about both. For the purpose of structure, I analyse implied Hutuness together with implied Tutsiness in *La promesse faite à ma soeur* and *Le passé devant soi* in Section 1.4.

1.3. Constructing Tutsiness

The construction of Hutuness discussed in the previous section is intimately linked to the construction of Tutsiness, since both Hutuness and Tutsiness seem to be two sides of the same coin in the novels of genocide that I am analysing. The question I try to answer here is: What elements do the novels provide to describe and portray Tutsi characters? The analysis below follows an approach similar to the one used in the previous section, namely one consisting of looking at the patterns that emerge from Tutsi-authored novels, before dealing with those emerging from Hutu-authored novels.

Mukasonga's (2012) *Notre Dame du Nil* clearly suggests that the Hutu elite in power and their daughters at Our Lady of the Nile Lyceum were abusing their power with the sole intention of harming the Tutsi, limiting their access to quality education, maintaining them in poverty and killing them if that appeared indispensable. In front of those Hutu leaders and their extensions at the Lyceum are the Tutsi, represented in the novel by Virginia Mutamuriza and Veronica Tumurinde, who happened to be in the same class as Gloriosa Nyiramasuka and other Hutu students. The two girls were confined in their roles of victims of different categories of Hutu they would come across. Gloriosa, the main Hutu character, kept reminding the two girls that they owed their presence at the Lyceum to the quota system and that, whatever they did, they remained snakes (Mukasonga, 2012: 33-34). This status of being permanent targets and victims pursued the two Tutsi girls even within the classroom, where knowledge was supposed to have no ethnic connotation. For instance, as Veronica was reading the Nile section in her geography textbook, Gloriosa interrupted her to compliment her that she had started looking for the shortcut to the place where she had come from. She even offered to make it easier for her by praying to Our Lady of the Nile to urge crocodiles to take care of her transport to that destination (*Ibid.*: 18-19).

Tutsi victimisation continued with Father Herménégilde, a Hutu ideologist who was amongst those who inspired the 1957 Hutu Manifesto and who happened to be part of the Lyceum management (*Ibid.*: 36-37). Father Herménégilde was unfair towards Tutsi students, as he always assigned them tough manual tasks (*Ibid.*: 105-106). What is more, he promised to reward them with underwear and dresses but only if they came to take them in his private apartment. When Veronica came for her reward, Father Herménégilde forced her to stand naked in front of him, allegedly to check whether the dress fitted her properly. Hutu students like Frida seemed to enjoy these invitations, whereas Tutsi schoolmates seemed to consider them as a form of torture (*Ibid.*: 106-109). In addition to these verbal and psychological attacks, Tutsi students suffered physical violence and massacres right before the coup d'Etat. Hutu militiamen and students led by Gloriosa hunted down Tutsi schoolmates and killed them. Veronica did not survive the violence (*Ibid.*: 220-221) but Virginia did, thanks to Immaculée Mukagatare.

Although *Notre Dame du Nil* is set more than two decades before the genocide, its victimhood-centred construction of Tutsiness is similar to the image of Tutsi characters that other Tutsi-authored novels provide. They all start by presenting Tutsi characters as passive victims of verbal and psychological violence on the part of Hutu characters and end with the same characters facing physical violence. That is more or less the image of the Tutsi that Rurangwa's (2006) *Au sortir de l' enfer* offers. Jean-Léonard was a Tutsi who had studied Law in Burundi and worked at the United States' embassy in Kigali as well as writing articles for pro-RPF *Kanguka* newspaper. He was also a member of the Tutsi-dominated party, PL[6] (Rurangwa, 2006: 31-32 & 47). Unlike Virginia and Veronica who knew about their status of being permanent targets and victims, Jean-Léonard seemed to be at war against that status. One evening, Jean-Léonard met Célestin Sembagare, the *Kangura* journalist who authored the *Ten Hutu Commandments*, at Hotel Chez Martin and both engaged in a dialogue that opened thus:

> -Good evening Snake *inyenzi-inkotanyi* [cockroach inkotanyi]! Says Sembagare to his 'enemy fellow journalist' of *Kanguka*.
>
> -Hi, mountain gorilla! How are CDR [Hutu party] animals doing? (*Ibid.*: 72. Brackets added).

---

6   The *Parti Libéral* was amongst the opposition parties that emerged in the early 1990s.

This opening shows that the two journalists knew the status of each other: obviously no one tolerated the presence of a snake or cockroaches in one's vicinity, whereas mountain gorillas referred to both strength and power. Jean-Léonard was the victim here and Sembagare was the powerful villain. Unlike Jean-Léonard who fought back, other ordinary Tutsi, like the bar-tenders at Hotel Chez Martin, heard Sembagare's announcement of the D-Day, about the time of gang-rapes and killing of the Tutsi, and kept about their business (*Ibid.*: 70-71). Like Gloriosa, whose predictions became true, Sembagare moved from verbal and psychological violence to physical violence that included killing Jean-Léonard's father and all of his family, killing his newly born child and raping his wife Jeanne-Laurette.

The image of the Tutsi as victims that Sehene's (2005) *Le feu sous la soutane* sketches is slightly different from the one in *Au sortir de l'enfer*. Perhaps the period in which it is situated, April to July 1994, explains this slight difference because the build up to ultimate violence is not provided in advance to see how Tutsi characters coped with their status of being victims before the genocide. Thus the Tutsi characters who sought shelter and protection at Sainte Famille parish were *ipso facto* victims and survivors, which was not so obvious for Veronica, Virginia and Jean-Léonard. The Tutsi characters at Sainte Famille suddenly found themselves in the situation in which Veronica, Virginia and Jean-Léonard were when the killings started. For that reason, my analysis of the victimhood-centred construction of Tutsiness begins with absolute victimhood of Tutsi characters rather than gradual but then leading to absolute victimhood.

One other important point in *Le feu sous la soutane* is that the main Hutu character, who was blamed for aggravating the absolute victimhood of Tutsi characters, is actually half-Hutu who was going through an identity crisis. As I discuss in Section 1.5, half-Hutuness, much more than half-Tutsiness, plays a significant role in understanding character dynamics and behaviour. For instance, when Father Stanislas told Spéciose that she was beautiful and invited her to come to live in the presbytery with him, Spéciose did not reject the invitation, as she would do if the man in front of her was like Sembagare or Father Herménégilde. Instead, she bit her lips and showed some hesitation, before packing her belongings and following him to the presbytery, where both slept in the same bed and had sexual intercourse (Sehene, 2005: 7-8 & 42-43). Father Stanislas did exactly the same with Dafrose (*Ibid.*: 63-64) and Assumpta (*Ibid.*: 91-93). The victimhood-centred construction of Tutsiness in *Le feu sous la soutane* is a dense one that culminates into two outcomes. On the one hand, within absolute victimhood, Tutsi characters at Sainte Famille followed a straight path to death when they fell in the hands of Damascène and other militiamen. On the other hand, within absolute victimhood, they managed to delay death by following a path of sexual abuse and immediate safety at the mercy of Father Stanislas.

Despite being situated in a post-genocide context where one could think that the idea of Tutsi characters as victims would disappear, Rusimbi's (2007) *The Hyena's Wedding* seems to rather give it another dimension. Tutsi victimisation in this novel maintains the permanent-target, permanent-victim status of the Tutsi in the background [discrimination and violence under previous Hutu regimes] whilst somewhat suggesting that the danger is still there. The case of Rucagu, the

Hutu who served under the previous Hutu regime, and who evicted Tutsi survivors so that Hutu criminals returning from exile could recover their properties, is a particularly interesting instance (Rusimbi, 2007: 30). Harriet, a young Tutsi girl who survived the genocide, heard from her aunt, another survivor, that the people who easily recovered her temporary home were the same ones who had killed her husband during the genocide. The aunt is obviously portrayed as a double-victim of Hutu misdeeds both before and after the genocide, with the sole difference being that physical death was not the culmination of the process in the post-genocide context. That same Rucagu seemed to have the intention to keep victimising the Tutsi using his powerful position. For instance, whilst choosing a site for the housing project for Tutsi survivors, Rucagu preferred a site with no easy access to water (*Ibid.*: 82). This choice can be interpreted as betraying his intentions to harm the survivors, which, in turn, maintains Tutsi characters in their position of being victims of abuse of power by Hutu characters.

The Hyena's Wedding offers another case of Hutu characters taking pleasure in victimising Tutsi characters, simply because they were Tutsi. One Tutsi woman travelling back to Kigali from the countryside was offered a lift by two men who, when they reached a quiet place, parked their car and attempted to rape the woman. When surprised by a military patrol passing by, the two men denied doing anything wrong but added that 'These arrogant Tutsis should have been wiped out' (Rusimbi, 2007: 47-49). This example might be understood as suggesting that even Hutu characters with apparent good intentions harboured hatred towards Tutsi characters, even in the post-genocide context in which power was controlled by a Tutsi regime. Here, like in *Notre Dame du Nil* and *Au sortir de l'enfer*, the Tutsi characters are inevitably victims of Hutu characters.

This notion of inevitable victimisation of Tutsi characters also dominates Rusimbi's (1999) *By the Time She Returned*, with the sole difference being that no one single Hutu character is blamed for it. As a matter of fact, there is no Hutu character in that novel. However, the Hutu are accused for having allied themselves with the colonial administration in the late 1950s to kill the Tutsi, and for chasing survivors from Rwanda. The Belgian colonisers had induced the Hutu into thinking that all Tutsi were in power, whereas only a small group were (Rusimbi, 1999: 25-26 & 144). Also, the Hutu are blamed for having rejected Tutsi refugees returning home following unrest in Uganda that specifically targeted Tutsi Rwandans. Seba's mother was one of those who crossed into Rwanda and was told that she was not welcome, as she was considered Ugandan. Kaitare told his brother Seba what their mother had gone through in Rwanda as follows:

> She was harassed in Rwanda. When she reached there, most of the young men and women were killed leaving only the elderly people. They were referred to as Ugandan exiles and put in camps. Poor supplies of relief aid and constant insults from the Hutu population couldn't allow them settle in their land peacefully. They had been rejected and killed by their brothers. They had to come back into exile in this country after the New Vision was in control (*Ibid.*: 124-125).

So Hutu characters are absent in *By the Time She Returned*, yet the Hutu are blamed for victimising the Tutsi, and by extension, for all other forms of victimisation that followed in exile in Uganda.

Apart from that historical context, *By the Time She Returned* constructs the Tutsi as a permanent victim at the mercy of Ugandans. Kaitesi, Seba's sister, epitomises the permanent victim, who finally realised that she had no choice but to join a military struggle to liberate Rwanda. Her biology teacher, Kwesiga, who happened to also be a zealous killer of Rwandans [Tutsi], intentionally humiliated her in public (Rusimbi, 1999: 9-10 & 99-100). When a rebellion broke out with Rwandan Tutsi support, an anti-Rwandan sentiment arose in schools and in the country at large, but this did not deter Kaitesi from going to school until she was officially dismissed from school together with other Rwandans (*Ibid.*: 106-107). Even later, when she became a housekeeper for Miss Queerwhite thanks to a Ugandan man named Musisi, she did not manage to escape from her position as a victim. Musisi raped her which pushed Miss Queerwhite to fire her when she realised that she was pregnant (*Ibid.*: 116-130). Obviously Musisi raped her to force her to be his second wife in secret, which exposed her to the fury of Musisi's first wife (*Ibid.*: 122). When the rebels finally took power with the support of the Tutsi, Kaitesi and other Tutsi refugees decided to attempt to end their permanent victimhood by preparing and waging a liberation war against Rwanda.

Multiple and repeated victimisation is the central, dominant theme of *Manifold Annihilation* (Twagilimana, 1996), as the novel's title itself indicates. Tutsi characters are constantly portrayed as being in a survival mode, whereby they are struggling to keep alive. Victor Kalinda, the old Tutsi man, incarnates manifold victimisation, as he went through so many sufferings imposed by the Hutu-dominated system that he ended up being a wreck and a good for nothing. He told Mahoro:

> Man, we suffered. Asking me a simple question opens volumes and volumes of files. I wish I could write books. I'm a wreck now. …. I've seen another world they won't even have a glimpse of… But strong, we emerged from annihilation. Strong, we emerged from the hand of the torturer. Those who died God took to the holy places of Heaven, for hadn't they been persecuted enough on earth? (Twagilimana, 1996: 34-35).

This quote sums up the victimisation that *we* suffered and clearly suggests the idea that the suffering was too much to describe in a few words. One needs books to be able to capture it all. Although the focus is on Kalinda's plight, his case is presented as just one amongst many. One French university professor who was jailed with Kalinda at 1930 Central Prison in Kigali and who had set out to collect fellow prisoners' stories to turn them into a novel, did not survive his release from prison. He left prison only to realise that his family had been massacred in his absence. He hanged himself as he could not bear it (*Ibid.*: 237). Another university professor was arrested and jailed for eight months for owning a book titled *The Chomskyan Revolution*, which the Hutu soldiers could not understand. The fact that it mentioned the term revolution without quoting the Enlightened Guide, the president, was enough to suspect him as an enemy preparing a revolution

(*Ibid.*: 131-132). Yet another university professor was jailed for 12 days for mentioning the rebels without insulting them. To the Hutu leaders, that meant that the professor was part of the invaders (*Ibid.*: 132).

All these cases, and many others, keep hammering home the idea that the Tutsi were inevitably victims, even though the Hutu from the south seemed to be part of the victims too. However, since no Hutu from the south is specifically named as a victim, whereas that is the case of Tutsi victims, one would not be wrong in concluding that the emphasis is on Tutsi victims, especially the intellectual elites (see *Ibid.*: 65; 66; 70-71; 72-73; 131-132; 237). In addition to university professors and other highly educated Tutsi, the novel includes ordinary Tutsi victims, namely the Bagogwe Tutsi in the northwest who were suspected of collaborating with the rebels (*Ibid.*: 134-135) and the Tutsi in Bugesera (*Ibid.*: 226-227).

After reading the above, one could challenge my claim that victimhood is systematically associated with Tutsi characters, arguing that there are a few cases in which Hutu characters are victimised. That is the case in *Notre Dame du Nil* where Modesta, a half-Hutu faced with an identity crisis (more in Section 1.5), seemed excluded from the group of 'True Rwandans' and had to deal with Gloriosa's fury when she suspected her of warning Virginia about the killings (Mukasonga, 2012: 219). I would not really call this a case of Hutu victimisation by the Hutu, because through Modesta's victimisation, one rather perceives the fury that is directed towards the Tutsi characters. A more interesting case is in *Au sortir de l'enfer*, where Jean-Pierre Basinga, an outspoken PSD [Social Democratic Party] Hutu militant who told President Habyarimana that he should negotiate with the RPF rebels, was grilled to death by Hutu extremists in his own bar (Rurangwa, 2006: 42-43). Here, Basinga's victimisation is presented as it having to do with his sympathy for the Tutsi. Therefore, his death rather confirms the association of victimhood with Tutsiness. The same is true for the brutal killing of Anastase Beninama [different from Jean-Léonard's father], by his own brother Casmir Kayiru, based on the motive that he was married to a Tutsi woman (*Ibid.*: 77-78).

Unlike the six Tutsi-authored novels which all equate Tutsiness with victimhood, three of the five Hutu-authored novels [Niwese (2001), Mbabazi (2007) & Bahufite (2016)], construct Tutsiness in a drastically different way. In Niwese's (2001) *Celui qui sut vaincre* Tutsiness is repeatedly associated with Machiavellianism towards the Hutu. Whenever a Tutsi character is mentioned or involved in any business, he is machinating and manoeuvring to harm the Hutu or at least to keep them under tight control. The most illustrative instances are those in the recording of a meeting of RPF insiders during which an expert evaluated the government policies. The expert-insider started with the remark that the RPF government was 'a minority system, undermined from all sides' (Niwese, 2001: 21), which rested on terror (*Ibid.*: 30). Evaluating the strengths of that system, the expert-insider mentioned the hundreds of thousands of Hutu prisoners whom he considered to be free labour force: 'those criminals work for us: they build houses for us and work on our farms. Others have been exported to the Congolese mines in the part under our control' (*Ibid.*: 31). Another association of Tutsiness with Machiavellianism is the suggestion made by one member of the RPF insider circle to intensify the war in Congo, and to ensure that the Hutu are on the frontline:

Let them kill the enemy and be killed… the members of the former [Hutu] army kill each other, since they are the ones fighting each other even though they stand on different sides of the front (*Ibid.*: 37. Brackets added).

All in all, the Hutu emerge from this novel as absolute victims of the Tutsi-dominated RPF system, whose maintaining seems to be based on making that victimisation tighter, more systematic, and permanent.

A similar portrayal of Tutsi characters as zealous killers of the Hutu, dominates Mbabazi's (2007) *Sheridan*. Apart from Kenya and her three stepsisters who were in the victim role, the sole Tutsi character who seemed to be an exception to the rule is Mihigo, Kenya's stepbrother, who was disgusted by the *unnameable* that the Tutsi rebels were committing against the Hutu (e.g., Mbabazi, 2007: 200-202; 290). In one instance, Mihigo agreed to pose as a rapist for Safari, a Hutu woman, so that the Tutsi rebels would not rape her as an appetizer, *amuse gueule* (*Ibid.*: 202). All other Tutsi rebels were enthusiastic Hutu killers and/or rapists. The champion of these mass killings was Colonel Karekezi, Mihigo's uncle, who seemed to find pleasure in killing the Hutu. Colonel Karekezi tortured and killed the Hutu without any distinction: pregnant women, children and the disabled were indiscriminately killed, usually with their head being smashed by a used hoe (*Ibid.*: 286). The same is true for Commander Salim who headed the *Kadogo* [child soldiers] unit. The more Salim child soldiers progressed, the higher the number of Hutu people they killed on their way (*Ibid.*: 233-234). What is more, all these killings were part of the instructions provided by the rebel supreme commander, General Ilunga (*Ibid.*: 206).

Unlike Niwese (2001) and Mbabazi (2007) who pointed at the Tutsi for having ill intentions towards the Hutu in an explicit way, Bahufite (2016) kept referring to the Rwandese Patriotic Army [RPA], or the Rwandan army or the Kigali army (e.g., Bahufite, 2016: 170, 173, 174, 176 & 178). For instance, when Nadine's family gathered in the Mugunga camp to decide which way to go prior to the RPA attack, one element that influenced their decision to run away from Rwanda and its troops, was that

> The survivors [of the massacres committed in other camps] told the stories of atrocities committed by the Rwandese Patriotic Army, the government army dominated by the former rebels of the Rwandese Patriotic Front headed by Paul Kagame… (Bahufite, 2016: 170. Brackets added).

Even though the term Tutsi is not used here – it is mentioned only once in the entire novel in passing (*Ibid.*: 172) – it is obviously and unambiguously implied, given that Paul Kagame is a Tutsi and that the RPF rebellion was an almost Tutsi-only one. So when one reaches scenes such as 'I didn't know that this time the enemy's ultimate goal was to exterminate all of us' (*Ibid.*: 176), or the one of a village where the Kigali troops had slaughtered the refugees and where 'hundreds of corpses littered the road' (*Ibid.*: 184), one understands that the Tutsi were systematically killing the Hutu.

In short, my attempt to grasp the main marker of Tutsiness in the six Tutsi-authored novels has led to the observation that victimhood signals Tutsi characters. Whenever a character is portrayed as being treated inhumanely or is being discriminated, brutalised, permanently threatened with death and abused sexually, that character is most likely Tutsi. In some cases, victims seem passive and co-operative, whereas in others they seem to resist and to find a way out. I have also stressed that the fact that a limited number of Hutu characters are shown in the role of being a victim confirms the victim status of the Tutsi characters, because the sole reason of their victimisation is their sympathy with the Tutsi. The three Hutu-authored novels included in this section have reversed this role. Tutsi characters emerge as Machiavellian villains whose mission is to ensure that the Hutu are killed or treated inhumanely or else submitted and exploited. The three novels present the Hutu as victims and the Tutsi as the killers and rapists. The next section takes the analysis further, but this time focuses on two novels that tend to resist the abuse of power and victimhood analytical frameworks I have used above.

1.4. Implied Ethnicity

The previous two sections have offered the analysis of the ways in which Hutuness (Section 1.2) and Tutsiness (Section 1.3) are constructed in a more or less straightforward fashion. In this section I use a different approach, namely one that searches for implied ethnicity based on deduction. The analysis focuses only on *La promesse faite à ma soeur* (Ndwaniye, 2006) and on *Le passé devant soi* (Gatore, 2008), the authors of which obviously, and perhaps intentionally, kept ethnicity far away in the background. In other words, the two novelists fictionalised a major historical event that involves ethnicity but did everything to conceal the latter. One could be tempted to add Bahufite's (2016) novel in this analysis, arguing that the term Hutu was not even used once in the novel. On its part, the term Tutsi was mentioned only once in passing and in general terms, without even attributing it to any character. In that specific instance, Nadine was remembering how kind her mother was, especially how she had risked her life when she 'hid the Tutsi during the events that cost the lives of thousands of Rwandans…' (Bahufite, 2016: 172). The cues provided here and in other references to the RPF, Paul Kagame, the refugee camps, to name a few of them, indicate that Nadine's family and those in the camps were Hutu, whereas those hunting them down were Tutsi. In that sense, ethnicity is rather explicit, even though it is not overtly named as such. In my analysis I proceed from the several cues that Ndwaniye (2006) and Gatore (2008) provide and make deductions as to what ethnicity might be hiding behind those cues.

Jean Seneza, the main character in *La promesse faite à ma soeur*, is half-Hutu (see Section 1.5), as his late father was a Hutu civil servant and his mother a Tutsi (Ndwaniye, 2006: 56). Except for this revelation about the ethnicity of Jean's parents, there is no other case in which characters are assigned ethnicity. The novel is set in the 1960s to the 1980s, and in late 2003, with the two periods of this novel being helpful in detecting the implied ethnicity of characters. I have to admit that the novel leaves no grounds whatsoever in guessing this in the 1960s – 1980s context: for instance, Edmond, the gardener at the Protestant mission (*Ibid.*: 7-8), Juvenal, the mission's nurse (*Ibid.*: 9), or Solomon, the all-around man at the hospital (*Ibid.*: 10) are not provided with any ethnic identity at all. Moreover, nothing of what they did, said, or thought gives any clue as to whether they were Hutu or Tutsi.

On the other hand, the post-genocide part provides material that can be subjected to analysis. For example, while at Zaventem Airport in Brussels in November 2003 en route to Rwanda after 17 years in Belgium, Jean met Georges, a Brussels-based taxi man, who told him the story of his ill father who was in jail for false genocide accusations (*Ibid.*: 42). He also came across Gabriel, whose father had been killed during the genocide, and who greeted him without any enthusiasm (*Ibid.*: 43). The only explicitly known ethnicity here is Jean's half-Hutuness, which makes him more Hutu than Tutsi in the Rwandan context (more in Section 1.5). Georges' story and enthusiasm to share it gives strong indications that he was a Hutu, whereas Gabriel's family history and lack of enthusiasm towards Jean send clear signs that he was a Tutsi. While in Rwanda, where he attempted to understand why his twin brother, Thomas, was accused of genocide, he met many people whose ethnicity is not revealed but can be implied. One of them is Nkundiye, a neighbour who knew about Thomas' actions and behaviour during the genocide. Jean seemed to not expect the whole story from Nkundiye in the presence of Charles, a survivor. He returned and met him *alone* and heard that his twin brother had done nothing wrong, as he had been forced to guard a roadblock a few days before going into exile in Congo (*Ibid.*: 102-103). A deduction here is that Nkundiye was likely a Hutu, whereas Charles was a Tutsi, which is also the case for all other survivors Jean came across in his search for the truth about his twin brother.

Contrary to Ndwaniye's approach that includes names that allude to real places, events, and dates which have a historical significance in Rwanda, Gatore (2008) did everything he could to avoid any direct link between places and events. However, the use of the names Isaro and Niko for the main characters, of the name Iwacu for a village, of an island in the middle of a lake from where one sees volcanoes, sends the reader to one country: the author's home country, Rwanda (Hitchcott, 2013: 80). Having situated the novel in space, it becomes possible to imagine the context and to start analysing how ethnic patterns emerge and interact within that context. In that respect, Isaro, the young girl adopted by a French family, was a half-Tutsi because, as her adoptive parents indicated, her father was killed because of who he was, whereas her mother could have survived if she had not been married to him. Her identity card indicated that she was not part of those who were targeted (Gatore, 2008: 151-155), which takes one to the conclusion that Isaro's mother was a Hutu, whereas her father was a Tutsi.

The other main character, Niko, is the opposite of Isaro, i.e., half-Hutu, as the killers in the novel suggested that his father 'is with us' but his deceased mother not, because she was a barbarian. That argument in favour of Niko's father is not completely convincing because the father later married another 'mole' (*Ibid.*: 126). This discussion seems to clearly indicate that Niko's father was a Hutu, whereas his late mother and his stepmother were Tutsi. It also seems to suggest that the killers were Hutu. With this in mind, it follows that the characters who happen to be targeted by the killers are Tutsi. In this respect, Hyacinthe, a young woman who passed near to Niko's pottery workshop, running for her life, with people armed with machetes and clubs after her (*Ibid.*: 125-126), is implicitly put in the barbarian category, which, as the above has suggested, could be understood as referring to the Tutsi. Despite Niko's efforts to divert the killers' attention, Hyacinthe was finally captured and added to the groups of those to be killed (*Ibid.*: 127).

The deductive analysis of the three fugitives who, together with Niko, sought refuge in the caves of the *Ile du Nez* leads to think that they were all Hutu. Uwitonze was an old righteous teacher, who was caught up in a serious dilemma: he hid 15 barbarians in his house and was not taking part in the collective effort to get rid of them. When the killers were about to search his house, he advised the fugitives to run away and provided them with food and drinks. They were all killed, hence the sentiment of guilt that pushed him to seek refuge in the caves of the *Ile du Nez* (*Ibid.*: 166-158). Interpreted in the genocide context, Uwitonze's character places him among the Hutu, as he was not hunted down like the barbarians. It is interesting here to note the similarity between Uwitonze, Juma [in *Au sortir de l'enfer*], Mukamana [in *Sheridan*] and Mukagatare [in *Notre Dame du Nil*]. These characters seem to have a humane perception of life, pretend to side with those who are abusing power against the Tutsi [all except Mukamana] and would take risks to rescue those in danger. These are the only Hutu characters who behave like this in all 11 novels I am analysing in this book.

Shema, another fugitive at the *Ile du Nez*, was a storyteller who used to entertain the village with stories about the past and even the present. During the 'unthinkable events', the killers locked him up to prevent him from telling stories about the killings (*Ibid.*: 171). When the killings stopped, he ran away, probably for fear of being killed by those who had locked him up. Here, too, the context pushes one to think of Shema as Hutu. His case becomes very interesting when one considers the communication power he had and the fear it provoked amongst the killers. Unlike Sembagare who used his power of communication to publish the *Ten Hutu Commandments* in *Kangura* (Rurangwa, 2006), Shema is presented as predisposed to use his power to counter the killings. In this respect, Shema together with Mukamana and Miko (Mbabazi, 2007), are part of the rare Hutu characters with good intentions and positive predispositions about helping the Tutsi. The fourth fugitive at the *Ile du Nez*, Uwera, was also a Hutu simply because, despite her mental issues, she was not targeted as a barbarian. Niko, who observed her from his own cave, wondered whether she had taken part in the killing campaigns during the 'unnameable period' (*Ibid.*: 168-169). If he thought that she could have been part of the campaigns, it is because she was a candidate, that is, not a barbarian.

In sum, the deductive analysis of the construction of ethnicity in Ndwaniye's (2006) *La promesse faite à ma soeur* and Gatore's (2008) *Le passé devant soi* leads more or less to the same observation as the ones made in Sections 1.2 and 1.3. This section, like the previous two, results in the observation that power and its abuse are an important marker of Hutuness and permanent victimhood as an important marker of Tutsiness. One major nuance, however, is that *La promesse faite à ma soeur* and *Le passé devant soi* do not systematically put all Hutu characters in the abusers of power category. Contrary to *The Hyena's Wedding*, *Le feu sous la soutane*, *Au sortir de l' enfer* [except for characters who married Tutsi women] , and *Notre Dame du Nil* [except for Mukagatare], *La promesse faite à ma soeur* and

Le passé devant soi offer a less simplistic categorisation. Nkundiye, the old man, seemed to be a man of honour and wisdom who had no single evil intention against the Tutsi. Although half-Hutu, Thomas, who was accused of killing his own sister and her Tutsi husband, is not painted as a criminal. Instead, he was given the opportunity to defend himself and demonstrate his innocence to his brother (Ndwaniye, 2006). Likewise, the killers who managed to recruit Niko are not the only Hutu characters in *Le passé devant soi*. Besides them, one also realises that there are characters like Shema, Uwera, and Uwitonze, who do not fit into the category of abusers of power. Despite these nuances, the two novels generally designate the Tutsi characters as victims and the Hutu characters as killers. They fundamentally differ from the other three Hutu authored novels [Niwese (2001), Mbabazi (2007) and Bahufite (2016)] in the sense that they contain no single case of Tutsi characters victimising the Hutu.

1.5. Identity Crisis

Rwanda's ethnic composition is not black and white, with the Hutu, the Tutsi, and the Twa [the latter group has not been included as it does not appear in any significant way in any of the novels] each confined in their own clearly defined corners. As a result of mixed marriages between these groups, a number of Rwandans found themselves with family roots in more than one ethnic group. As Rwanda is a patrilineal society, children automatically inherit their father's ethnic identity. Hence the appellations of half-Hutu for those with Hutu fathers, and half-Tutsi for those with Tutsi fathers. In the social and political context of Rwanda, people with mixed identities might be on either side, depending on the circumstances. However, when the situation is violent and so polarised as it was in the 1990s, those people are caught up in between, feeling safe neither amongst the Hutu nor amongst the Tutsi. The role that half-Hutu and half-Tutsi played during the 1990 to 1994 war, the 1994 genocide, during the Hutu refugee massacres in DR Congo, the status assigned to those amongst them who were killed and the label given to those accused of committing crimes, have been largely neglected in the now extensive Rwanda scholarship. The latter has rather focused on the Hutu who are often divided into moderates and extremists, and the Tutsi, who are never categorised. That neglected theme has been at the heart of six of the 11 novels I am analysing in this book. In fact, that theme is prominent in all six and absent in *By the Time She Returned* (Rusimbi, 1999), *The Hyena's Wedding* (Rusimbi, 2007), *Celui qui sut vaincre* (Niwese, 2001), *Sheridan* (Mbabazi, 2007) and in Bahufite's (2016) *Une vie qui n'est pas mienne*.

The question that arises and which this section explores is: How is half-Hutuness constructed in those six novels of genocide? I am excluding half-Tutsiness from my analysis because it appears only once in all six novels. It also seems to play no role at all in the story that that novel tells. That case is Isaro in *Le passé devant soi* (Gatore, 2008), whose father was a Tutsi and whose mother was a Hutu. Moreover, Isaro lived in France most of the time and when she came to Rwanda, she interacted with a few people whose ethnic identity cannot be detected. The absence of half-Tutsiness and the abundance of half-Hutuness in those novels might be interpreted as reflecting a certain social, cultural and political reality in Rwandan society. However, as that subject falls outside the scope of my analysis, I will not discuss it further. In my focus on half-Hutu characters, I argue that they seem lost and hesitant about where they should stand and how they should behave.

The most prominent case of half-Hutuness is Father Stanislas' in Sehene's (2005) *Le feu sous la soutane*. Father Stanislas' mother was a Tutsi and had sought refuge first at Sainte Famille church, and later on at Hotel des Mille Collines, a few meters away (Sehene, 2005: 19). Father Stanislas described his mother as having always been a single parent, *femme libre*, and as someone who would be the prey of the first man knocking at her door (*Ibid.*: 133). His mother never told him about his father or about the ethnic group to which he belonged: 'Is she ashamed of having conceived me with a Hutu…What if my father was a Hutu?', Father Stanislas wondered (*Ibid.*: 35; see also 133-134). It is with this vague ethnic identity that Father Stanislas grew up, with the deduction that if his mother refused to reveal his father's identity, it is because he was Hutu. This deduction was confirmed in his mind in the 1970s during his junior seminary years, when Damascène, the future militiaman, told him that he should not consider himself as a Tutsi because he was sure he was a Hutu (*Ibid.*: 35-36). For that reason, Father Stanislas considered himself a Hutu and forced himself to behave accordingly, following his perception of Hutuness.

It is with this confusion that Father Stanislas became a regular killer of the Tutsi who had sought refuge in his parish. He seemed to enjoy the scenes of militiamen slaughtering the fugitives he was supposed to protect. The frequent presence of Damascène, the former schoolmate turned militiaman, kept reminding him that he had to prove his Hutuness. Damascène kept calling him 'Tutsi-Hutu' (*Ibid.*: 46), and often reminded him of his resemblance to his mother (*Ibid.*: 57). As Damascène's pressure increased, Father Stanislas deemed it vital to prove him wrong. One day, from behind the pulpit, Father Stanislas asked the Tutsi to go on his left and the rest on his right. He collected all identity cards from the Tutsi in the presence of Damascène and his fellow militiamen, before asking them to stand in the church courtyard:

> Suddenly, Damascène hands the machete over to me and orders me to accomplish my duty as a true Hutu. I walk back because I was not expecting that. The militiamen immediately stop their chats, intrigued by my reaction. I can no longer hear the refugees' supplications. The hesitation that petrifies me seems endless. I admit fighting an intense envy to shoot Damascène down with my pistol. Yet I prefer to reach out to the machete (*Ibid.*: 103).

Among those he killed was Deogratias, the brother of Assumpta, the woman who, at that very moment, served as his sexual slave at the presbytery. What is interesting here is the mentor role played by Damascène, whom Father Stanislas considered as the representative of the Hutu. If he managed to prove to him that he deserved the title of a true Hutu, then no one could doubt his loyalty anymore. He wished he was like Damascène, with a firm identity that allowed for no scrabbling around, no hesitations and for no doubts (*Ibid.*: 61).

Despite his quasi conviction that he was Hutu, Father Stanislas was haunted by the idea that he had some Tutsi traits in himself. During his seminary years, he had already realised that his flat nose could not be one of a Tutsi, but his tallness could not be one of a Hutu either (*Ibid.*: 35-36). For him, both the Tutsi and the Hutu should consider him one of them, but he had a feeling that neither group welcomed him whole-heartedly. Even his Tutsi sexual slaves did not show enthusiasm in bed, as they thought they were 'too beautiful, too outstanding for a Hutu' (*Ibid.*: 43). His conclusion was one of a profound identity crisis, as he felt rejected both by the Hutu and the Tutsi: 'I hate the entire world', he said (*Ibid.*: 93).

Like Father Stanislas, Niko, one of the two main characters in Gatore's (2008) *Le passé devant soi*, was also caught up in a profound identity crisis, as his father was a Hutu and his mother, a Tutsi. Niko never saw his mother because the latter, left alone by all including her husband, died during delivery (Gatore, 2008: 79-80). Due to his dumbness, Niko grew up in social isolation, as no one wanted to have a relationship with him except uncle Gaspard. His stepmother, also a Tutsi, was the cruellest of them all: she would never call him 'my son'; she would rarely hold him in her arms, and would always chase him away from the kitchen. Turning to his Hutu father also did not help, as the latter's sole duty was making children (*Ibid.*: 81-82), not taking care of them. Having no place in society whereby both the Hutu [father] and the Tutsi [stepmother] rejected him, Niko sought refuge in his frequent daydreams where he spent hours every day (*Ibid.*: 83-84) and in his cordial relationship with the goat that he had received from Gaspard (*Ibid.*: 48-49).

All this time, Niko is presented as a victim with whom one should sympathise. His ethnic identity played no significant role until he, like Father Stanislas, was reminded that he was not a full Hutu, given that his mother was a Tutsi, i.e., a barbarian. Militiamen armed with Kalashnikovs rounded up several barbarians and their accomplices as well as people like Niko whose loyalty had to be proven. In their discussions the militiamen referred to the latter group as those who were 'a little bit with us' and who were required to prove that they deserved our trust (*Ibid.*: 127). People in this group were individually called up, given a club or another weapon, and were asked to smash the head of a barbarian. When it came to Niko's turn, he 'pretended to hesitate, to not hear that he was the one being called' (*Ibid.*: 129). Knowing that his own life was at stake, he moved nearer to the victim, who was none other than his own father, and smashed his head despite his father's supplications. With that 'heroic' deed, Niko had proved beyond any doubt that he was not a barbarian, and for that, he received a round of applause from the public. (*Ibid.*: 129-131). His cousin Anastase, Gaspard's son, who happened to be amongst those who needed to prove their non-barbarian status, failed to kill an old woman and was shot dead on the spot.

What is worth noting in the cases of Niko and Father Stanislas, is that once they passed the initial test, they whole-heartedly embraced the killer status and became fully-fledged Hutu. However, the two half-Hutu characters experienced their identity crisis differently. Father Stanislas' identity crisis lasted a long time [since the 1970s] and seemed to underlie most of his actions and reasoning. In the case of Niko, his identity crisis was sudden: the same society that had rejected him as a member suddenly told him that his life hung on his choice between siding with those associated with his mother's identity or with those associated with his father's identity. His choice for his life and thus for the death of the barbarians, became the only criterion for social acceptance. Contrary to Father Stanislas who still felt rejected by both the Hutu and the Tutsi, Niko was fully accepted and was even promoted to commander of the militia (*Ibid*.: 132-133).

Identity crisis also plays an important role in Mukasonga's (2012) *Notre Dame du Nil*, where Modesta epitomised a half-Hutu student whom neither the Hutu nor the Tutsi trusted. Modesta's father was Hutu, but because of her Tutsi mother, she could not pretend to be a full Hutu. To avoid being considered as a spy and a traitor, she had to avoid hanging out with the Tutsi (Mukasonga, 2012: 87-88). Before experiencing an identity crisis at school, Modesta went through it at home and on a daily basis. Her own father, Rutetereza, had wished to make himself Tutsi under the Tutsi monarchy before independence. He worked for a Tutsi chief and had a lot of cattle. Given his wealth [cattle], a poor Tutsi family had accepted to marry one of their daughters to him. He even wanted to join the pro-monarchy party in the late 1950s, but his Tutsi boss reminded him that he had never been a Tutsi. Because of that, he should join his fellow Hutu's party. Under the Hutu-dominated Republic, he lived with an uncomfortable situation, as people would frequently remind him of his willingness to become a Tutsi (*Ibid*.: 88-89). To repair his past mistakes, Rutetereza started humiliating his wife, Modesta's mother, by forbidding her to serve beer to visiting Hutu friends and to accompany him to church on Sundays, amongst other measures. 'Since he became a Hutu again', Modesta told Virginia, 'my father is ashamed of my mother. He hides her'. Her own sons hated her because they could not be like other young Hutu. They were mulattos, i.e., half-Hutu (*Ibid*.: 93-94).

Gloriosa, the defence minister's daughter, was obviously aware of Modesta's situation and Modesta knew it. She had to constantly prove to Gloriosa and other Hutu who did not trust her that 'she is a true Hutu' (*Ibid*.: 89). One way of proving that was staying in Gloriosa's vicinity and serving her as her 'dog'. One day, as the killings were underway, Gloriosa realised that Virginia had vanished and blamed Modesta for having warned her 'friend'. Gloriosa poured her fury on her:

> Dirty bastard, you warned her and told her to run away; she was your friend, your true friend, you spied me for her; I am going to punish you like a parasite because you are one…you are decidedly your mother's daughter (*Ibid*.: 219).

Gloriosa's accusations and emphasis on Modesta's true friendship with Virginia might lead to the wrong deduction that she, indeed, had the trust of her Tutsi classmates. It is true that she felt at ease with, and often talked to, Virginia and Veronica, but this did not mean that she had won their trust. One day Virginia, to whom she had once told about her mother's plight, told Veronica to be very careful about her: 'Even though her mother is Tutsi', she said, 'you know very well on which side she will always stand' (*Ibid*.: 206). This suggests that the choice of half-Hutu characters is predictable when it comes to siding with the Hutu or with the Tutsi. The choices made by Father Stanislas and Niko, though under totally different circumstances, confirm this predictability. Indeed, Modesta chose the

Hutu side when the killing started, as she felt no need to run away, to hide, or to rescue her Tutsi classmates.

Lack of trust in half-Hutu characters amongst Tutsi characters is exacerbated in Rurangwa's (2006) *Au sortir de l'enfer* in more explicit terms. When Jean-Léonard announced the news of his engagement with Jeanne-Laurette, fierce discussions followed about the fiancée's ethnic identity. The father and the mother seemed happy but hastened to ask about who she was. Jean-Léonard provided the name, the school she had attended, etc., but Marie, his sister suddenly interrupted him to ask: 'Is she a Tutsi or a Hutu?', to which Jean-Léonard could not answer, because he did not know about Jeanne-Laurette's ethnic identity. Marie insisted: 'So you're going to marry someone without knowing whether she is a Tutsi or a Hutu?' (Rurangwa, 2006: 56-57). Biologically speaking, Jeanne-Laurette was Tutsi but she was Hutu on paper. She was born from two Tutsi parents in the early 1970s and was forced into exile in 1973, when anti-Tutsi violence broke out. Her father died during that violence. After President Habyarimana took power and pacified the country, Jeanne-Laurette and her mother returned to Rwanda in 1975. Her mother got married to Anastase Benimana, a Hutu, whose Tutsi wife had also died in 1973. Jeanne-Laurette became Benimana's daughter and became *ipso facto* Hutu on paper (*Ibid.*: 62). Despite this rather reassuring piece of information, Marie was not convinced. For her, Jeanne-Laurette was *genetically* a Tutsi but *culturally* a Hutu. Moreover, in her eyes, Anastase Benimana was a Hutu extremist, which Jean-Léonard denied, and that alone turned his stepdaughter into a Hutu extremist (*Ibid.*: 63). As already mentioned, Anastase Benimana and his wife were killed during the genocide by Casmir Kayiru, Benimana's own brother. Finally, Jean-Léonard and Jeanne-Laurette married each other and soon after welcomed their first child. The type of identity crisis presented here is different from the ones described in previous paragraphs. This time the crisis is not observed from the perspective of the character who experienced it. No one single time did Jeanne-Laurette wonder who she was and what type of behaviour that implied. At not a single moment did she fake her attitude and pretend to be someone else. It is rather Marie and parts of her family who were in a deep crisis as their received idea of what Tutsiness meant was suddenly challenged. Even when it became clear that Jeanne-Laurette was *genetically* Tutsi, Marie still smelt Hutuness in her and rejected her. In other words, she was lost, as rejecting Jeanne-Laurette based on her alleged cultural upbringing meant rejecting her own brother and parts of her family. I should add here that a similar crisis is observed in Mbabazi's (2007) *Sheridan*, but this time with a Hutu family that was opposing marriage with a Tutsi girl. When army officer Miko presented Kenya as his fiancée to his sisters, the latter categorically rejected the idea of having a Tutsi in the family. For Zuba and Masaro, it was a scandal that Miko had even thought of marrying a Tutsi, knowing that the Tutsi had attacked the country to re-conquer power (Mbabazi, 2007: 116).

Like Gatore's (2008) *Le passé devant soi* and Sehene's (2005) *Le feu sous la soutane*, Ndwaniye's (2006) *La promesse faite à ma soeur* turns around a half-Hutu character, Jean Seneza. Unlike Niko and Father Stanislas, he manifested no signs of an identity crisis. This might be explained by Jean's 17-year long absence from Rwanda.

Another reason could be that Jean's visit to Rwanda came in a less tense period, when there was no direct ethnic confrontation. It is when there are ethnic tensions such as in the early 1970s and in the 1990s that ethnic identities and identity crises were likely to be exacerbated. However, like the scene at Zaventem airport suggests, Jean seemed aware of the identity dilemmas to which he was exposed. When he approached George, a Hutu character, he felt more warmth (Ndwaniye, 2006: 42), as opposed to the distance he felt when he met Gabriel, a Tutsi character (*Ibid.*: 43). An assumption that could be speculatively made here, is that Jean's twin brother, Thomas, might have experienced a deep identity crisis when he held a machete and stood at a roadblock (*Ibid.*: 71-72), or when, if the accusations were correct, he helped the killers of his sister and her Tutsi husband (*Ibid.*: 73). I should once again remind that Ndwaniye's novel does not provide enough clues regarding ethnicity, hence the difficulty in the analysis of an identity crisis.

Fortunata Uwera also seemed to be going through an identity crisis, albeit beneath the surface (Twagilimana, 1996). Her mother, Celia, was a Tutsi but her biological father, Joseph Nduru, was a Hutu. The novel provides some clues about this crisis when Fortunata told her lover, Mahoro, that she hated her Hutu biological father. Her brothers Miki and Toto went even further to say that they would kill him when they grew up (Twagilimana, 1996: 59). Nduru was the biological father of Fortunata and her three siblings, though the four of them were administratively Kalinda's children. Nduru had broken their family by dating their mother for more than two decades, preventing Kalinda from having even one child with Celia. It is probably this under-the-surface crisis that motivated half-Hutu Fortunata to accept to have sex with her childless, official Tutsi father, to avenge him on her mother, on her biological father and on society at large. This explains why she did not regret the incestuous intercourse, as she had the conviction of assuming 'the role of prophetess of life. She was the voice of vision, the incarnate refusal of annihilation. She was the right person for a vision of life' (*Ibid.*: 255). This crisis is definitely different from the previous ones, because it culminated in an act perceived as heroic – giving life – whereas, the other crises were about killing the Other or torpedoing other people's plans.

The main point from this section is without doubt that whenever a character is described as hesitating about what to do, where to stand, whom to kill or whom to betray, that character is mostly likely a half-Hutu. This type of character dominates Gatore's (2008) *Le passé devant soi* and Sehene's (2005) *Le feu sous la soutane,* and plays a significant role in Mukasonga's (2012) *Notre Dame du Nil*. The first important point to note from these three novels, is that all of the half-Hutu characters, Father Stanislas, Niko, and Modesta, knew that what the Hutu were doing was bad, and yet they still chose to side with them. The second is that the choice was not enough, as each of them had to undergo a test to prove that they were worthy of trust. Even though half-Hutuness does not play a major role in Rurangwa's (2006) *Au sortir de l'enfer*, it nonetheless reveals another interesting dimension relating to mixed identity. Some Tutsi characters do not trust people who are genetically Tutsi with a Hutu cultural upbringing. The same is true in Mbabazi's (2007) *Sheridan*, where some Hutu characters seemed categorical in rejecting a relationship between a Hutu and a Tutsi. A subtler identity crisis is in

Twagilimana's (1996) *Manifold Annihilation*, with a half-Hutu child born into an extra-marital relation, taking an extreme move to give herself a positive role in society.

1.6. Summary and Discussion

This chapter opened with the observation that the characters' main role is to represent human behaviour. For that to happen, they need attributes and a value system that constitutes their identity and defines their perception of the surrounding environment and of society. However, it should be stressed that characters are just characters and not humans. They are rather human-like in the sense that they have names, think, walk, kill and have feelings amongst other attributes. What makes them non-human is the simple fact that they have no existence outside the novel. One important observation is that if they do what humans do in the real world, then they should also be able to recollect the past in their fictional world. This is where cultural memory comes into play and influences the construction of ethnic identities.

The analysis of the construction of Hutuness as an identity was put into five categories that mainly revolve around power and its abuse: [1] Hutu characters who seem systematic in using their power to harm the Tutsi under the Hutu regimes; [2] very few Hutu characters under Hutu regimes who pretend to side with powerful Hutu but do their best to help the Tutsi; [3] Hutu characters under a Tutsi regime who still have some power and use it to harm the Tutsi as well as those who are powerless and confess to abusing their power in the past. These three patterns dominate the construction of Hutuness in Tutsi-authored novels. Unlike them, two of the Hutu-authored novels portrayed [4] Hutu characters as using power in a positive way to rescue the Tutsi, and [5] as possessing the power to resist hardship and injustice and live with them.

The analysis of the construction of Tutsiness resulted in two main conclusions: on the one hand, the six Tutsi-authored novels are unanimous in presenting Tutsi characters as victims. On the other hand, three Hutu-authored novels either portrayed simultaneously some main Tutsi characters as victims and others as zealous Hutu killers, or presented them as Machiavellians keen on killing a maximum amount of Hutu and on subjecting them to suffering.

Two novels, namely Ndwaniye's (2006) *La promesse faite à ma soeur* and Gatore's (2008) *Le passé devant soi* necessitated a different interpretive approach as they do not explicitly assign ethnic identities to its characters. The analysis resulted in conclusions similar to the ones about Hutuness and Tutsiness: power and its abuse seem to be associated with Hutu characters, whereas victimhood seems to be reserved to Tutsi characters. The only difference that these two novels bring is that some Hutu characters are not presented as abusers of power or as people who play a double-game.

The analysis of character identities has also revealed that mixed-identity played a certain role in six novels. What all these characters have in common is confusion about who they were and how their behaviour betrayed that confusion. In some of the cases, they were forced to choose a side and, when they chose the Hutu side as most of them did, they were put to the test. In other cases, a crisis loomed in the background, with families refusing to accept the idea of mixed marriages. In one case, a mixed-identity character engaged in an incestuous relation as a result of that crisis.

I would like to close this chapter with some discussions about a few important points that stem from the analysis presented above. The first point relates to the authors' ethnic identities and their possible interference with the construction of Hutuness and Tutsiness in the novels. Five of the ten authors are Tutsi: Mukasonga, Rusimbi, Rurangwa, Sehene and Twagilimana, and five are Hutu: Gatore, Mbabazi, Ndwaniye, Niwese and Bahufite. If one aligns authors' ethnicity with their construction of Hutuness and Tutsiness in the novels, one comes to the following tables:

Table 1.1. Tutsi authors and their general approach to character ethnic identities.

Tutsi Authors	Hutu characters	Half-Hutu characters	Tutsi characters
Twagilimana (1996)	-Hutu from the north hate the Tutsi -Hutu from the south associated with the Tutsi & victimised	-1 secondary character who behaves like the Tutsi	-All victims, targets
Mukasonga (2012)	-All main characters hate the Tutsi except one	-1 secondary character who is friendly to Tutsi characters	-All victims, targets
Rurangwa (2006)	-All hate the Tutsi except very few	-Absent	-All victims, targets
Rusimbi (1999)	-Absent	-Absent	-All victims, targets
Rusimbi (2007)	-All hate the Tutsi	-Absent	-All victims
Sehene (2005)	-All hate the Tutsi except one	-Main character who hates and kills the Tutsi	-All victims, targets

Table 1.2. Hutu authors and their general approach to character ethnic identities.

Hutu Authors	Hutu characters	Half-Hutu characters	Tutsi characters
Niwese (2001)	-No hatred against the Tutsi	-Absent	-Machiavellian intentions: they killed the Hutu and plan to continue
Ndwaniye (2006)	-No hatred against the Tutsi -Implied victimhood	-1 main character, who shows compassion with Tutsi characters -1 secondary character, who denies genocide allegations	-Implied victimhood
Gatore (2008)	-Anonymous actors who hate the Tutsi -A few sympathise with the Tutsi	-1 main character : forced to hate and kill the Tutsi	-All victims
Mbabazi (2007)	-Many well-intentioned towards the Tutsi -Some hate and kill the Tutsi	-Absent	- Some victims - Some Hutu killers
Bahufite (2016)	-No hatred against the Tutsi	-Absent	-Absent -General reference to the Tutsi

The 'Hutu characters' column in Table 1.1. shows that Tutsi authors tend to emphasise the Hutu's absolute hatred against the Tutsi. Only rare exceptions amongst secondary characters seems to have any sympathy for the Tutsi. The 'Hutu characters' column in Table 1.2. offers the opposite, as Hutu authors tend to choose Hutu characters who rather have sympathy for the Tutsi. Those who engage in killings are anonymous militiamen or a few named militiamen. More interestingly, three of them, excluding Niwese (2001) and Bahufite (2016), converge in portraying Tutsi characters as victims. As for the 'Half-Hutu characters' columns, one realises that Tutsi authors offer a mixed portrayal. Half-Hutu characters are either absent or friendly with Tutsi characters or hate Tutsi characters. In the Hutu authors' novels, the half-Hutu shows either empathy with the Tutsi, faces accusations of genocide or is a ruthless killer. It is interesting to note that both tables contain two extremes: half-Hutu's friendliness/compassion with the Tutsi on the one hand, and their lethal hatred against them on the other.

The main conclusion to which these tables come, is that the 'Hutu characters' and the 'Tutsi characters' columns reflects more or less memory dynamics in post-genocide Rwanda. On the one hand the dominant, government-sponsored narrative categorises all Hutu as collectively guilty of genocide and all Tutsi as victims, which is the stance that all Tutsi-authored novels have taken. On the other hand, there is a counter-narrative, dominant in three of the five Hutu-authored novels [Niwese, 2001; Mbabazi, 2007 & Bahufite, 2016] that rejects that black-and-white simplification and points a finger at the Tutsi as killers of Hutu civilians. The conclusion that the government-sponsored narrative dominates or is present in one way or another in eight out of the 11 novels, is in line with the theories about the relationship between literature and memory, especially the observation that 'literary works resort to culturally predominant ideas of memory, and, through their literary techniques, represent these ideas in an aesthetically condensed form' (Neumann, 2008: 335). The recent launch of the so-called *Ndi Umunyarwanda* [I am Rwandan] campaign exacerbates in a more explicit way this 'all Hutu are killers and all Tutsi are victims' politics of memory.[7] Tutsi authors seem to have followed the dominant narrative to the letter, whereas two of their Hutu counterparts [Ndwaniye (2006) & Gatore (2008)] seem to have inserted some nuances.

---

7   Launching the *Ndi Umunyarwanda* campaign during a youth gathering on 30th June 2013, President Paul Kagame (2013) suggested that all Hutu people were guilty and explained what they should be doing collectively (more about this in Section 2.5).

Chapter 2

Character Names

Names in the Rwandan culture play a very important role and reflect to a great extent the zeitgeist that prevails at the time when they are given. As such, they function as memory instruments, as they condense into a few syllables or in full sentence formulations, what the parents, usually the father, want everybody else to remember when they see, talk or refer to the name bearer. For this reason, brothers and sisters do not automatically inherit their father's name, which is the case in many western cultures. In addition to archiving a certain moment in the past, names often serve as mission statements that assign certain tasks to be accomplished by the bearer in the future (see extensive discussion on Rwandan names in Nyirubugara, 2013: 97-116).

Naming as a memory mechanism is central to this chapter, as it investigates character naming patterns in the 11 novels under scrutiny. If novels represent human behaviour as explained at the beginning of the previous chapter, what would logically follow is that character naming patterns would show most of the characteristics of names in the real world. The reader is frustrated when cultural basics such as naming patterns are not respected. One good example is Diop's (2000) novel *Murambi*, which is set up in post-genocide Rwanda but violates one key Rwandan naming principle. At a certain point one comes across a business*man* called Abel *Mujawamariya* (*Ibid*.: 380) and feels betrayed by the author who, by deciding to write a novel of memory about Rwanda, tacitly agreed to respect that society's cultural rules. A man can *never* be called Mujawamariya, *Mary's Servant*, in Rwanda, as *Muja-* automatically indicates, without any possible exception, that the bearer is a woman. *Muja-* is like the prefix *Muka-*, which means *wife of…* such as in *Muka*mugema, *Mugema's wife*. Naming a male character Mujawamariya is like naming him Mukamugema, which becomes like a stone in the reader's shoe.

This chapter investigates the character naming patterns and attempts to answer the following question: What memory messages do character names convey? This question contains a number of assumptions, namely that character naming has a purpose and that that purpose bridges the past and the future. I open this chapter with a short theoretical discussion about character naming, before analysing names assigned to Hutu, Tutsi and half-Hutu/half-Tutsi characters.

2.1. Beyond the Name

Novelists rarely, if at all, choose their names by accident. They have a reason to select a specific name for a specific character, to whom they attribute a certain behaviour and assign a specific task. The name has to fit the behaviour, otherwise there will be dissonance. Theorists converge in considering the name as a crucial element in understanding characters and their behaviour in the novel. In this section, I want to briefly review relevant academic discussions around character naming. My goal in doing so is to pave the way for my analysis of character names in the 11 novels.

Character naming works more or less like naming in real life (Hochman, 1985: 37) and fulfils a number of functions. If, in a given society, a name functions as an indicator of someone's descent, then naming in novels about that society should follow the same rules. If a name signals someone's gender and circumstances under which one was born in a given culture, such as in Rwanda, then character names in novels about that culture should fulfil the same function. The most important function of character names is without doubt 'individuation', because characters need to be easily distinguishable from one another (Docherty, 1983: 43). By mentioning a character name in a novel, the author wants the reader to immediately think about all the attributes he or she has assigned to the character (Bal, [1985] 1997: 123). So the name is a condensed way of evoking one's qualities and, because of that, is a way of creating expectations in the reader's mind about how that character behaves.

Novelists often choose names with a historical or emblematic connotation for their characters (Lamarque, 2009: 177; Bal, [1985] 1997: 119-120). Those names send the reader to the reputation of the figure, who is usually a public figure whom people should know, or to the popular image that a specific emblematic figure has in popular culture, e.g., in a tale, a myth or a legend. For instance, De Villiers' (2000) *Enquête sur un genocide* [*Investigating genocide*] names one character Charles Lizinde, who is a former colonel in the intelligence department of the RPF army (De Villiers, 2000: 29). Even though Charles was not the first name of the historical Colonel Lizinde – his was Théoneste – all the rest, e.g., his disgrace from the RPF, his exile in Nairobi and his assassination on the street in that city, inevitably sends the reader to the historical Colonel Lizinde. If a name like Ngunda was to be used in a novel, one would immediately expect the character bearing that name to behave like the emblematic Ngunda in popular tales in Rwanda. He would work hard and eat and drink until his stomach explodes.

Historical characters like Colonel Lizinde have one advantage: they make the reader confident about the character's identity. They also make it easy for the author to be creative about his or her behaviour, provided that it fits in with the set of behaviours his or her reputation permits him or her to have. This could also be considered to be a disadvantage because, once one has chosen a ready-made identity from real life, one's creativity is limited as real-life reputation imposes restrictions (Bal, [1985] 1997: 120). In this respect, if De Villiers had made Colonel Lizinde a Tutsi rather than a Hutu, his novel would have lost all credibility, because the historical Colonel Lizinde was an anti-Tutsi officer before breaking up with President Habyarimana in the early 1980s. Despite close resemblance between novel characters and historical characters, the former are still symbolic as they are deprived of any existence in the real world (Hochman, 1985: 117; Schmid, 2010: 31-32).

One important aspect of character naming for the novels I am analysing in this book is what I would like to call *semiotic names*. These are names that are crafted in such a way that they have both a literal meaning and a figurative one. Eco (2011: 101-102) held that proper nouns, including character names, should not be considered as self-contained but rather as pegs on which certain properties hang. Like other semiotic objects, thus, character names have referents and provide clues that guide the reader in his or her search for those referents (*Ibid.*). The reader obviously plays an interesting role as a co-creator of the character (Docherty, 1983: 15; Hochman, 1985: 32 & 36) and that co-creation heavily depends on the command, [or lack of it], of the language, the culture and the history/memory that is underlying in the novel. As the name is a linguistic, cultural construct that means more than the few letters put together, it allows for the opportunity that some names can ring a bell in the mind of the readers who are able to retrieve the implied referent, whereas they pass by unnoticed for those who do not or cannot retrieve the referent. As a consequence, the outer description of the character that the name encapsulates leads to different conceptualisations of characters' innermost motives (Docherty, 1983: 7), depending on what the reader does, or does not do, with the name.

In short, this section has suggested that character names are not another detail in character descriptions. They are rather crucial cues that invite readers to keep the real world in the back of their mind, whilst staying in the possible world of the novel. This interference between the real world and the fictional world through character names involves, to a great extent, the reader's background and prior knowledge. Managing to retrieve the figurative meaning of a character name requires more than the willingness to read the novel. One has to consider each name as a semiotic object, before proceeding to search for what it might mean and connecting its meaning to the character's behaviour. That is what I want to do in the next three sections where I build on my argument in *Complexities and Dangers* (Nyirubugara, 2013), that naming in Rwandan culture is a complex memory-archiving mechanism. Since novels represent human behaviour and culture, logically, it would follow on that naming in Rwandan-authored novels about Rwanda would reflect similar memory functions. So in the next three sections I systematically analyse names attributed to the main and secondary Hutu, Tutsi, half-Hutu and half-Tutsi characters, in search of possible memory referents. My aim in analysing those character names along ethnic lines is to find out if there are ethnic patterns, and if so, to compare them.

2.2. Hutu Character Names

After the analysis of the main patterns in the construction of Hutuness (Section 1.2), I would like to identify the patterns that the naming of Hutu characters followed and discuss their memory implications. Since the name, the Self, and identity are intimately linked to one another in the Rwandan culture, my hypothesis here is that there should be some correlation between the abuser of power and the Tutsi-killer markers of Hutuness and the names the Hutu characters receive. Similarly, I would expect those novels that constructed Hutuness around victimhood, rescue, and resistance to hardships, to provide Hutu characters with corresponding names. In other words, one should be able to identify a character's ethnic identity and predict their behaviour based on the name that character is given. This analysis does not include Rusimbi's (1999) *By the Time She Returned* for the simple reason that it does not have a single Hutu character.

The first type of Hutu character names is one that includes names that fall under what I call the *land-work name category*. These names explicitly or implicitly refer to agriculture and related land work in general. For instance, in Mukasonga's (2012) *Notre Dame du Nil*, the main Hutu character is named Gloriosa Nyiramasuka, which the author rightly translates in the novel as *Celle-de-la-houe* or 'The one belonging to the hoe' (Mukasonga: 2012: 28). It is crucial here to discuss both the first name and the surname simultaneously, because the combination has a memory, political and ideological significance. The first name, Gloriosa, implies the Hutu glory during the First Republic [1961-1973] in which the novel is set, whereas the surname clearly refers to the Hutu as a soil-tilling ethnic group. This reference is reinforced by the many passages in which Nyiramasuka repeated that her anti-Tutsi rhetoric and actions made her worthy of her name (e.g., *Ibid.*: 31-32 & 203). In other words, her name made her a 'true Hutu' and gave her the mission to do what a true Hutu had to do, i.e., harm and kill the Tutsi.

Rurangwa's (2006) *Au sortir de l' enfer* contains many other examples that followed the same logic, as almost all Hutu characters bear loaded names. The *Kangura* journalist who killed the Benimanas, a Tutsi family, is named Célestin Sembagare, a name that literally means, *The one who belongs to weeds*. Weeding is a crucial step in the agricultural system in Rwanda and, because of that, refers explicitly to land work and its association with Hutuness. Also, the Hutu extremist who wanted to recruit Juma, the houseboy at the Benimanas', is called Butihoro, a name whose last part, *horo*, is the radical of the Kinyarwanda word for machete [Umu*horo*] (Rurangwa, 2006: 16-17). Like the hoe, the machete in Rwandan culture is an essential tool for land work [e.g., clearing the bush before tilling the soil, harvesting sorghum, etc.], and is associated with Hutuness. Another Hutu character, whom Jean-Léonard came across in a pub in Brussels, is named Gervais Sefuku, with the surname literally meaning, *The one who belongs to/looks like the mole* (Rurangwa, 2006 :131-132). That animal is known for the ravages it causes by digging beneath the surface and mostly eating up the tubers it finds there. In a way, it tills the soil like the Hutu.

The name Sefuku, *The one who belongs to/looks like the mole*, is interesting in the sense that it implicitly refers to land work, but also because it gives an animal name to a Hutu character. Rurangwa used names from this *animal name category* several times throughout his novel. For instance, while discussing with his Tutsi friend in a pub in Brussels, Jean-Léonard showed him another Rwandan in the bar named Jérémie Kajangwe, *The small cat*, a Hutu who studied chemistry in Brussels. Jérémie, or Jeremiah, is also highly meaningful here, because when Kajangwe heard that his parents had been killed in Tingi Tingi refugee camps [Democratic Republic of Congo], he started *lamenting*, like the biblical Jeremiah, to whoever would be willing to listen to him, blaming the Tutsi for the killing of his family (*Ibid.*: 134). Jean-Léonard and his friend also came across Théodore Gakwavu, *The small rabbit*, a former Physics professor at the National University of Rwanda, who had gone mad because of the death of a Tutsi family that was killed by his own brother as they hid in his own home. Gakwavu would spend his days haunted by that killing and begging for forgiveness (*Ibid.*:135-136). Mukasonga also named one Hutu character Kabwa, *The small dog*. Dog in Rwandan culture refers to any person who has no sense of honour and is not brave and trustworthy. On her way to Rubanga, a Tutsi sorcerer who used to be a royal adviser, Virginia stopped to enquire about the way. That is when Kabwa came into play. He took her to Rubanga but only after she had given him some donuts and a bottle of soda (Mukasonga, 2012: 132-135). The boy is a *small dog*, because it is not honourable to ask for a reward before showing the way to a stranger.

Unlike Rurangwa and Mukasonga who crafted loaded names themselves or borrowed animal names, Rusimbi (2007) used names that fall under the *historical/emblematic name category* for two of his three Hutu characters. One is named Rucagu, the one who brutally evicted Tutsi survivors from Hutu properties (Rusimbi, 2007: 30) and made some wrong decisions about the location of the survivors' new homes (*Ibid.*: 82). Rusimbi explicitly sent the reader to the historical Rucagu, currently in charge of The *Intore* [patriotism training] programme, when Harriet [Tutsi survivor] wondered if Rucagu was the one she had read about in the media and in human right reports:

> The name Rucagu appeared on the human rights list of people who had planned and executed genocide in Rwanda. Was he the man or someone else with a similar name? It must be a cursed name I thought to myself (*Ibid.*: 30).

The same is true for the name Karamira, given to the Hutu character accused of having led a militia that killed a lot of Tutsi in the village. Once again, Rusimbi provides enough explicit cues that send the reader to Frodouald Karamira. Like the historical Karamira, the fictional Karamira is arrested, tried, found guilty of genocide and shot by a firing squad in public (*Ibid.*: 67-68 & 107-108). The difference between the historical Karamira and the fictional Karamira is that the former was Frodouald rather than Joseph. Another difference is that Frodouald was a prominent member of the MDR [*Mouvement Démocratique Républicain*] whereas Joseph was a member of *Interahamwe* militia.

Even though Twagilimana's (1996) *Manifold Annihilation* named only a few Hutu characters, or simply named some characters without specifying whether or not they were Hutu or Tutsi, it nonetheless offered at least one instance of a Hutu character named with an emblematic name. However, before reaching that emblematic name, one has to do some interpretive gymnastics. One man is [nick-]named Omega and is described as a powerful Hutu from the north, serving as prefect [governor] of Ruhengeri in the early 1990s (Twagilimana, 1996: 165). The description takes the reader to the historical figure of *Z* or *Grand Z*, the short name for Zigiranyirazo. From here, the link between Z and Ω as the last letters of the Roman and Greek alphabets, respectively, becomes obvious. However, Omega seems to add a symbolic dimension, especially if one associates it with the following biblical statement: 'I am the Alpha and the Omega, the First and the Last, the Beginning and the End'. In the novel, Omega behaved like someone who had the last word, someone who could not be contradicted or defied. For instance, when he ordered all the stock of plaster to be taken from Ruhengeri hospital's pharmacy to his house that was under construction, neither the French director nor the chief pharmacist could prevent it from happening (*Ibid.*: 166-168).

Another emblematic name is Saligoma, which Rurangwa (2006: 49) gave to Jean-Léonard's houseboy, and which falls under the emblematic names that has a negative connotation. It is derived from the French *sale gamin*, or dirty boy, and the word is used in everyday language and popular culture to refer to young [street] boys with deviant behaviour. That is what Saligoma reflected in *Au sortir de l' enfer*, when he guided Sembagare to Jean-Léonard, his own boss (*Ibid.*: 87).

The third Hutu character in Rusimbi's (2007) *The Hyena's Wedding* falls under the *Tutsi-the-Other name category* as it refers in some way to the Tutsi without explicitly naming them. That character is named Mbarimombazi, a loaded name that literally means *I live among them* [enemies] *and I know them*. This character was not explicitly identified as a Hutu but his description and the comments that Kiroko, the Tutsi local leader made, put him in the Hutu category. Poor and hungry, Mbarimombazi reported to the counter where young volunteers were registering to build houses for Tutsi survivors. Mbarimombazi wanted to join the solidarity camp together with his wife and six children, not because he wanted to help, but because he wanted his family to have something to eat. Kiroko's comment revealed his Hutuness when he said: 'I envied him, for his family was never affected by genocide yet he was a Hutu or Tutsi, for it was our responsibility to uproot the differences' (Rusimbi, 2007: 86). The fact that he was unknown to Kiroko, that his family had not been affected by the genocide, that he did not associate his poverty to genocide and that he was not in need of a house, places him amongst the Hutu characters. Mbarimombazi's name suggests that there was an enemy around and leads to the deduction that he would eliminate them as soon as possible, if he had the means. This takes us back to power and abuse of power that is associated with Hutuness in most novels (Section 1.2). This name implies that if he had the power to annihilate the enemies, he would do so.

Ngendabanga, *I walk forward but they push me back*, the name of the former Hutu minister in exile in The Empire [Belgium] (Niwese, 2001), falls under the same category. However, 'they' in this name does not seem to exclusively refer to the Tutsi Other. All the efforts he made seemed in vain because some other forces would prevent him from succeeding. When he was arrested on the suspicion that he had killed Lemaître, the Tutsi-dominated government rejoiced and published a press release to congratulate itself for the arrest of a renowned genocide criminal (Niwese, 2001: 57). In addition, his reflections on a better Rwanda always referred to the Tutsi system as an obstacle. 'They' can also be associated with the system in The Empire that prevented him from having a legal status, which, in his eyes, meant life.

The name of Sylvestre Nagahima, *The small Hima*, that Rurangwa (2006: 114-116) gave to the Hutu character who abducted Jean-Léonard's wife, Jeanne-Laurette, and turned her into his sexual slave even in the refugee camps in eastern Zaïre [DR Congo], falls under the same category. The surname pejoratively refers to the Hima, a Tutsi subgroup in north-eastern Rwanda [also present in southern Uganda and north-eastern DR Congo], and suggests that the Tutsi/Hima are, or should be, inferior and should submit to the Hutu. This explains in part the sexual enslavement of Jeanne-Laurette. Hutuness is also present in this name through Sylvestre which, despite being a Christian name, refers to the wood or forest and, by extension, to land work. Nagahima, like Mbarimombazi, refers to the Tutsi as the Other who deserves no humane treatment and who is inherently ill-intentioned.

It is worth noting here that names like Nagahima, *The small Hima*, Kajangwe, *The small cat*, and Gakwavu, *The small rabbit*, all have in common the fact that they are pejorative. So is the name Casmir Kayiru, *The small servant*, given to a Hutu character in Rurangwa's (2006) *Au sortir de l' enfer*. Old Kinyarwanda borrowed the term *umuyiru*, the servant of the royal drum, from Ankole, a region in southern Uganda. That term became *umwiru*, a title given to the guardians of the esoteric code [like a Constitution] of the monarchy. The name Kayiru here is used in the primary sense of 'servant' associated with intensive and tiring work. One finds it in the term *Icyumweru*, meaning *ikiruhuko cy'umuyiru*, or resting day for the servant. Icyumweru in modern-day Kinyarwanda means Sunday, a day on which most people rest. Kayiru, then, becomes *the small servant* or *the small Hutu*. He is described in the novel as an extremist militant of the CDR, the Hutu-only *Coalition pour la Défense de la République* (Rurangwa, 2006: 57-58). He is the one who killed his own brother, Anastase Benimana, before raping his sister-in-law (*Ibid.*: 77-78).

One name that is negatively connoted but does not fall into any of the categories outlined above, is Joseph Nduru, *The noise maker*, which is the name of the man who broke Kalinda's family by appropriating his wife and producing four children with her. Nduru was a powerful and rich Hutu from the north, and his name fits perfectly to his behaviour. Making noise usually means preventing two or more people from communicating. It interferes with good communication. That is exactly what Nduru did by causing separation between Celia and Kalinda, thereby causing distress and misfortune in that family (Twagilimana, 1996: 56 57). He did the same with another couple after Celia's death, but this time he was caught red-handed and was shot by the cheated husband (*Ibid.*: 255-256).

The next category is one that comprises *names with positive connotations*. These names can be divided into two sub-categories: firstly, one can distinguish those names provided to exceptional Hutu characters who happened to be friendly to the Tutsi against all odds. Secondly, one can identify names with positive connotation without any apparent motivation or explanation. Immaculée Mukagatare, *Pure-hearted girl/woman*, falls under the *exceptional-good-Hutu name category* because, unlike all other Hutu characters, she warned her Tutsi classmates, told them where to hide, and even took them to safety during the massacre (Mukasonga, 2012). The name Immaculée Mukagatare is very interesting because of its meaning and its relation to the bearer's behaviour. The fact that both the first name and the surname mean the same thing – purity of the heart – suggests that Mukasonga wanted to present her as an exceptional Hutu, who confirmed the rule that all the others were, in principle, not pure-hearted. Juma, a Muslim name that refers to Friday, the day dedicated to prayers, falls under this exceptional and rare Hutu category. His name relates to piety and his behaviour in saving Jean-Léonard was coherent with that name (Rurangwa, 2006).

Like Mukagatare and Juma, Mukamana, *The one who belongs to God* or *The divine woman*, received a positively connoted name and behaved accordingly in Mbabazi's (2007) novel. Mukamana was a Hutu woman from the north west (Mbabazi, 2007: 191) and, contrary to what Twagilimana's novel suggests about the Hutu from that region, played the good Samaritan role when badly wounded Kenya and Gatete came to her (*Ibid*.: 177). She called another Hutu anaesthetist to come and help heal their wounds, allowed them to make a call with her telephone and pleaded in favour of Gatete and another Tutsi woman whom militiamen came to take in her home (*Ibid*.: 184-185). Mukamana's *divine* heart inspired her to give the identity card of her diseased sister to Kenya, allowing her to cross all roadblocks on their way to Mukamana's parents in Gisenyi (*Ibid*.: 186).

It could be argued that *Sheridan* presents the good Hutu as the rule and the bad ones as the exception. This is embodied in the name of one of the main characters, Miko. The name Miko refers to the sacred tree of *umuko* or Erythrina, whose religious name is *umurinzi*. It is under this tree that Ryangombe, the founder of the cult of *kubandwa*, took his last breath after a buffalo killed him. Since then, all initiation rites had to take place under that tree, which is believed to have protective and healing powers. The religious name *umurinzi* itself means 'the tree that protects'. That tree can never be used as firewood.[8] With this background, the name Miko emerges as a sacred one that means 'The protector'. As a commander of a special unit within the government army, Miko is presented as carrying out Superman-like operations behind the Tutsi rebels' lines to *protect* his country (Mbabazi, 2007: 181; 213 & 235-236). As a lover, he is described as someone who was ready to protect his Tutsi fiancée, Kenya, against his sisters and against the killers.

The other positively connoted names do not have any obvious motivation and some are even inconsistent with the behaviour of their bearers. The names used in Gatore's (2008) *Le passé devant soi* and Ndwaniye's (2006) *La promesse faite à ma soeur*, seem to contain no specific meaning, as both novels avoid to explicitly discuss ethnicity. As I suggested earlier (Section 1.4), both novels tend to camouflage ethnicity or to hide it altogether, even though they provide a few cues that permit to draw some conclusions about characters' implied ethnicity. Another important aspect is that both authors are Hutu, which might have played a role in their choices. The fact is that Gatore named three Hutu fugitives on the mysterious island Uwitonze, *The Quiet*, Uwera, *The Pure*, and Shema, *The Proud* (Gatore, 2008: 14), without any relation to their behaviour vis-à-vis the Tutsi characters. As for Ndwaniye, only the main character, Jean Seneza, *The kind-hearted* (Ndwaniye, 2006: 33) which I discuss in Section 2.4, and Nkundiye, *The one who loves*, the old man who believed in jailed Thomas's innocence, are given positively connoted Rwandan surnames.

It is worth mentioning the inconsistency that is observable in the names Zuba, *The Sun*, and Masaro, *Pearls*, that Mbabazi (2007) gave to Miko's sisters. The idea of the sun is that it gives light, warmth and life to living beings, whereas the idea of pearls is that they are beautiful and provoke pleasure. Instead of behaving as people who provided light, warmth and pleasure, they instead had evil thoughts

---

8 See Pauwels (1958: 112-139) for an extensive discussion about Ryangombe and the cult of *Kubandwa*.

about the Tutsi in general, and about Kenya and her stepsisters in particular. They pledged to do all they could to prevent Miko from marrying Kenya. Masaro even plotted to have Kenya killed, whereas the latter naively counted on her as a future sister-in-law (Mbabazi, 2007: 116-119). The same seems to be true with the name Hogoza, *The beautiful and awe-inspiring woman*, given to Ngenda's wife (Niwese, 2001). The name suggests that the bearer is not only beautiful but also reasonable. Hogoza's behaviour, marrying Ngenda because he was a minister and abandoning him because he was poor in exile, contradicts the mission conveyed in that positively connoted name.

The last category of Hutu character names is the one I call the *no-meaning name category*, which includes first names that are not accompanied by Rwandan surnames and other names that have no obvious meanings. Apart from the two main characters, Niko and Isaro, both of whom I discuss in Section 2.4, and the fugitives on the island, all other Hutu characters in Gatore's (2008) novel are called by their Christian names such as Gaspard, Antoine, Alphonse. The same is true for Damascène in Sehene's (2005) novel, for Frida, Goretti, Godelive as well as Herménégilde in Mukasonga's (2012) novel and also for Mama Jackie in Rurangwa's (2006) novel. On its part, Bahufite's (2016) novel does not provide any single character with a Rwandan name. The main character is Nadine, her daughter Aline, her best friend Céline, his 50-year-old protector in the Zairean farms, Vianney, etc. However, in a few cases, Christian names seem to fall under historical names, especially when all other indices impose a clear association between the first name and the last name or between the first name and the circumstances and context in which the character is evolving. This is the case for Paul in Sehene's (2005) *Le feu sous la soutane*. By giving the first name of 'Paul' to the director of the Hotel des Mille Collines where Tutsi refugees found shelter and by suggesting that Paul is married to a Tutsi wife, Sehene wanted the reader to think about Paul Rusesabagina (Sehene, 2005: 37), whose story is told in Terry George's film *Hotel Rwanda* (2004). The no-meaning names also include names like Amato, Kadeyi, *Old piece of cloth*, and Matamata which Mbabazi's (2007) novel attributed to Hutu characters.

The foregoing has shown that the names given to most Hutu characters are not fortuitous. They seem to have a meaning beyond their surface, and that meaning often has a link to Rwanda's cultural memory. Through their names, some Hutu characters are associated with land work which is traditionally thought to be a Hutu activity. Other names bring back to mind historical figures who played a role in Rwanda's recent politics and genocide memory. Yet others refer to the relationships between the Hutu and the Tutsi and the tensions that underlie them. It was also pointed out that several names falling under the above-mentioned categories are either animal names or formulated in a pejorative way. One major conclusion one could draw at this stage is that apart from the Christian and other no-meaning names that some novelists used, most Hutu character names have a negative connotation or are cast in a negative light. The few that are positively connoted either imply that good Hutu are exceptional and rare or are inconsistent with the characters' behaviour. This analysis partly confirms my hypothesis that there is some correlation between the abuse of power aspect and its negativity with the names given to Hutu characters. It also supports the observation that the few novels that constructed Hutuness in a positive way have provided Hutu characters with names that correspond to that identity construction. I have to add that I have refrained from discussing the names borne by the few Hutu characters married to Tutsi women. I thought it would make more sense to discuss them in Section 2.4, when I analyse the names given to half-Hutu and half-Tutsi characters.

2.3. Tutsi Character Names

So far, character names have been approached as a central element in revealing ethnic identities and related memories as they appear in fictional Rwanda. This section aims to take the analysis further by attempting to categorise Tutsi character names and to identify ways in which they relate to cultural memory. The working hypothesis in this section is that the names given to Tutsi characters are in harmony with their victimhood status or consistent with the Machiavellian and zealous-Hutu-killer status' they have in two novels. My analysis follows the same logic that guided the previous section, which means that firstly I identify the overarching categories before comparatively discussing individual names and how they fit into specific categories.

Some of the authors of the novels under scrutiny tend to give Tutsi characters names which suggest their innocence and all other related attributes. This is the case in Mukasonga's (2012) *Notre Dame du Nil*, where the sole Tutsi students in the novel are named Virginia Mutamuriza, *Don't make her cry* or *Don't hurt her* [because she's innocent] (Mukasonga, 2012: 126-127) and Veronica Tumurinde, *Let's protect her* [because she's innocent] (*Ibid.*: 69). These two surnames clearly indicate that the bearers were exposed to danger and that they needed protection. They also imply that no one could have a reason to make Virginia cry, because she was innocent or to harm Veronica, as she was supposed to be protected. Another name closely related to Mutamuriza and Tumurinde is Umutesi, *The well treated child,* born by one of Kenya's stepsisters in Mbabazi's (2007: 100) novel. The same is true for Gatete, *Let the small girl be well treated*, in the same novel (*Ibid.*: 176). The implication behind these names is that the bearers are so pure and innocent that nothing could justify any bad treatment being brought against them. What is even more interesting in relation to Mutamuriza and Tumurinde is the use of Christian names that equally bring to mind the notion of innocence. Virginia brings to mind the idea of virginity, which reinforces the observation that she is equally impeccable in the sexual sense. In the same vein, Veronica sends one to Saint Veronica, the woman who wiped Jesus' face with a towel as he was carrying his cross. Veronica brings innocence to mind because, unlike most other women in Jerusalem, Saint Veronica believed in Jesus' innocence and went forward to help him, which, in a sense, was protecting him from sweat and blood which were flowing down his face.

The idea of protection and victimhood is also contained in the names of Victor Kalinda in Twagilimana's (1996) novel. The name Kalinda stems from the verb *Kurinda* or *kulinda*, which can either mean 'to protect' or 'to wait for someone'.[9]

---

9   This verb is also used to refer to female mammals [cows, goats, etc.] coming into heat and seeking a male for mating purposes. This meaning is irrelevant to the discussion.

Kalinda, thus, can both mean *The Protector* and *The one who is waiting*. Kalinda's behaviour was consistent with these two meanings, both of which imply the ideas of protecting himself against death under the yoke of the oppressive Hutu regime and of waiting for the moment he could produce a child to rescue his blood from extinction. Talking to Mahoro, Kalinda summed up this double-meaning of his name by saying: 'They killed us, but many refused to die. They can do anything they want now. I've conquered the sublime. ...But strong, we emerged from annihilation' (Twagilimana, 1996: 34-35). This quote shows that Kalinda not only refused to die by protecting himself, but also because after a time of waiting, they could come and kill him. He had won, hence the first name Victor.

It is worthwhile noting the way in which Sehene used many first names, without ever adding surnames. Most of those names relate to the Roman Catholic faith, perhaps because his novel is about a Catholic priest and contains a certain notion of innocence about them. For instance, one of the Tutsi women whom Father Stanislas took to the presbytery to abuse her sexually, was named Assumpta (Sehene, 2005: 102-104). This name refers to the Virgin Mary, whose fidelity and virginity are believed to have been rewarded with the Assumption of her body to Heaven. With this name, a suggestion is made that what Father Stanislas did to Assumpta is the opposite of what the name suggests. In the same vein, another woman abused by Father Stanislas was named Dafrose (*Ibid*.: 63-64), a name that takes the reader to Saint Dafrose who, in 362 A.D., was martyred because of her faith.[10] Martyrdom supposes that one is trying to do the good, or has done nothing wrong, and that someone else with ill-intentions punishes one with death.

Innocence is also implied in the name Hyacinthe that Gatore gave to a Tutsi girl whom Hutu militiamen hunted down and captured before killing her (Gatore, 2008: 124-125 & 127). Before being associated with a first name, the hyacinth is a 'pleasant-smelling plant with a lot of small flowers that grow close together around one thick stem'.[11] All in all this flower seems pleasant and beautiful and there is no obvious reason that would justify cutting such a plant.

Unlike Sehene who used first names alone and very rarely in combination with Kinyarwanda surnames, Rurangwa seems to play more with the implicit meanings of his Tutsi characters' names. As the previous section has shown, he did the same for his Hutu characters. The main character, who is a Tutsi, is named Jean-Léonard Benimana, *The children of God* (Rurangwa, 2006: 15). Obviously, unlike the children of the Devil, the children of God are innocent by definition. The same name was given to a Hutu character but I will discuss this in the next section.

Rurangwa chose the name Emmanuel Sakindi, *The uncertain* (*Ibid*.: 66-67), for another Tutsi character who was a successful businessman before the genocide. *Sakindi* is the beginning of a popular proverbial expression, *Sakindi izaba ibyara ikindi*, that means 'the future will tell [as no one is certain about what the future reserves]'. Despite his intelligence, Sakindi was not admitted into secondary education, because he was a Tutsi. He ventured into business in eastern Congo

---

10 Martyrologe Romain publié par l'ordre de Grégoire XIII (Paris: Adrien Le Clere et Compagnie, 1830), p. 5.
11 Cambridge Advanced Learner's Dictionary. 3rd Edition (Cambridge: Cambridge University Press, 2009), p. 708.

and in Burundi and started an ironsmith business in Kigali. His wealth allowed him to lend money to President Habyarimana's cabinet ministers and to senior army officers, but the latter never paid him back. Instead, they threatened him with imprisonment. This uncertainty was confirmed when he was imprisoned as an accomplice of the RPF rebels in October 1990. What is clear here is that Sakindi lived in a constant state of victimhood (Section 1.3) marked by constant uncertainty. In addition to that innocence, he was even 'kind', perhaps naïve, as he would lend money to those who would never pay him back. All he got in return was jail and probably death during the genocide. For this particular character, Rurangwa seems to have chosen the first name Emmanuel – God is with us – on purpose. Emmanuel refers to Jesus, Son of God [Benimana = children of God], and its combination with Sakindi, *The uncertain*, might be interpreted as Innocence confronted with constant uncertainty.

Another combination of first and last names that perfectly reflects this idea of innocence and uncertainty is Jean Mahoro, the name of the main Tutsi character in Twagilimana's (1996) novel. Mahoro means *Peace* or *Peace-maker*, or *The Peaceful*, or *Pacific*. This name suggests that there is turmoil and some fighting that victimises innocent people. In this case, the Tutsi and, to a lesser extent, the Hutu from the south, are presented as the innocent victims of the violence and injustice imposed by the Hutu from the north. Adding Jean brings the notion of uncertainty in the name. Like the Biblical Jean [John], Mahoro received a revelation at the beginning of the novel and a mission to denounce injustice. The hanging dead man in his nightmare wanted him to write a book that would contain 'The revelations I couldn't reveal':

> I couldn't share my vision with anybody. Share it with everybody. Share the suffering of the past, the wreckage of the present, and the hope for the future. Don't distort my vision. The past was mine to suffer. I offer you the future. I'll haunt you until the completion of the task (Twagilimana, 1996: 14).

As this quote shows, the dead man is sure about the past but uncertain about the future. He is sure about violated innocence in the past, but needs a preacher [Evangelist like John] to prevent it from happening in the future.

A similar notion of innocence coupled with uncertainty can be observed in the name Harriet Uwaje, *The one who came*, the cousin and wife of the main character, Kiroko, in Rusimbi's (2007) *The Hyena's Wedding*. Usually Uwaje is the short form of Uwajeneza, *The one who came under perfect circumstances* [e.g., right after famine had ended; right after the father had secured a job; etc.]. Harriet never knew who her father was, as her mother got pregnant before even completing high school. The father had preferred to continue his secondary education rather than starting a family. He later became the principal of the school that Kiroko and Harriet were attending when the genocide broke out. Harriet and Kiroko learnt from the former's aunt that their fathers, both of whom died during genocide, were brothers (Rusimbi, 2007: 35-36). This story tells us implicitly why the author used Uwaje, *The one who came*, rather than Uwajeneza, *The one who came under perfect circumstances*. It also tells us that Harriet was *innocent* in all that, because, as the aunt told her, 'I do not blame you. Perhaps it is your mother, myself and the society that has lost values' (*Ibid.*: 35). It is interesting to note here that *society* was blamed for what happened between Kalisa, Harriet's father, and her mother. Society was so unfair to the Tutsi at that time that Kalisa could not permit himself to jeopardise his future by halting his studies. Aware of that, the mother accepted the sacrifice to enable Kalisa to keep studying. Considering that Harriet was 12-years old (*Ibid.*: 17) when the genocide broke out, one concludes that Kalisa's adventure with her mother took place in the early 1980s, a peaceful period marked by Tutsi exclusion in certain sectors. So the name Uwaje not only takes the reader to that time, but also grants absolution to all Tutsi characters involved.

Another important category is one that comprises names that imply bravery or heroism. One recurrent and popular type of names that falls under this category is one that ends with -*gabo*, a radical name that implies manliness. 'Man' [umu*gabo*] in Kinyarwanda has nothing to do with gender [*Umuhungu* refers to the masculine gender], but rather refers to a set of values: bravery, courage, trustworthiness, honour, etc. Its opposite is *imbwa* [dog. See discussion about Kabwa in Section 2.2]. More than any other novelist, Rusimbi used -*gabo* names for his Tutsi characters in his two novels. In *By the Time She Returned*, Rusimbi (1999) named the brother of the main character Kaitesi, Seba, which is the shortened version of Seba*gabo*, *The one who belongs to men*. Despite his poor refugee life in a slum of Kampala, Seba is described as a man of honour, who kept visiting and assisting his mother in the refugee settlement and who reminded everyone that Rwanda and its values should keep guiding the refugees (Rusimbi, 1999: 18-19). In that same novel, one comes across Mugabo, the Rwandan with the highest rank amongst the victorious Ugandan rebels who became the army chief. Mugabo's senior position in the army and those occupied by other Rwandan officers provoked jealousy and animosity amongst indigenous Ugandan officers, pushing Mugabo to launch a Welfare Foundation that initially concerned itself with cultural activities. This foundation turned into a political and military platform, raised funds, trained Tutsi fighters and waged war against the homeland Rwanda. Describing Mugabo to Seba, Gasana proudly said:

> Mugabo is one of our top commanders. *He is a brave man* and a real technician. He is one of the few combatants the chief rebel *trusts*. Whenever he goes on an operation, *success is certain* (Rusimbi, 1999: 102. Emphases added).

The description of Mugabo and his story in Uganda are very similar to the history of General Fred Rwigema, the first RPF commander who was killed on the battlefield on 2nd October 1990, a day after launching the war from Uganda.

The same name is given to a former catholic priest and RPF officer in *The Hyena's Wedding*. Stanislas Mugabo had built a reputation of being an heroic fighter who 'had passed through fire – terrible fire' (Rusimbi, 2007: 1). He lost one leg on the battlefield when he was attempting to rescue tens of thousands of Tutsi trapped in the Nyamata church. After the genocide Mugabo became an administrative chief and continued his brave mission to ensure the well-being of the survivors in particular and for all Nyamata residents in general.

It should be noted that two Hutu characters in all 11 novels bear a *-gabo* name. One is Kagabo, *The small man*, in Mukasonga's (2012) *Notre Dame du Nil*. Kagabo is a traditional healer and sorcerer who kindly welcomed the two Tutsi girls, Virginia and Veronica, when they came to him for his services. As love affairs were not his domain, he offered to take them to another Hutu sorcerer, Nyiramongi but only if they paid him one hundred francs (Mukasonga, 2012: 57-58). It is important here to stress the similarity between Kagabo's and Kabwa's (Section 2.2) attitudes. Both were willing to help strangers but both posed a condition. When that condition was met, they helped. When the massacres started, Kagabo played a crucial role in rescuing Virginia by taking her to safety in Nyiramongi's hut (*Ibid.*: 211-215). The name Kagabo falls under the category of pejorative names given to Hutu characters (see Section 2.2). It implies that Kagabo could be helpful, trustworthy and brave, provided that one paid him little money. He was definitely not like the Tutsi character named Mugabo who sacrificed a leg to rescue innocent people that were trapped. The other Hutu character with a *-gabo* name is Alphonse Mugabo, *The man*, in Sehene's (2005) *Le feu sous la soutane*, but his case is discussed in the next section.

The name Michel Mivumbi, *The torrent*, that Rurangwa gave to the RPF captain also has a direct link to heroism and bravery (Rurangwa, 2006: 105-106). Captain Mivumbi is Jean-Léonard's former pupil in Burundi, where part of his family was killed in 1972. Three of his brothers died on the battlefield fighting for the RPF rebels. The rest of his family were killed during the genocide in 1994. The name Mivumbi implies two things: [1] irresistible strength that destroys everything in its way and [2] speed. The name becomes more interesting when combined with the officer's military rank and his first name. Michel [Michael] the archangel is mentioned in the Bible as leading an army of angels that fights against the Dragon (*Revelation*: 12) and prevails and as facing the Devil in a dispute (*The Letter of St. Jude*: 9).

I should mention that only a few novelists preferred to name Tutsi characters using historical or emblematic names. These names create immediate association with a known historical figure, with a popular person from the past or from myths and legends. When Rusimbi gave the name of Paul to one of the Tutsi commanders who had fought alongside Ugandan rebels (Rusimbi, 1999: 154) and whom a spy, sent by the Rwandan regime, nearly killed in a hotel ahead of an imminent attack against Rwanda (Rusimbi, 1999: 154-156), he probably wanted the reader to think about Paul Kagame, a former RPF commander who is now president of Rwanda. Rusimbi also named Seba's mother Mukakigeri, *The wife of Kigeri* [Kigeri is a royal dynastic name] (*Ibid.*: 17), which is a name that falls under emblematic names, as it immediately brings to mind a close relationship with the royal family. Seba was indeed a nephew of the last King of Rwanda, Kigeri V Ndahindurwa (*Ibid.*: 19).

In a similar vein, the names of Kami-kaze, *Let the King come* [back] and Yuhi given to Kenya's stepsisters in Mbabazi's (2007) novel, have a strong symbolic and emblematic dimension. The former name clearly connects an ordinary Tutsi girl to the monarchy, whereas the latter is simply a dynastic name borne by the Kings of Fire, *Abami b'umuriro*, i.e., those tasked with ensuring the sustainability of the dynasty. There were in total four monarchs with Yuhi as a royal name.[12] The only problem here is that a male name was given to a female character. Even so, the novelist's intention seems to be keeping in the reader's mind the idea that both girls and their siblings had some links with the deposed monarchy and the rebellion. The strong link to the monarchy is also reflected in the name of Musinga, given to the RPF commander's adviser (Mbabazi, 2007: 249). Musinga is the name of the last Tutsi monarch with the royal name of Yuhi. As it will be observed later (Section 5.2.), this novel considers the RPF rebellion as an effort to recover the power that was lost when the monarchy was toppled.

The case of Martin Kayihura in Rurangwa's (2006) *Au sortir de l' enfer* also calls for some reflection. It can be associated with the historical Michel Kayihura, a Tutsi chief in the late 1950s who, together with other Tutsi leaders, rejected the official [colonial] account of the 1959 Revolution. I am discussing this as a separate case because the name is neither historical nor emblematic, but seems to have a strong historical dimension. Like the historical Kayihura, who was a prominent member of the Tutsi-dominated *Union Nationale Rwandaise* that was opposed to colonial administration, Martin Kayihura was a prominent member of the equally Tutsi-dominated *Parti Libéral* that was opposed to President Habyarimana's regime (Rurangwa, 2006: 65-66).[13]

The last category of Tutsi character names comprises those that imply *extraordinariness*. This extraordinariness usually resides in the character's capability to accomplish what other ordinary people cannot accomplish. For instance, the name Musonera, *The one who tolerates*, in Rusimbi's (2007) *The Hyena's Wedding* reveals the intention of the author to portray someone who lost all his relatives during the genocide and yet preached no revenge even from a position of power (Rusimbi, 2007: 10-11). Musonera had promised himself that if Karamira, the Hutu who had killed all of his relatives, was to come back from exile, he would 'tear him to pieces' or 'throw him into a deep hole and bury him alive' (*Ibid.*: 12). Yet, when Karamira returned from exile, none of this happened. Karamira was offered a chance to defend himself in court before being found guilty and executed. Musonera's position as a leader of the Kayumba sector gave him the power to avenge himself but, being extraordinary, he kept control over his emotions.

The name Rubanga, *Heavy secret*, in Mukasonga's (2012) *Notre Dame du Nil*, also tells the reader that the bearer was an exceptional person. He managed to keep a secret and was ready to die rather than reveal it. Rubanga was *umwiru*, a guardian of the dynastic esoteric code, under the monarchy. After independence, he lived in disgrace in a cabin far from a society that considered him a poisoner. Virginia visited him to ask about the rituals surrounding the queens' death and burial. Rubanga answered:

---

12 See Kagame (1951: 30-50) for a more extensive discussion about Rwanda's monarchs.
13 All other details, the owner of Hotel Chez Martin [Chez Lando], his white wife, his academic education, obviously lead the reader to Landouald Ndasingwa, who was killed during the genocide.

> Don't ask me that. It's a secret. Ibanga [Secret in Kinyarwanda]. A secret of the Kings. I am one of the guardians of the secrets of the Kings. I am an umwiru. You know *my name, my name holds the secret* (Mukasonga, 2012: 136. Brackets & emphasis added).

Rubanga is presented as a man of principle and honour and his name is nothing but a stamp that confirms that. He was extraordinary because he managed to resist the temptation of revealing the secrets, which was not the case for the Catholic priest who pretended to be *umwiru* and who divulged the secrets of the kings through his books.[14]

Following a similar pattern, the name Mihigo, *The record breaker*, borne by Kenya's stepbrother fighting amongst RPF rebels, indicates that the bearer behaved in an extraordinarily different way (Mbabazi, 2007). However, Mihigo's record-breaking behaviour is used in a sarcastic way in Mbabazi's novel, as all other Tutsi rebels, except Mihigo, seem keen on massively killing, torturing and raping innocent Hutu people. On one occasion,

> He had just been confronted with the slaughter of about two scores of tied-up, defenceless, civilians, whose sole wrong was that they were Hutu. He cursed himself. He had not dared to defend them. He had preferred to look away, because of fear, because of weakness or simply because of hatred, he didn't know anymore why (*Ibid.*: 159).

Mihigo witnessed many similar scenes whereby his companions broke the record of killing the Hutu in the cruellest way. His own record-breaking resided in resisting the temptation to do the same and even in envisaging defending the defenceless Hutu. He once managed to pose as a rapist to prevent the rape of a Hutu woman by the real rapists (*Ibid.*: 202).

Other names given to Tutsi characters follow the same extraordinary character without necessarily motivating them with a particular behaviour. This is the case for Kamanzi, *The one who can't be equalled*, the member of parliament who taught the government's version of history and preached genuine reconciliation amongst Kayumba populations in *The Hyena's Wedding* (Rusimbi, 2007: 91-93). Spéciose, the name of the first sexual victim of Father Stanislas in Sehene's (2005) *Le feu sous la soutane*, also reflects a certain extraordinariness in the sense that she looked indescribably beautiful and irresistible (Sehene, 2005: 6-7). The Latin origin of that name, *speciosus* [good or pretty appearance], confirms this extraordinariness. The same notion of extraordinariness is also present in Kamali, *Little wealth*, the name of the Tutsi survivor who advocated a tougher approach to so-called moderate Hutu, but was countered by Musonera who was more tolerant (Rusimbi, 2007: 24).

It should also be noted that a few Tutsi characters' names do have a positive connotation that is not consistent with the behaviour of their bearers. The case of Kamali mentioned in the previous paragraph is one example. Another example is the name Mukagatare, *The pure-hearted girl/woman*, in *By the Time She Returned*, whose bearer behaved in a way that contradicted the prescriptions in her name.

---

14 Rubanga is most likely referring to Mgr Alexis Kagame, whose publications include many references to, and analysis of, the esoteric code.

Mukagatare, shortened in the novel as Muka, was Seba's wife, but she hated her sister-in-law Kaitesi (Rusimbi, 1999: 4, 6-7). The same is true of the Muslim/Arabic name Salim, *Peace*, that one RPF commander bore in *Sheridan*. Salim headed battalions of *Kadogo* [child soldiers] that ravaged the south and centre of Rwanda, where they committed indescribable crimes against the Hutu (Mbabazi, 2007: 231-234). The name of Salim's colleague, Colonel Karekezi, which can mean both *The shepherd* [who takes cattle to water springs far away] and *The shooter*, [15] also falls under these sarcastic names. Given the role that Colonel Karekezi plays in the novel, one can maintain that the name refers to both meanings, *The shooting shepherd*, as the colonel is in charge of a battalion, thus a shepherd, and has a gun to shoot. Usually, a shepherd's task is to take good care of, and protect, cattle under his charge. Instead of doing that, Colonel Karekezi encouraged his men to massively kill innocent Hutu (e.g., *Ibid.*: 286 & 288) and to rape Hutu women (e.g., *Ibid.*: 200-202). Here, like in the case of Salim and Mihigo, the name was used to mean the opposite of its initial meaning.

The analysis in this section has shown that Tutsi character names could be divided into five broad categories: [1] those that evoke innocence and attempts to protect it, [2] those that evoke or imply bravery or heroism, [3] those that have a historical or emblematic dimension, [4] those that evoke extraordinariness and [5] those positively connoted ones used in a sarcastic way. What most of these categories have in common is their positive connotation, which is the opposite of what was observed in the previous section. Even when character behaviour includes hatred or discrimination, the name keeps its positive connotation. The findings presented in this section confirm in various ways the hypothesis presented in the introduction of this section. *Innocence names* are the most explicit in suggesting that the Tutsi characters are usually presented as being permanent victims of the Hutu characters. *Bravery names* confirm that state of victimhood by showing the other side of the coin, namely those Tutsi characters who managed to escape victimisation and were fighting to free or rescue other Tutsi. *Historical* and *emblematic names* on their side do not contain a strong notion of victimhood, though some cases might be argued as doing so. Finally, the *extraordinariness names* add a new dimension, namely the extraordinary capability to avoid falling into various traps despite past victimisation. The *sarcastic names* seem to be in the minority and are mostly meant to show that the Tutsi rebels were far from liberators. I would like to end this section with a note that some names appear to be non-Rwandan and for that reason, meaningless. These include Kenya and Ilunga [the name of the commander-in-chief of the Tutsi rebellion] both used in Mbabazi's (2007) novel.

---

15 The name Karekezi comes from the verb *Kurekera*, one of the many Kinyarwanda verbs with multiple meanings. In one sense *Kurekera* means taking cattle to a far-away water well. In another sense, it means shooting an arrow with a bow. Another verb that falls under this category of double or triple-meaning verbs is *Gukira*, which can mean [1] 'becoming rich', [2] 'recovering from illness' and [3] 'overcoming a danger'.

2.4. Half-Hutu, Half-Tutsi Names

I keep discussing half-Hutu and half-Tutsi as two distinct categories because five of the 11 novels, excluding Rusimbi (1999 & 2007), Niwese (2001), Rurangwa (2006), Mbabazi (2007) and Bahufite (2016), give them a peculiar status and a distinctive identity (see Section 1.5). Other authors have generically referred to these characters as *hybrids* (e.g., Hron, 2009), but that appellation does not seem fitting for my current analysis because it conceals all nuances relating to the dominant ethnic identity, i.e., the father's ethnic identity. Section 1.5 has shown that hybrid Hutu characters, i.e., Hutu with Tutsi mothers, tend to identify more with the Hutu, even though they seem confused about who they really are. The sole hybrid Tutsi character, Isaro, whose father was a Tutsi and mother a Hutu, is also presented as if she were hundred percent Tutsi (Gatore, 2008). One hypothesis is that half-Hutu characters tend to have names that combine both the features of Hutu names (see Section 2.2) and those that relate to their identity crisis (see Section 1.5). Another hypothesis is that the sole half-Tutsi character, who did not experience any apparent identity crisis, has a name that is close to those of most other Tutsi characters, i.e., an *innocence name*. For practical reasons, I also discuss the names attributed to characters in mixed couples, whom I could not discuss in previous sections. This is because they tended to have special names that deviate from the broader patterns. It makes more sense to insert them in this section, where subjects relating to the coming together of the two ethnicities are handled.

It is important to start with the remark that the main characters in three of the five novels I am focusing on in this section, have parents from two different ethnic groups. Niko is half-Hutu and Isaro is half-Tutsi (Gatore, 2008); Jean Seneza is half-Hutu (Ndwaniye, 2006), which is also the case for Father Stanislas (Sehene, 2005). To these, one should add other secondary characters like Modesta (Mukasonga, 2012) and Fortunata Uwera (Twagilimana, 1996) who were both born from mixed relationships. This relatively significant presence of characters with mixed ethnicity suggests that this category of characters needs special attention. In many cases, they tend to stand out in their behaviour and in their naming. The questions that need to be put here are: Do their names match their behaviour? In what ways do their names reflect their half-Hutuness/half-Tutsiness?

Gatore's (2008) naming of his two main characters, Niko and Isaro, is very interesting to begin with, because it offers an immediate case of the two possibilities of mixed ethnicity. The name Isaro, *The pearl*, given to the girl born from a Tutsi father and a Hutu mother, thus half-Tutsi, clearly brings to mind the notion of innocence and pure-heartedness, amongst other attributes. The pearl in Rwandan culture, and elsewhere, is something beautiful and precious that offers no one a reason to break or damage it. In a way, it contains the same idea as the one in Mutamuriza, *Don't make her cry* or *Don't hurt her* [because she's innocent] (Mukasonga, 2012: 126-127) and in Tumurinde, *Let's protect her* [because she's innocent] (*Ibid*.: 69). In the last analysis, the name of the sole half-Tutsi character in all 11 novels puts her amongst the Tutsi, which is in line with her story.

Niko's case is more intriguing because initially it was not a name, but rather a 'You-there!' call to the mute child, who never received a name from his father. As everyone called him *You there!* he ended up receiving 'Niko' as a proper name

(Gatore, 2008: 81). Even though the process of his naming contains something unheard of in Rwandan culture, the name calls for a deeper reflection. Why would one be denied the right to have a name, the one that tells who one is or ought to be, the one that tells about one's personal past and identity, the one that serves as one's mission statement? The answer is in the novel: Niko seemed to have no place in society (Section 1.5), as the latter, through his father and his stepmother, had rejected him, refusing him all rights to be its member. By refusing him the right to a name, his father and by extension, society, signalled to him that he did not deserve to have any identity. Nameless Niko was like an animal which has no need to be distinguished from other similar animals. Indeed, Niko felt more comfortable with his goat, to which he gave his own name [Niko], than with fellow humans (*Ibid.*: 48-49 & 87-88). Gatore's choice to use this no-name approach might be interpreted as part of his strategy to provide a minimum of cues. He probably wanted to challenge the reader to find his or her way through the story behind the novel. Niko's crimes were somehow not committed by a human being. They were committed by someone whom both the Hutu [the father] and the Tutsi [the stepmother] had rejected, whereas he had the blood of both [his mother was Tutsi]. In this sense, the *You there!* call used as a name was addressed to the Rwandan society that creates the Nikos, the neither-Hutu-nor-Tutsi, and forces them to make difficult choices in order to be accepted. The fact that Niko could not speak is also important, as it tells us that he could be called, yet he could neither respond nor call out to anyone. The implied idea is that Rwandan society should respond.

Another strategically chosen name is Stanislas, that Sehene (2005) gave to his main character born from an unknown Hutu father and a Tutsi mother. For any readers familiar with the 1994 genocide, the association between Father Stanislas and Father Wenceslas Munyeshyaka is more than obvious (Hitchcott, 2012: 27). Father Wenceslas Munyeshyaka was at Sainte Famille parish during the genocide and he, indeed, welcomed hundreds [thousands?] of refugees, mostly Tutsi. When he came to France in 1995, he was arrested and accused of genocide. Also, the novel seems to include a significant number of documentary elements, especially news reports and interviews that can be found on the Web.[16] The similarities are so self-evident that Hitchcott (2012: 22) considered the novel to be 'a thinly veiled fictionalisation of the tale of the now infamous priest'.

The name Stanislas seems to convey two messages: the first message is in *-slas* at the end of the name which tells the reader that Sehene wanted the character to be as close to Father Wence*slas* as possible without having to craft a Rwandan name. Moreover, both Stani*slas* and Wence*slas* have three syllables, the last of which is *-slas*. The second message is that when one pronounces Stanislas the Kinyarwanda way, *Sitani*silasi, one comes very close to the name given to Satan, *Shitani*. The combination Father + Satan would be in line with the title of the novel [*Fire under the Cassock*], where the cassock, the external sign of piety, is coupled with satanic sexual appetite. This name, then, is probably not as *neutral* as it appears at first

---

16 E.g., 'Rwanda : Munyeshyaka, un curieux homme d'église – Part. 1'; uploaded on 1st November 2006 by AmatekaRwanda. https://www.youtube.com/watch?v=7HdsuE2FFzs [Accessed 11 March 2016] & 'Rwanda : Munyeshyaka, un curieux homme d'église. Part.2'; uploaded on 1st November 2006 by AmatekaRwanda. https://www.youtube.com/watch?v=V_O5pUd-FUg [Accessed 11th March 2016].

sight. On the one hand, it takes one back to an historical person with an infamous reputation and on the other hand, it leaves room for some interpretation that implies a negative connotation.

Unlike the names Isaro, Niko, and Stanislas, that require some complex interpretations, the name Jean Seneza, *The kind-hearted*, that Ndwaniye (2006) gave to his half-Hutu character, seems straightforward in its meaning. Indeed, Seneza is presented as a kind person who had friends in both ethnic groups and was willing to enthusiastically interact with all of them. He was also kind to his twin brother, Thomas, who was accused of committing genocide, as he did not hesitate to visit and embrace him in jail and to show compassion and understanding towards him. When his Tutsi mother told him that Thomas was accused of helping the killers of their own sister, Jean Seneza hastened to ask: 'But what does he respond to that?' (Ndwaniye, 2006: 73). This question is central to the process of understanding the name Seneza in the context of genocide. Jean wanted to have the response of someone whom society considered as a criminal. He seemed to believe that he might be innocent. Giving him a chance to respond to those serious accusations became his main mission in Rwanda. While visiting him in prison, Jean told his brother that he wanted to hear, from his mouth, what he was accused of, as if he did not trust what his [Tutsi] mother had told him. Thomas' story corroborated what Nkundiye, the old man, had told Jean a few days earlier: When President Habyarimana's plane was shot down, local leaders forced everyone to set and guard roadblocks. In those days, no one took the small path near their home and houses were burnt on hills on the other side. In those days, RTLM journalists called on all Hutu to not trust the *Inyenzi,* the Tutsi fighters and their accomplices (*Ibid*.: 179-180). Jean persisted in his search for the exact accusations that Thomas faced:

> -THOMAS: Murder. When I came back from Congo in 1995, a former neighbour, the sole survivor in a family of five, accused me of not having done anything to rescue her. Yet, she knew I had no power to do anything. Who was I to save anyone? …I had to keep a low profile so that no one can harm my wife and children…
>
> Sometime later, the neighbour added another allegation: the murder of her brother.
>
> …
>
> -JEAN: I believe you, I said. I hope the popular court, the Gacaca, will prove your innocence (*Ibid*.: 180-181).

This excerpt reveals that Jean's kind-heartedness resided primarily in understanding the other, whatever they might be accused of. In a few other novels, accusations are almost equated with guilt and no one single suspect is allowed to respond. For instance, in Rusimbi's (2007) *The Hyena's Wedding*, all genocide suspects are portrayed as guilty and there seems to be no room for possible innocence. As Kiroko and Mugabo, both local Tutsi leaders, visited the overcrowded communal prison, they saw several genocide suspects escorted by security forces and angry survivors:

-KIROKO: 'You mean...they find it better to stay in prison cells?' I was surprised.

-MUGABO: 'Yes, they fear retribution. If survivors have to see justice, genocide suspects or criminals would be no more. They are protected in here.'

-KIROKO: 'Protected by...'

-MUGABO: 'Warders, policemen, the courts...the law with its procedures and protocols... (Rusimbi, 2007: 64).

What the dialogue presented above tells the reader is that no innocence is allowed when it comes to genocide. That seemed to be the opposite of Jean Seneza's view. Despite his reluctance to explicitly engage in discussions and debates around ethnicity and genocide, Ndwaniye has used his novel to denounce the idea of automatic collective guilt. Jean's mixed ethnicity has the advantage of placing him at the centre of the genocide, as a brother of both a victim and a suspect. As a half-Hutu, he mourned his sister and her family, yet he believed that the brother accused of those crimes was innocent. Considered from this angle, the novel suggests that kind-heartedness in post-genocide Rwanda is not a simple virtue: it implies the capability to simultaneously manage sorrow and clear-sightedness, mourning and justice.

Another interesting name is Modesta, which Mukasonga (2006) gave to one of her secondary characters. As Section 1.5 has shown, Modesta's father was a Hutu, whereas her mother was a Tutsi. The situation at home and in public, where the father was openly ashamed of having a Tutsi wife, affected her behaviour at school. She was caught between her fear of Hutu extremists led by Gloriosa Nyiramasuka and her friendship with the two Tutsi classmates, Virginia and Veronica, in whom she could safely confide. The name Modesta seems to tell a lot about what is going on in the novel and, by extension, in Rwandan society. Someone is said to be modest when that person is not keen on talking about or displaying their success[17] and that seems to be the case in Modesta's situation. The actors around her were either hostile [Gloriosa and most other Hutu classmates] or mistrustful [Veronica and Virginia]. Managing to please the former while 'clandestinely' building friendship with the latter was quite an achievement. The name and behaviour of Modesta suggest that people in her situation are often caught in dilemmas whereby they have to keep quiet about their achievements, especially when these are favourable towards the Tutsi. This name then has both a positive and a negative connotation. On the one hand, the modest character accomplishes success but on the other hand, that success has to be kept under the radar.

Amongst all half-Hutu characters, Fortunata Uwera, *The pure-hearted* [girl], is the one who chose to side with the Tutsi characters, although nothing was said about her attitudes towards the Hutu (Twagilimana, 1996). Biologically, Fortunata Uwera is a half-Hutu, born from Joseph Nduru [a Hutu] and Celia [a Tutsi]. Officially and culturally she was a Tutsi as she grew up with the knowledge that

---

17 Cambridge Advanced Learner's Dictionary. 3rd Edition (Cambridge: Cambridge University Press, 2009), p. 918.

Kalinda was her father, since he was the man living with her mother in the house. Also, her attitude towards Kalinda, e.g., taking and executing orders from him, taking care of him when hospitalised, etc. (Twagilimana, 1996: 122-123), made her Kalinda's daughter. She would call him 'papa' all the time and Kalinda would call her 'my daughter' (e.g., *Ibid.*: 39). The name Uwera sends the message that the girl was not to be blamed for any misfortunes that had befallen their family, namely the affair between her mother and Nduru. She was just the outcome of an unfortunate situation she could not have controlled. In a way, the name implies both innocence and victimhood, the villain being the powerful Hutu man who misused his power to destroy her family. It is at this level that her first name, Fortunata, becomes interesting. She was the only one to symbolise good fortune for her official father, Kalinda. Against all odds, she accepted to have a child with the man she called 'papa', so that the latter could at least leave behind someone with his blood when he died (*Ibid.*: 248-249).

The last category of names I would like to discuss comprises those names given to Hutu characters married to Tutsi women. This category of Hutu stands out and behaves in a peculiar way that distinguishes them from other Hutu characters. These characters, who share the experience of paying with their lives for the 'mistake' of marrying a Tutsi, appeared only in two novels, namely Sehene's (2005) *Le feu sous la soutane* and Rurangwa's (2006) *Au sortir de l' enfer*, and seemed to play a relatively significant role. Hutu men married to Tutsi women can be spotted in some other novels, but in those cases they are either not named (e.g.: Ndwaniye, 2006; Gatore, 2008) or mentioned in a story told within the novel (e.g.: Mukasonga, 2012). Such characters are absent in Twagilimana (1996), Rusimbi (1999 & 2007), Niwese (2001) and Mbabazi (2007).

The use of Hutu husbands being married to Tutsi women plays an important role in Rurangwa's (2006) *Au sortir de l' enfer*, as Jean-Léonard's father-in-law was a Hutu married to a Tutsi. That Hutu father-in-law was named Anastase Benimana, *The children of God*, a name that he shared with Jean-Léonard's father, Ildefonse Benimana. In the previous section, this name was categorised as an *innocence name* and as implicitly evoking the state of permanent victimhood in which Tutsi characters are set in most novels. One could wonder why the same name, with the same connotation, is used twice for characters with two different ethnic identities. One explanation could be that the author wanted to remind the reader that there were exceptions amongst Hutu characters. There were a few who considered the Tutsi as children of God and who decided to marry them, despite the risks that decision implied. Benimana's first wife, Agnes Mukamurenzi, was a Tutsi, too, which, in a sense, confirmed his closeness to the Tutsi. Mukamurenzi was killed during the anti-Tutsi pogroms in 1973, the same pogrom during which the first husband of his second wife, Irène Mukangira, was also killed. In a sense, by marrying Mukangira, Anastase Benimana wanted to confirm that the Tutsi were the children of God who deserved love and fair treatment (Rurangwa, 2006: 62-63). In the end, he was killed by his own brother, Kayiru, who reminded him of the risk he took in marrying a Tutsi woman twice (*Ibid.*: 77-78). It is worthwhile noting the difference in the naming patterns between the two brothers: one was given an *innocence name* that implies victimhood, whereas the other was given a *land-work name* that signals Hutu characters and their abuse of power (see Section 2.2).

Sehene (2005) also briefly used a Hutu man married to a Tutsi woman and named him Alphonse Mugabo, *The Man*. As discussed in Section 2.3, *The Man* means the same as *The Courageous, The Brave, The Trustworthy, The Honourable*, amongst others, and has nothing to do with gender or sex. Section 2.3 has also shown that most *-gabo* names used in novels were used for Tutsi characters. Alphonse Mugabo in Sehene's novel and Kagabo in Mukasonga's, were the sole Hutu characters with *-gabo* names. However, as already observed, Kagabo, *The small Man*, is the pejorative form of Mugabo. As for Alphonse Mugabo, he was amongst the refugees at Sainte Famille church when an RPF commando came by surprise to the church during the night and took a few Tutsi to safety in the area that they controlled. Damascène, the Hutu militia commander and Father Stanislas were so furious that they started shouting to the refugees, asking them to denounce the traitor who had opened the door to the rebels. A Hutu woman, who had seen it all, came forward and denounced the culprit, Alphonse Mugabo, who immediately tried to explain his gesture: 'Father', he said, 'I did it for my [Tutsi] wife and children…If it were you, what would you have done if the lives of your wife and children were at stake?' (Sehene, 2005: 87-88). Mugabo was obviously a *courageous man* who did what all husbands and fathers should do for their wives and children. He was also courageous and brave because, when unmasked, he stood up and confronted the mighty Damascène and Father Stanislas, rather than apologising for having done the right thing. Faced with this unshakeable courage, Father Stanislas started doubting Mugabo's Hutuness: 'Despite his Hutu peasant appearance, Mugabo is certainly Tutsi. Probably an infiltrated rebel' (*Ibid.*). Father Stanislas handed him over to Damascène and his militiamen and 'I know exactly what they reserve[d] for him' (*Ibid.*). The core of the message in Mugabo's name and story seems to be in Father Stanislas' doubt. A man as courageous as Mugabo could not be a Hutu, which infers that courage, honour, bravery, etc., are Tutsi values. Only a few Hutu could claim to have those values.

The main conclusion of this section is that no new pattern has emerged from the analysis of the names given to characters with mixed ethnicity or those in mixed couples. All the names fit into the patterns outlined in the previous two sections and seem to depend on the role that the novelists assigned to each individual character. In one case, the character who ill-treated the Tutsi and even killed them, was given a name with resemblance to a historical name with an infamous reputation. In another case, a half-Hutu character was given no name, and that no-name became his name, which somehow makes society responsible for his future crimes. Yet in other cases, half-Hutu characters and those in mixed couples who showed sympathy to the Tutsi, were given names that evoked bravery or innocence. It is also important to stress that the name of the sole half-Tutsi character entirely falls under the *innocence name* category, under which most Tutsi character names fall. These conclusions seem to partially contradict my initial hypothesis that the names of characters with mixed identities would reflect their identity crisis. The novelists seem to have used them to introduce some of the subtler nuances in the relationships amongst people from different ethnicities.

2.5. Summary and Discussion

The aim of this chapter was to explore the character naming patterns in the 11 novels in order to find out what possible memory messages were behind those names. The initial assumption was that character names in Rwanda's cultural context would reflect the same naming patterns observed in Rwandan society. The review of theories on character naming has shown that names are rarely neutral as novelists use them as part of their plot. By giving a name to a character, novelists invite readers to decode it and to find connections between that name and the behaviours assigned to the character in the novel. This becomes very interesting in the Rwandan cultural context, where names are often crafted based on the message one wants to convey through that name.

The analysis of the names assigned to Hutu characters has resulted in six broad patterns. [1] Some names explicitly or implicitly evoke land work, which popular belief and culture associate with the Hutu in general. [2] Other names are derived from animal names and tend to suggest that the behaviour of some Hutu characters has nothing human about them. Yet, [3] other names show clear similarities with historical or emblematic figures, all of whom have a rather negative connotation in post-genocide Rwanda. A few [4] other names tend to refer to the Tutsi as the Other who should be mistrusted or [5] refer to the good Hutu as an exception rather than the rule. The last pattern includes [6] first names that have no obvious or specific meaning, except for one, Gloriosa, whose combination with the surname takes one back into the memories of the 1960s and the 1970s. All in all, the first category contains memory names that directly fetch from cultural memory, whereas, the second, third and fourth categories comprise names with negative connotations. Names in the fifth category reinforce those in the previous three, as they serve as the exceptions that usually confirm the rule. The sixth category of names could be labelled as fillers.

A similar analysis of the names attributed to Tutsi characters resulted in five patterns: [1] those that refer to innocence and victimhood, [2] those that imply bravery or heroism, [3] those with an historical or emblematic dimension, hose [4] that contain the idea of extraordinariness and [5] a few with a sarcastic dimension. What all these names have in common is their positive connotation. They contain values that Rwandan society cherishes. They also include Christian names which, unlike those given to most Hutu characters, seem to have a certain meaning when considered in their biblical context. The combination of such first names with surnames often results in memory-loaded names and coincides with the construction of Tutsiness discussed in the previous chapter.

The analysis of the names given to half-Hutu and half-Tutsi characters as well as Hutu characters in mixed couples, did not culminate into any new categorisations. The only clear point was that the sole half-Tutsi character in all 11 novels has a name that completely falls under the Tutsi name categories, as it clearly evokes *innocence*. For the rest, names seem to be attributed depending on the role and behaviour the character was assigned. In this respect, names that fall under any category mentioned above could be borne by half-Hutu characters and Hutu characters in mixed couples. Those characters who showed sympathy towards, or closeness with, Tutsi characters received names that fall under the Tutsi name patterns. The Hutu characters with these positively connoted names are presented as exceptions that confirm the rule that the Hutu have ill intentions towards the Tutsi.

The reader who is not familiar with Rwandan names might wonder why an entire chapter should be dedicated to character names, rather than the artistic or literary merits of the novels. From a cultural memory perspective, names seem to tell the reader more than most other aspects of the novel. In the specific case of Rwanda's cultural memory, especially in the context of genocide, character naming reveals what the dominant narrative is and how the various components of post-genocide Rwandan society are framed in that narrative. In that vein, the names attributed to Hutu characters suggest that the Hutu are perceived as having ill intentions towards the Tutsi. When in power, they misuse it to harm and even kill the Tutsi. Other Hutu characters' names refer to animals, some in a pejorative form. This might suggest that the Hutu are equated not with a bigger rabbit or bigger mole, but with the smaller ones. The few positively connoted names in Tutsi-authored novels tells us that there are very few Hutu who fall outside the above mentioned rule. This idea of collectively turning Hutu characters into villains is reversed in two Hutu-authored novels, where positively connoted names are given to Hutu characters. As for the names given to Tutsi characters, they generally tell the reader that the Tutsi have never had evil intentions towards anyone and are inherently victimised. From that victimhood position they accomplish heroic and extraordinary deeds. In all 11 novels, not one single name suggests the contrary or any other negative connotation. In a minority of novels [two], a few positively connoted names are used sarcastically. In one Hutu-authored novel, sarcasm is used to stress criminal behaviour amongst Tutsi characters.

The messages behind most character names look like a copy of the dominant, government-sponsored memory narrative in post-genocide Rwanda, where the Hutu are constantly designated as collectively guilty of the genocide (see Nyirubugara, 2013: 59-73). Recently [30th June 2013], as he was launching the so-called *Ndi Umunyarwanda* [I am Rwandan] campaign, President Paul Kagame (2013) set in stone what the place of the Hutu is in the grand narrative:

> …a true hero confesses his crime and even helps others confess theirs. Helping others means that he can take the responsibility for their crimes because he is linked to that crime or its consequences in one way or another. That is how it works. People should overcome fear and renounce evil. All people should renounce evil and say it aloud. Will you keep quiet when someone has killed in your name? Why? Even if you have not killed, you still have a problem with me. [You should say:] 'I am not part of the killers, how come that you used my name to kill? I should kill you! Yes! I should not let you live in peace'. Those who are shy, why being shy about speaking out? If you haven't killed and haven't confessed to that, stand up and apologise for those who killed in your name. Tell the killer: 'You don't deserve to live'. The killers must say: 'We committed the unnameable. We're sorry'. The one who did not kill, but in whose name the crime was committed, should say: 'Sorry. I won't let the killer do it again'.

This speech pronounced in the real world reflects many aspects discussed in fictional Rwanda as portrayed in the novels. There seems to be no way to imagine a well-intentioned Hutu. All of them have to apologise, including those who were not yet born during the genocide. Even the true heroes, like Alphonse Mugabo (Sehene, 2006), Mukagatare (Mukasonga, 2012), and Mukamana (Mbabazi, 2007), to mention a few, are guilty in the sense that the crimes were allegedly committed in their *names*. This confirms fictional theories that reality and fiction are connected in some way. Both are often so close to each other that fiction becomes a way of conveying reality (Docherty, 1983: xi; Genette, 1983: 11; Schmid, 2010: 30; Eco, 2011: 79).

It is also worth checking differences in the ways in which remembering and forgetting processes take place through character names. This chapter has shown that two Hutu authors, Gatore and Ndwaniye, followed a subtly different path compared to the one followed by their Tutsi counterparts. Gatore somehow blames society for having created a neither-Hutu-nor-Tutsi character, who ended up killing the Tutsi. That character was rejected by both the Hutu and the Tutsi, and his no-name name perfectly embodied that situation. In a way, the Hutu share the blame with the Tutsi. Also, the allegorical names that Gatore gave to his other Hutu characters do not have any negative connotation. In a similar vein, Ndwaniye counters the grand narrative, both through his choice of positively connoted names for the few Hutu characters he identified as such and through the compassionate attitude of his main character towards a genocide suspect. The other two Hutu authors, Niwese (2001) and Mbabazi (2007), offered a completely different narrative that challenged almost all points in the official narrative. The names they used for the main characters cast a rather positive light on Hutu characters. Names being language codes, this finding confirms my earlier observation that in Rwanda, the Hutu tend to use language to overcome imposed amnesia (Nyirubugara, 2013: 54-58). By giving positively connoted names to Hutu characters, four Hutu authors [Niwese (2001), Ndwaniye (2006), Mbabazi (2007), and to some extent Gatore (2008)] expressed what they wanted to be remembered now and in the future. Obviously what their Tutsi counterparts wanted to be remembered now and in the future was very different. For the latter, the Hutu, except for a few, are ill-intentioned animals and criminals, whereas, the Tutsi are innocent and brave, without any exception.

Part Two

Stereotyping

Chapter 3

Beauty, Handsomeness, and Ugliness

Stereotypes, as this chapter and the next will show, play a significant role in most of the 11 novels of genocide that I am analysing in this volume. The aim of these two chapters is to map the most recurrent and dominant stereotypes, namely those relating to the physical appearance of individual characters and to their level of intelligence. In doing so, I would like to map these stereotypes in fictional Rwanda before discussing their implications in real life.

The concept of 'stereotype' originated from the printing press industry back in the 18th century, when printers/publishers found a new technique to make matrices that enabled them to reproduce similar pages without having to re-key the text (Rosello, 1998: 21-22). Before the invention of this technique, compositors spent days and weeks in front of a linotype or monotype machine that enabled them to key one letter at a time, until all the text had been keyed (Fèbvre & Martin, [1958] 1976: 61). The meaning that stereotype later received figuratively, implies that what applies to one [page] applies to all [other similar pages in different volumes of the same title]. Stereotypes are often used in mass media as 'quick picture messages that tell readers, listeners or viewers how they should think about an individual or group' (Aldrich, 1999: 6). By definition, stereotypes are simplifications, positive or negative, that deny any individuality to human beings (Pieterse, 1992: 11; MacIver, [1948] 1970: 198). When a community or a group uses a given stereotype in reference to another, it does two things: On the one hand, it identifies itself collectively as homogeneous and on the other hand, it rejects the stereotyped group as a threat to that homogeneity (Semujanga, 1998: 39).

Despite their simplifications and generalisations, theorists in cultural and literary studies consider them to be half-truths, as they reflect ways in which a given society perceives itself. For instance, while theorising culture as being the result of collective mind-programming, Hofstede (2001: 14) argued that 'Stereotypes ... always reflect the mind-sets of those judging and sometimes also something real about those being judged'. In other words, even if the simplified image of a given group might be unfounded, there is still some truth in stereotypes as they reveal part of the mind-set of the one who utters or uses them in a novel. Discussing specifically artistic productions, including novels and their use of stereotypes, Rosello (1998: 17; see also Semujanga, 1998: 40) suggested that stereotypes are not 'the opposite of truth', but rather part of 'the narratives that a given power wants to impose as the truth at a given moment'. Again, here, one sees a link between the simplified image and a certain truth, namely the truth about those in a dominant position and whose aim it is to impose a certain narrative. This aspect is closely connected to the discussion with which I concluded the previous chapter when I drew a parallel between the dominant, government-sponsored memory narrative with the dominant narrative in Tutsi-authored novels. A hypothesis that emerges from this is that the same novels that embraced the dominant narrative would logically include stereotypes that credit and reinforce that narrative, whereas, the few that challenged it would do the reverse. In other words, Tutsi characters are likely to be positively stereotyped in most novels, whereas Hutu characters are likely to be negatively stereotyped, except in the two Hutu-authored novels [Niwese (2001) & Mbabazi (2007)] that openly challenged the official narrative.

The questions that this chapter is going to attempt to answer are: How do the novelists portray the physical appearance of their characters? How do these portrayals relate to ethnicity? What memory implications do these portrayals have? To simplify my analysis in this chapter, I solely focus on the notions of beauty for female characters and handsomeness for male characters and their opposites, i.e., ugliness, for both genders. The next chapter focuses on the notion of intelligence and its opposite.

3.1. Beauty

What are the beauty traits in Rwandan culture? This is an extremely difficult question as beauty, like colour and taste, is strictly a matter of personal preference. However, it is essential for this analysis to find a way to define beauty in the Rwandan cultural context before I can proceed with my investigation of its use in the novels. Even though the perception of beauty is a matter of personal preference, it is possible to put together a non-exhaustive list of beauty traits based on popular adages, proverbs, myths, legends, historical tales[18] and artistic productions. Generally speaking, a beautiful Rwandan girl has calf's eyes [*amaso y'inyana*], tender skin, is soft and usually fair-complexioned, has white teeth and black gums and more or less a large behind, amongst other attributes. In the biography she wrote about her mother, Mukasonga (2008) described her as a beauty expert who would scout for possible fiancées on behalf of young men. One day, she was inspecting a girl named Mukasine, *The brown-skinned cow*, who, according to Mukasonga's mother, was the incarnation of Rwandan beauty: She was tall, fair-complexioned [*inzobe*], had long hair like Mukasonga's [the author herself] and a glorious bottom, legs, and thighs:

---

18 Historical tales abound with cases of beautiful women and girls and some provide details of what is meant by beauty, whereas others stay on the surface. For instance, in the historical tale that gave birth to the popular proverb *ntabyera ngo de* [Nothing is ever perfect], a young girl named Karira is described as 'the most beautiful girl of all contemporary women and girls' (Mulihano, [1980] 2005: 92). She was so beautiful that Prince Rujugira abducted her by force just to see her taken away by his own father, King Yuhi III Mazimpaka. The latter returned her but Rujugira preferred to flee the country to avoid being killed by his father. In another historical tale about King Ndahiro II Cyamatare and Hutu rebel King Nkongoro, the former's servants are described as beautiful, elegant, well-dressed and clean, whereas the latter's servants looked vulgar and wore dull ornaments. One of Nkongoro's servants approached the royal servants and asked them to take her with them so that she also could look beautiful (Coupez & Kamanzi, 1962: 210-212). A similar tale is about a young girl named Bwiza – Beauty – described as 'so beautiful that everyone agrees she was unrivalled' (Smith, 1975: 290). A man called Rugayi son of Buzi from Burundi had offered scores of cattle to reserve her as his fiancée. However, when they finally got married, Gahindiro, the King of Rwanda abducted her and made her his wife (*Ibid.*: 290-313).

> Mukasine had all the traits that Rwandans attribute to the cow, but she displayed all of them to perfection. She is an *Inyambo* [prestigious type of long-horned cow], a royal cow. By the way, is she not named Isine, the brown-skinned cow? My mother kept repeating it: She had found an *inyambo* (Mukasonga, 2008: 102. Brackets & emphasis added).

This fragment gives one a glimpse of what Mukasonga and her mother and probably many other Rwandans, consider to be the ideal beauty of a Rwandan girl. In this section, I want to systematically find out which female characters are portrayed as beautiful on the one hand and on the other hand, to identify eventual patterns as to how the notion of beauty relates to ethnicity.

Of all the novelists I am considering, Mukasonga (2012) is the one who uses the notion of beauty the most frequently. Perhaps this has to do with her mother whom she presented as a beauty expert in her biography (Mukasonga, 2008). For instance, Gloriosa Nyiramasuka openly hated and was jealous of Veronica Tumurinde's beauty and promised to make her name – *Let's protect her* – mean its opposite (Mukasonga, 2012: 33-34). The notion of beauty comes back when the two Tutsi girls visited Mr. de Fontenaille, a white man who lived near the school. Mr. de Fontenaille adored the two girls and the Tutsi in general. He believed that they belonged to the same family as the Jews or the Romans. In any way, they were not negroes and must have come from Ethiopia or Alexandria (*Ibid.*: 71-75). Mr. de Fontenaille used to tell the two girls that when his friends visited him, he welcomed them with beautiful girls, mostly Tutsi. He would reproach the Tutsi to have lost the memories of where they came from, but would admit that despite all the distance they had walked, 'they had kept their cattle, their sacred bulls, their nobility, and their daughter had kept their beauty' (*Ibid.*: 75).

In addition to beauty-centred jealousy amongst the Hutu schoolmates and the irrational fascination by Mr. de Fontenaille, Veronica seemed to have idealised a Tutsi historical figure as the incarnation of beauty. This was clearly apparent when the school was preparing for the official visit of Queen Fabiola of Belgium. The students were discussing Queen Fabiola's beauty, some finding her beautiful, more beautiful than their female white teachers and others were disagreeing. Veronica was amongst those who had a different opinion, as she found Queen Gicanda, the [Tutsi] wife of King Mutara III Rudahigwa, to be more beautiful (*Ibid.*: 178-179). On hearing this, Gloriosa became furious:

> You, the Tutsi, always think you are the most beautiful in the world, but, as I speak, beauty has switched sides. Your alleged beauty will bring you bad luck (*Ibid.*: 179).

A similar confrontation between Veronica and Gloriosa around the issue of who was beautiful and who was not, occurred when the selection of dancers began ahead of Queen Fabiola's visit. The numerous journalists and photographers showed a great amount of attention to Veronica's performance. They asked her to stand alone on the podium so that they could take pictures of her from all sides. They told one another that she could be on the front pages of their outlets. Furious, Gloriosa asked them why they would only look at Veronica. They laughed aloud and offered to take pictures of her, too (*Ibid.*: 172).

What emerges from the instances cited above is that beauty seems to be a Tutsi girl attribute. The Hutu students seemed to agree about that and were jealous. Foreigners, whom one can call neutral observers [after all, they were not Rwandans] like Mr. de Fontenaille and the journalists, also found the Tutsi girls beautiful. Veronica, a Tutsi herself, identified a Tutsi historical figure, Queen Gicanda, as the incarnation of beauty. The conclusion is that there seemed to be absolute unanimity about the beauty of Tutsi girls.

Beauty is also frequently mentioned in Rurangwa's (2006) *Au sortir de l' enfer*, where Jeanne-Laurette, a Tutsi girl, is constantly referred to as beautiful. When Jean-Léonard saw her for the first time during a church service at Sainte Famille parish, he observed her from head to toe: 'A beauty! Never before had any girl dazzled his eyes and set his senses ablaze' (Rurangwa, 2006: 38). She had beautiful eyes, sensual lips and pretty hands (*Ibid.*: 44). Even later, when she had been sexually abused and lost all her pride, Jeanne-Laurette, who had changed her name to become Immaculée Manzi[19] and lived in eastern Congo after the genocide, kept dazzling the eyes of those who looked at her. While at the Nyiragongo Night Club, she managed to conquer the heart of Orlando Padovani, an official of the UN High Commission for Refugees, to the detriment of a Congolese woman, who had initially come with him to the club. In Padovani's mind, Immaculée was 'pretty' and was obviously not a prostitute (*Ibid.*: 110-111).

Besides the specific focus on Jeanne-Laurette/Immaculée as the incarnation of beauty, Rurangwa's novel also offers a few generalisations. For example, while describing the Hotel Chez Martin in Kigali, Jean-Léonard said that it offered an ideal environment for those who wanted to rest away from daily hassles. Apart from music and African and European cuisines, the hotel's young Tutsi waitresses had the physical attributes that made white clients in search of exotic pleasures, mad (*Ibid.*: 65). In a similar vein, Jean-Léonard portrayed Claudine, a young Tutsi working behind the counter at Le Tanganyika bar in Brussels, as 'so pretty, so young and so smart' (*Ibid.*: 130). It appears from Rurangwa's novel, like in Mukasonga's, that beauty and Tutsiness are intimately associated. The difference between Mukasonga's (2012) *Notre Dame du Nil* and Rurangwa's (2006) *Au sortir de l' enfer*, is that Mukasonga has many Hutu female characters, none of whom is given any beauty trait, whereas Rurangwa simply has no single female Hutu character expect for Sabine Gahigi, known as Mama Jackie, whose role is insignificant in the novel. She happened to be the manager of the bar where Jean-Léonard and Jeanne-Laurette once went for a refreshment (Rurangwa: 2006: 44).

Sehene's (2005) *Le feu sous la soutane* also uses the notion of beauty exclusively in relation to Tutsi female characters. The reason is that they were the only ones that Father Stanislas fished out of the masses to be his sexual slaves in the presbytery. Father Stanislas described his first sexual victim, Spéciose, as 'a beautiful woman, a very beautiful woman'. She was slim and dignified, her hair was cut short, her forehead was high and her lips were black and sensual. Despite the dire conditions within the church, Spéciose was still elegant and coquette (Sehene, 2005: 6-7).

---

19 It is interesting to note how this name falls under the categories of Tutsi character names discussed in Section 2.3. Manzi [like Kamanzi] means 'The one who can't be equalled'. Combined with Immaculée, Immaculate, the name suggests both innocence and extraordinariness.

Sehene uses a lot of detail when describing Spéciose's beauty traits through Father Stanislas' eyes:

> What beautiful buttocks she has! Round and firm, their upper part shakes like two independent and loose globes. Irresistible, really. I am tempted to touch them each time she walks past me (*Ibid.*: 9).

In short, Spéciose was so pretty that Father Stanislas openly told her: 'You are very beautiful, you know and I spotted you long ago' (*Ibid.*: 8). This detailed and long description with several superlatives and overstatements explains why that woman was named Spéciose, a name whose Latin origin, *speciosus*, refers to pretty appearance. It also explains why that name falls under *extraordinariness names* discussed in Section 2.3, in relation to Tutsi character names.

Sehene seems systematic in his portrayals of Tutsi female characters. They all receive a detailed description that outlines their prettiness. One day, as the faithful were lining up for the communion, Father Stanislas spotted out a newcomer, 'very pretty' with a willowy body, a giraffe neck (Sehene, 2005: 39) and interminable legs (*Ibid.*: 52). In Father Stanislas' thoughts, that young woman was an incarnation of beauty:

> Doubtless she embodies, once again, the inaccessible Tutsi woman, that creature, delicate, languorous, elegantly walking like a royal cow. The woman whom all men dream of having (*Ibid.*).

Dafrose, another woman abused by Father Stanislas, also receives an extensive description that revolves around her beauty traits. As he caressed her, Father Stanislas found her skin 'tender' and 'silky'. She was dark-complexioned and 'as the Rwandan beauty canon requires', has 'black gums' (*Ibid.*: 68-69). Assumpta, whose mother had requested Father Stanislas to protect her against the rapists and who ended up in the priest's bed, was also described as 'a beautiful young girl, tall, thin and timid. I spotted her pretty buttocks, well pulled up, perfect for my taste' (*Ibid.*: 78). Interestingly, Sehene extends his beauty-centred description of Tutsi female characters to Father Stanislas' mother. Even though she was already old with stretched traits like withered fruit, she used to be a pretty woman 'the prettiest of our [Father Stanislas'] hill' (*Ibid.*: 123. Brackets added).

What appears from Sehene's systematic and extensive beauty-centred descriptions of Tutsi female characters, is that he overwhelmingly imposes the image of the Tutsi woman as embodying beauty itself. Even Father Stanislas' mother, who somehow unwillingly found herself on the killer's side, receives the beauty traits that all other Tutsi women receive in the novel. This could have been an exception, but the message of the novel seems to be that all Tutsi girls and women are extremely beautiful. It is also interesting to note that the sole Hutu female character in the novel is the one who denounced Alphonse Mugabo, the Hutu character who opened the door to the RPF rebels so that his Tutsi wife and children could be rescued. That woman does not receive a name or a portrayal of her physical appearance (Sehene: 2005: 87-88).

Twagilimana's (1996) *Manifold Annihilation* follows a similar approach and uses superlatives to highlight the beauty of Tutsi women. The novelist fetched all imaginable overstatements to sketch the beauty of Victor Kalinda's wife Celia. As he was describing his wife to Mahoro, Kalinda said that she was *'ikibasumba'*, the unequalled beauty (Twagilimana, 1996: 40). She was 'perfection itself' and seeing her was like seeing a vision. She was 'as bright as this light in a dark house. She [was] beauty incarnate' (*Ibid*: 41. Brackets added). Mahoro was even more laudatory when she saw her for the first time:

> Her curled hair shone as if tinted with invisible diamonds shining lights on the surface. Her face was illuminated by two electrifying eyes. They looked like the tropical milky sky, with two blue spells whose charm led to infinite spaces. She had inviting lips. Her breasts were still tender and stood erect, despite her age and fourfold maternity. She had those big buttocks that Rwandans love so much, and her legs were of movie star's perfection (*Ibid*.: 57).

What is interesting in *Manifold Annihilation* is that beauty is also associated with a half-Hutu girl, Fortunata Uwera, Celia's daughter. Her official father, Kalinda, introduced her to Mahoro as 'perfection from toe to hair, by any standards…[as] a beautiful woman!' (*Ibid*.: 41). However, before doing that, he provided a premise that she was a 'replica' of her mother (*Ibid*.), which stresses the idea that Tutsiness and beauty are one. Whoever claims beauty must have some Tutsi blood in herself. This observation is supported by Mahoro's own remark, when he discovered Celia for the first time. He compared Furtunata and Celia and came to the conclusion that the latter was more beautiful than her eldest daughter (*Ibid*.: 57). In other words, what the above suggests is that a half-Hutu girl is beautiful, but her beauty stems from her Tutsi mother's beauty and remains inferior to it.

In the remaining seven novels – Rusimbi (1999 & 2007), Niwese (2001), Ndwaniye (2006), Mbabazi (2007), Gatore (2008) and Bahufite (2016) – the notion of beauty is present but does play a minor role. For instance, in Rusimbi's (1999) *By the Time She Returned*, Seba's wife Mukagatare is presented as a pretty woman. When she and Seba met, they were both attending the Kitante Hill School and 'She was the most beautiful girl at school. We used to call her Miss Kitante (the beauty queen)' (Rusimbi: 1999: 20). Seba's sister, Kaitesi, is also portrayed as a beautiful woman, which exposed her to sexual harassments, not only from her teachers (*Ibid*.: 9-10), but also from married men who preferred her to their Ugandan wives (*Ibid*.: 116-117). One Ugandan businessman named Musisi raped her and made her his second wife. He once told her: 'You [not my Ugandan wife] are the one I love most Kaitesi, you are more beautiful and appealing to me' (*Ibid*.: 136. Brackets added). Another Rwandan female character in that novel is Jane Namusisi, whose real Rwandan name used to be Kaitesi (*Ibid*.: 141). She sold food stuff at a Kampala market and was active in recruiting women for the liberation movement that was preparing war against Rwanda. When Kaitesi [Seba's sister] described her, she stressed that her beauty made her stand out:

> *She didn't look to be a Muganda* [Uganda's majority ethnicity] though she spoke Luganda fluently… She always spoke politely to me. *She was not ugly like most of her fellow market women* (*Ibid*.: 140. Emphases & brackets added).

The two italicised parts of this quote suggest that almost everyone else is ugly except for a Tutsi woman. Namusisi was 'extremely smart and [more] beautiful' (*Ibid.*: 141. Brackets added), which might explain why she seduced so many lovers in the past (*Ibid.*: 146). The last female Tutsi character that is described as pretty, is Jenipher, 'a beautiful girl' who was part of the cultural group that served to camouflage fundraising activities and military trainings amongst refugees (*Ibid.*: 153). Despite being a Tutsi refugee, Jenipher turned out to be a spy of the Rwandan government, which enabled her to live a luxurious life in exile. She managed to seduce Paul, a leading commander of the liberation movement, into a bed in a hotel where she nearly shot him (*Ibid.*: 154-156).

As I explained in previous chapters, Rusimbi's (1999) *By the Time She Returned* does not include one single Hutu character. What is essential to note in this respect, is that three out of four female Tutsi characters in this novel are portrayed as beautiful and superior to local Ugandan girls. The sole female character who is not described in detail, is the old Mukakigeli, Seba's mother, who is rather presented as a wise, patriotic woman, who urged her children to never give up Rwandan values (Rusimbi, 1999: 18-19 & 52-53).

In his other novel, *The Hyena's Wedding*, Rusimbi (2007) slightly touches upon the notion of beauty and associates it with Tutsiness (see Section 1.3). One day, as local leader Mugabo was guiding government officials in the Nyamata church and its tunnel where the bodies of genocide victims were laid to rest, he commented upon 'a beautiful lady', whom Interahamwe militiamen had gang-raped after killing her husband. When they were done, they pushed a sharp stick into her body to kill her (Rusimbi, 2007: 60). What is suggested here is that the woman's sole sin in the militiamen's eyes was her beauty, which takes one back to Gloriosa Nyiramasuka warning that Veronica's beauty was going to bring her bad luck (Mukasonga, 2012: 179).

Unlike the cases described above, where the beauty of Tutsi women explains their raping or their brutal and humiliating death, beauty is not an important theme in Gatore's (2008) *Le passé devant soi*. The few times the novelist mentions or refers to beauty, he applies it to Isaro, the half-Tutsi girl, whose parents were killed during the genocide. One such instance is when Isaro realised that the concierge of the building where she lived in Paris was observing her. Despite the fact that her hair looked like 'a pile of iron wires' and her face was puffy, the concierge gave her a compliment: 'What a beauty!…How has God managed to concentrate that amount of gracefulness in one person?'(Gatore, 2008: 70-71). By the time Isaro finally decided to take care of her hair and to dress smartly, she realised herself that she, indeed, was beautiful. Looking at herself in a mirror, she wondered if the person in the mirror was herself: 'For the first time, she found herself beautiful' (*Ibid.*: 72).

So far, the analysis of the use of beauty in the novels of genocide shows that that attribute is overwhelmingly assigned to Tutsi women and girls and to those with mixed ethnicity. In both cases, beauty is associated with Tutsiness. The sole novels that associate some beauty traits to Hutu female characters are Niwese's (2001), Mbabazi's (2007) and Bahufite's (2016). When Marc Ngenda ended his studies in Europe and returned to Rwanda to become a minister, he came across Hogoza, a

25-year-old Hutu girl working as a secretary at the French embassy. Ngenda, who was still a bachelor, found her to be

> a young comely girl…charming and beautiful to watch…Her eyes were large and when she smiled, nice dimples would show on her cheeks. Her breasts stood upright in her chest. On top of her beauty was flawless behaviour (Niwese, 2001: 63).

In a similar vein, Bahufite's (2016) novel attributes beauty traits to two Hutu female characters. Martin, the son of Nadine's Zairian boss, found her beautiful despite the dire conditions in which she lived in the refugee camp. The first time Martin saw her, he approached her and started talking to her. At some point he said: 'Wouldn't you find it great if both of us could marry? I find you so beautiful and you are a hard-working girl…' (Bahufite, 2016: 80). Also, Nadine describes Céline, her best friend aged 17, as 'the most beautiful pregnant woman I have ever seen' (*Ibid*.: 127), without providing any specific beauty trademark she had.

Unlike Niwese (2001) and Bahufite (2016), who discussed beauty once or twice and only in relation to Hutu female characters, Mbabazi's (2007) *Sheridan* included both Tutsi and Hutu female characters. In this novel beauty is discussed at three levels: firstly, in relation to the Tutsi main character Kenya and her sisters; secondly, in relation to Hutu characters Zuba and Masaro; and thirdly, in relation to Rwandan women in general. The novel describes Kenya as a pretty girl, who, 'without being a super beauty, … managed to be in a pole position place amongst the most beautiful women' (Mbabazi: 2007: 7). In this respect, Mbabazi joins the novelists who used superlatives and overstatements to describe the beauty of Tutsi female characters. He even used more overstatements to let the reader visualise the beauty of Kenya's stepsisters: Kami-Kaze was like Kenya's replica [thus equally beautiful] but added a fairer complexion and a 'subliminal face' (*Ibid*.: 100). As for Mutesi, she was so beautiful that there were traffic jams each time she found herself at a crossroads (*Ibid*.). More beautiful than all the others was Yuhi, who 'incarnated beauty par excellence for Africans' (*ibid*.). Orange, the youngest, still in her adolescence, was also beautiful as she, like her sisters, would make the Pope defrock if the latter had a chance to see her (*Ibid*.: 101).

The difference between these descriptions and the ones provided by Twagilimana (1997), Sehene (2005), and Rurangwa (2006), is that they are coupled with one Hutu character's beauty. However, compared to the exaggerations used to describe the beauty of the Tutsi characters, the description of the Hutu character beauty is more modest. Without a detailed portrayal, Miko's sister Zuba is generally presented as a beautiful girl with a small, slender body that would make her eligible for any model contest. The only problem was that she had a small and snubbed nose that she wanted to correct with surgery. In short, she met the western standards of beauty rather than African ones that imply more flesh and fat (Mbabazi, 2007: 122). Here, one notes that Zuba's beauty has a lot of 'buts'. She was beautiful *but* her nose needed correcting; she was pretty *but* not according to African standards. Compared to Kenya's sisters who caused traffic jams in Africa and would make the Pope defrock, Zuba's beauty is insignificant. The same 'beautiful but' description also applies to another minor character called Mbeba, *The mouse*,[20] who was one of the Hutu women whom the Tutsi rebels used as an appetiser. When Mihigo saw her after a night in a rebel's bed, he could not recognise the former Miss Rwanda. Because of her husband's frequent beatings and other ill-treatments, she had become a 'fat, dowdy-looking, black-skinned woman' (*Ibid.*: 200-201). Mbeba used to be beautiful *but* that was not the case anymore when Mihigo saw her. The same was true for Nadine's mother who 'used to be a very beautiful woman, with a dignified posture' (Bahufite, 2016: 32), but whose beauty had vanished following aging.

The other difference between Mbabazi and the Tutsi novelists is that, despite his hyperbolic descriptions of the Tutsi characters' beauty, he goes beyond ethnicity and attributes beauty to Rwandan women in general. For instance, when Kenya visited parts of Rwanda, she noted the 'stunning beauty of Rwandan girls' (*Ibid.*: 104-105). A Belgian UN peacekeeper made a similar observation in a letter to his family, when he observed that 'Rwandan girls are so so beautiful', though not as beautiful as Somali, Ethiopian, and Fulani [*Peuls*] girls, who are reputed to be the most beautiful on the African continent. However, the Rwandan girls have a considerable advantage in that they are not excised (*Ibid.*: 134-135).

Ndwaniye's approach to beauty, like his opaque approach to ethnicity, is totally different from the ones that the other authors have adopted. His novel does stress the physical traits of the female characters, often in an erotic way, but it systematically refrains from associating those traits with ethnicity. So when Jean Seneza remembered his early years when he used to come to the local hospital to contemplate the 'beautiful, very beautiful' nurses in white skirts, he did not reveal whether they were Hutu or Tutsi (Ndwaniye, 2006: 12). The same is true for Stéphanie, the woman he gave a lift to on his way back to Kigali from Kabengera. Stéphanie was

> very beautiful, tall with a pretty straight neck, a true gazelle, as we say in my country…She had a generous chest and the zigzag form of her blouse made in Dutch wax fabric showed the forms of her breasts. Their shape was perfect. I haven't yet talked about her hips!… (*Ibid.*: 110-111).

The contrast between Ndwaniye's approach and that of the other authors is significant. He likes erotic details like Sehene but, unlike him, he does not leave any clue as to whether the characters in question are Tutsi or Hutu. This is consistent with his general strategy of giving Kinyarwanda names to a minimum of characters, only two, and not revealing his characters' ethnicity.

To conclude, all 11 novelists used the notion of beauty in their novels, but some tended to use it as a central theme, whereas others only slightly included it. The main finding is that most novels – eight out of 11 – converge in exclusively associating beauty with Tutsiness. In other words, whenever beauty is mentioned, it is either in relation to a Tutsi female character who is perceived as pretty, or in relation to a Hutu character who contests or challenges it. When one Hutu female

---

20 This Hutu character was given this animal name to divert Death's attention away from the baby girl. Her mother had repeatedly had miscarriages and when the latest was born, the father named her The mouse [Mbeba], which made her uninteresting to Death. The latter is always looking for human beings (Mbabazi, 2007: 201-202).

character in Mukasonga's (2012) novel attempted to challenge Tutsi beauty and to claim beauty herself, her move provoked laughter that suggests that the idea of a beautiful Hutu girl is unthinkable, at least in that novel. Another interesting conclusion is that in some cases, there seems to be some consensus about the association between Tutsiness and beauty. The people around the Tutsi female characters, usually the Hutu characters, do admit that Tutsi girls are beautiful, which makes the former jealous. In addition to this, foreigners, whom one would consider as neutral observers, confirm that Tutsi girls are indeed beautiful. It is also important to note that only three Hutu-authored novels [Niwese (2001), Mbabazi (2007) and Bahufite (2016)] slightly and sparingly associate Hutuness with some form of beauty. I should also mention that some novels have associated beauty with half-Hutuness and half-Tutsiness. This association can be explained by the principle that beauty and Tutsiness are linked and, as a consequence, any character with mixed ethnicity stands a chance to take some beauty traits from her Tutsi parent. Finally, it should be noted that this *beauty is a Tutsi attribute* pattern, is challenged by Ndwaniye, who refuses to categorise his female characters as belonging to either ethnic group. The next section takes the analysis of stereotypes further and considers handsomeness and its use in the novels.

3.2. Handsomeness

Rwandan culture seems to accord little, if any, significance to handsomeness, as men are rather expected to strive for manly attributes such as physical strength and toughness. The story of Bisangwa, son of Rugombituri, a member of the Ingangurarugo [The very first militia[21]] militia under King Kigeri IV Rwabugiri [1853-1897] is illustrative, as it clearly reflects the preference of manliness to handsomeness. Bisangwa, a Hutu fighter, had won the favours of King Rwabugiri, who appreciated his courage. This situation had created tensions and jealousy amongst the fighters, who thought that the King favoured him because of his pretty face, i.e., his handsomeness. Aware of this, Bisangwa included his response in his war poem, *Icyivugo*, saying:

> The Ingangurarugo [fighters] do not love me because I am handsome.
> They love me because I [bravely] fought alongside them on multiple occasions.[22]

Unlike women's beauty, men's handsomeness seems to be a minor detail in comparison to their strength and bravery in war [difficult] situations. At this stage, one might wonder why I decided to investigate men's handsomeness in novels of genocide if handsomeness does not seem to be a common and cherished attribute for Rwandan men. The reason is that handsomeness happens to be amongst the

---

21 According to Alexis Kagame (1952: 23), when King Kigeri IV Rwabugiri came to power around 1853, he started setting up new militias. The first of them was Ingangurarugo, a name that means, The First [militia to be set up]. It was followed by Inshozamihigo, those who provoke, and Ibisumizi [The Body-to-Body Fighters/Wrestlers], etc.
22 Original text:
Ingangurarugo ntizinkudira ubwiza
Zinkundira ko nazikubitaniye uruguma gatatu.

dominant themes discussed in the novels. What is more, this theme keeps coming back in popular music and in mass media where it is coupled with other non-related subjects. One can claim that handsomeness has gradually gained prominence in Rwandan culture in the last few decades. One example is a song titled *Mushimira mute Imana?* [How do you thank God?] by Impala Orchestra, which dominated Rwandan pop music throughout the 1980s and in the early 1990s. The storyline of the song is that a man could not find a lover and wonders what other men did to find lovers. He was a true *umugabo* with all the values that a Rwandan man should have: He had no hatred in his heart; he was not a thief and he never engaged in gossip. 'Perhaps am I not handsome?', he wondered, before providing the following reflection:

> Handsomeness! Does anyone eat it?
> Not at all
> By the way, I am not even very ugly
> There are many who have lovers and who are uglier than me.[23]

What this popular tune tells us is that handsomeness is secondary to the values attributed to *umugabo*. However, it also recognises that handsomeness is gaining more prominence in relationships between both genders.

Another example comes from a newspaper called *Igihe*, which recently published a news story about reforms to be conducted at the faculty of Law at the University of Rwanda. That story provoked dozens of comments that related, not only to the content of the story, but also to the handsomeness of one man whose picture was published in the article (Hagenimana, 2016). The very first comment was: 'What a handsome man, my goodness!…I thought he was an old man…You're great in discussing Law'. The second comment was: '…you're an absolutely handsome boy'. Another went as follows: 'Besides speaking well, you also look pretty/handsome'. My approach is not to exclusively discuss what has long existed in Rwanda's culture and oral traditions, but to also find out how new stereotypes are being created. The Tutsi-girl/woman-is-beautiful stereotype seems to be deeply rooted in oral traditions and, as the previous section has shown, is being perpetuated in modern day novels. In this section I attempt to answer the following questions: What does a handsome man look like? How is handsomeness connected to ethnicity? The aim here is to find out how novelists constructed the handsome man and whether the attribution of handsomeness follows any ethnic lines.

Bahufite's (2016) novel slightly mentions the shift in mentalities in the mid-1990s, when handsomeness seemed to have become an important criterion in choosing one's lover. Young adolescent girls, including Nadine and Céline, would wonder what requirements they would consider before choosing their future husbands, and 'handsomeness' would unanimously emerge as the most important one. However, they immediately realised the absurdity of this criterion: 'Handsomeness? Which handsomeness? As a result of working like slaves, the boys' skin had hardened, their eyes were bloodshot, their hands were covered with scales' (Bahutife, 2016: 46-47). With such a desperate description, one cannot expect any

---

23 Author's personal archives.

Hutu character to be handsome in this novel. However, it is suggested that those Hutu boys had had a chance to be handsome before coming to the refugee camps.

Of all the novelists, Rurangwa seems to be the one who described his male characters the most, based upon their physical appearance. Obviously the main character, Jean-Léonard, a Tutsi, received the most attention and was described as 'handsome, young, rich, intelligent and born into a well-to-do and intellectual family' (Rurangwa, 2006: 51). Later on, while in a pub in Brussels, his handsomeness drew the attention of Julie Charrot. This Mauritian girl asked a friend in the same pub: 'He is very handsome, isn't he?...He also seems very sexy' (*Ibid.*: 150). Julie managed to secure a conversation with him where she heard the story of his survival. This story inflamed her even more. She told herself: 'I will do all it takes to be his wife...I'm going to conquer his heart. He is too handsome to let him escape me' (*Ibid.*: 156). Julie took Jean-Léonard on holidays to Mauritius to let her family discover this irresistible man. Her family did not believe that Jean-Léonard was a black African:

> From time to time the latter [Julie's family] quickly glanced at Jean-Léonard. They were impressed by his fineness and regular physical traits. The stereotype of the African with a flat nose, thick lips, and dark complexion did not apply to Jean-Léonard. Everybody wondered whether part of the blood flowing in his veins was not white (*Ibid.*: 176. Brackets added).

Jean-Léonard's handsomeness seems indescribable and beyond any understanding. His handsomeness-based superiority comes back in the novel when Orlando, the white man who married Jeanne-Laurette [renamed Immaculée], told his wife about Jean-Léonard [thus her husband during the genocide], an

> ...extraordinary young man...different from other Africans whom I come across in Matonge [Brussels neighbourhood]. He is handsome, intelligent, courteous, sincere. As soon as he opens his mouth, he sparks sympathy (*Ibid.*: 185. Brackets added).

The two quotes presented above are worth commenting upon, especially the suggestion they make that Jean-Léonard was more handsome and more intelligent than all other black Africans. What is interesting is that the Tutsi-man-is-handsome stereotype is put in the foreigners' mouths, Julie's family and Orlando's, who are considered to be neutral observers. The deduction would be that if foreigners find Tutsi men to be the most handsome men in Africa, then that must be the case. What is more, Rwandans themselves seem to come to the same conclusion as they, too, find the Tutsi man handsome. In this respect, Rurangwa portrayed Captain Michel Mivumbi, another Tutsi character, as a 'handsome young officer, slim like a nail' (*Ibid*: 96-97), who blew up girls' hearts in Kigali. For instance, a girl found him at Intsinzi Bar and, as soon as she saw him, her face radiated with joy: 'She was crazy about that so handsome and intelligent young officer' (*Ibid.*: 99). This approach creates a sort of consensus around the Tutsi-man-is handsome stereotype.

Rusimbi also attributed handsomeness to his Tutsi characters in his two novels, even though he did not do so as extensively as Rurangwa. In *By the Time She Returned*, Paul, a Rwandan Tutsi senior army officer, who fought alongside victorious Ugandan rebels, was described by Jenipher, a Tutsi girl spying for the Hutu regime in Kigali, as 'a handsome man…generous' whose 'personality is rare' (Rusimbi, 1999: 154). The association of handsomeness and Tutsiness is also observed in *The Hyena's Wedding*, where Kalisa, Harriet's biological father, is presented as 'handsome and a good singer' (Rusimbi, 2007: 35). In the eyes of Harriet's aunt, Kalisa was so handsome that two sisters, including Harriet's mother, fell in love with him at the same time (*Ibid.*).

Amongst all of the novels, Mbabazi's (2007) *Sheridan* is the only one that attributes handsomeness traits to a Hutu character. What is more, this novel does not attribute handsomeness to any Tutsi character. Hutu army officer Miko is portrayed as a handsome man both by foreign and Rwandan observers. When French army officer Linda Hammel saw him for the first time in the Judo hall in Paris, she was immediately overwhelmed by this 'handsome guy' – *beau mec* (Mbabazi, 2007: 21). In Linda's eyes, Miko was of 'remarkable elegance' (*Ibid.*: 20) and had a face with regular traits (*Ibid.*: 23). It was certainly because of his handsomeness that Linda fell in love with him, despite her being his instructor (*Ibid.*). It also partly explains why Kenya was easily seduced by that man, despite their different ethnicities and political affiliations (*Ibid.*: 82-83).

Mbabazi (2007) also described some of the other African army officers attending the training together with Miko in France. At the end one realises that Miko was the most handsome of all: Rawiri, the Gabonese, was 'more or less stocky and heavily muscled' (*Ibid.*: 26); Khaled, the Tunisian, had 'a flat nose and sunken eyes' and was 'as hairy as a monkey' (*Ibid.*: 27); Demanya, the Togolese, had 'an enormous mouth…' and a large scar across his right cheek' (*Ibid.*: 56); as for Pekine, the Senegalese, he was 'as black as anthracite' and had 'a small, hunchbacked nose and very badly aligned teeth' (*Ibid.*: 56).

To end with, this section has only focused on five novels out of eleven, because the other six do not discuss the notion of handsomeness. As explained in the introduction, men's handsomeness seems to be marginal, as Rwandans tend to favour manliness and mental attributes rather than physical appearance. This is perhaps the reason why only five novels mention men's handsomeness, whereas all 11 mention women's beauty (Section 3.1). From the five novels that refer to handsomeness, one major pattern has emerged: three out of five attribute handsomeness to Tutsi male characters, with one even suggesting that the Tutsi man is absolutely superior to other black African men. One novel – Mbabazi's – reversed the situation by presenting a Hutu male character as not only handsome, but also as exceeding other African men in handsomeness. It is worth noting here that the three novels that stereotype the Tutsi man as handsome were all authored by Tutsi authors, whereas the sole novel that portrays a handsome Hutu character was authored by a Hutu novelist. This finding joins the one I have already presented in the previous section, where the Tutsi-woman-is-beautiful stereotype dominated the Tutsi-authored novels, even though it also slightly appeared in two Hutu-authored novels. Further conclusions in this regard will be drawn after the notion of 'Ugliness' has been discussed in the next section.

3.3. Ugliness

Unlike 'beauty' and 'handsomeness' which are gender sensitive, 'ugliness' applies to both men and women. Defining ugliness seems mission impossible, even though it is often easier to distinguish the ugly from the beautiful. Historical tales, myths, legends and proverbs that often sketch ways in which Rwandans conceptualise the world around them, are not so helpful in this respect. However, one popular anecdote about a woman named Bakayishonga, reveals one aspect of ugliness. Close to King Mutara III Rudahigwa [1931-1959], the woman visited the royal palace in Burundi and, as she was speaking with her hosts, one of them asked in Kirundi:[24] '*Nta ndya?*' [Is there anything to eat?]. The Rwandans who had accompanied Bakayishonga understood the Kinyarwanda '*ntandya?*' [Is she not going to bite me?]. They were chocked by that 'lack of courtesy', because they knew that Bakayishonga was obviously ugly. Her excessively long teeth ostensibly prevented the two lips from touching each other, which explains the assumption that the Burundian thought that she would bite her. One of the Rwandan visitors answered in Kinyarwanda: '*Ntaryana! Ni ububi gusa!*' [She does not bite anyone! She is just ugly!]. In his autobiography, artist Corneille (2016: 24) also described his grandmother on his father's side as 'ugly', as her almost toothless mouth, her 'burst, dead, misshapen and grey eye' made her look like a witch. Like these anecdotal examples, some of the novels I am analysing explain ugliness using one or many specific physical traits, but some of the others just use it without elaborating upon it. The objective of this section is to analyse the use of ugliness amongst female and male characters and to find ways in which it is associated with ethnicity, if at all.

Amongst all the novels on which I am focusing, Mukasonga's (2012) *Notre Dame du Nil* is the most explicit and detailed in portraying ugly characters. Gloriosa Nyiramasuka, the Hutu main character, is presented as the incarnation of ugliness. Because of her 'imposing posture', her 'brawny calves' and 'huge circular glasses', Gloriosa had received the nickname 'Behemoth' (Mukasonga, 2012: 28).[25] As described here, Gloriosa's stature brings to mind Miko's sister Masaro, who had a flat stomach and nice behind *but* had the problem of being beefy (Mbabazi, 2007: 115). What is more, according to the local mayor who also knew Gloriosa's father, 'she is a perfect copy of her father' (Mukasonga, 2012: 28). Despite her obvious ugliness, Gloriosa still thought she was beautiful. That is why she became so furious about her Tutsi classmate, Veronica, when the latter monopolised the journalists' attention during Queen Fabiola's visit. The fact that the journalists laughed out loud when Gloriosa asked them why they were focusing on Veronica, suggests that the journalists, too, found her ugly and not worth profiling on the front cover of their magazines (*Ibid.*: 172). Also, Gloriosa's recurrent remark that the Tutsi were beautiful or that their beauty would bring bad luck, betrays a complex she had that she, unlike her Tutsi classmates, was inherently ugly.

---

24 Kirundi is so close to Kinyarwanda that Burundians and Rwandans speak each their own language when they talk.

25 It is worth pointing out that Mukasonga used a similar description in her mother's biography to describe a Tutsi girl named Claudine. Like Gloriosa, Claudine was exceptionally vigorous and so strong that she would carry water jugs on her head that no man could lift. Her thighs were massive and haired and she would mightily walk like an elephant (Mukasonga, 2008: 134).

One observes a similar complex in the conduct and thoughts of Godelive, another Hutu classmate. She was constantly enquiring about how to look beautiful and smart. At one point she asked Immaculée, another Hutu student, about tips for her to appear beautiful. She wanted to know about nail varnish, like the one their white teacher used and whether she could also get some 'lip varnish' (*Ibid*: 167-168). Godelive's efforts to become beautiful are similar to those made by Masaro, who spent a fortune on beauty products 'in order to have a fair-complexioned skin close to that of white people' (Mbabazi, 2007: 115). Masaro would smear her body with carcinogenic products that would strip layers off her skin. To her sister Zuba, who mocked her, she would say: 'Let me alone! If I am lightening my skin, it's because I want to become luminous' (*Ibid*.).

Godelive's ugliness became a subject of conversation amongst classmates when she informed them that President Kayibanda had chosen her to accompany his youngest daughter to Belgium. The president had decided to offer his daughter to the childless royal family of Belgium. Despite Godelive's close relationship with President Kayibanda's family, her Hutu classmates thought she did not deserve to accompany the president's daughter, because she was so ugly:

> -Is it you that he [the president] is going to offer to the King of Belgium? At your age! With your fatness! With your [poor] grades! You already see yourself as [Queen] Fabiola's daughter!
>
> -No, he is offering one of his daughters, Merciana, the youngest. She is nine and she's fair-complexioned, she looks like her [Tutsi] mother. She is almost a white girl.[26]
>
> -…
>
> -I am just accompanying her to Belgium… (Mukasonga, 2012: 164. Brackets added).

Goretti, a Hutu classmate, did not believe Godelive's story. She wondered: How can the president choose 'the ugliest and most stupid girl of the entire lyceum to accompany his daughter?' (*Ibid*.: 165). On hearing this, Gloriosa defended Godelive saying that she was going simply because she was

> a true Rwandan girl, and no one can be mistaken about that; that [her true Rwandanness] is not assessed based on her grades or on her beauty; she will valuably represent the majority people (*ibid*. Brackets added).

The dialogue amongst Hutu students and the exchange between Goretti and Gloriosa, both Hutu, is very important for my analysis. Firstly, all these Hutu characters agreed that Godelive was ugly. Godelive herself did not even try to defend herself, which suggests that she agreed that she was ugly. Secondly, her ugliness was immediately contrasted with the beauty of President Kayibanda's youngest

---

26 In her mother's biography, Mukasonga (2008: 112-113) dismissively presents the Tutsi-as-almost-white-people idea as an invention of early European historians and anthropologists who wanted to create divisions. Yet, her use in this dialogue seems to betray a complex of superiority. The author lets her Hutu character refer to the Tutsi as 'almost white people' probably because she wants to spread that complex.

daughter, who looked like her mother [Tutsi[27]]: she was almost like a white girl. The novel presents the half-Hutu daughter of the president as owing her beauty to her Tutsi mother, which brings to mind Fortunata Uwera's beauty that she had also taken from her Tutsi mother (Twagilimana, 1996). Thirdly, Gloriosa, the one who embodied and defended Hutuness, also agreed that actually what counted was not beauty [not even intelligence, see Section 4.3] and seemed to suggest that despite her obvious ugliness, Godelive still valuably represented Hutuness.

What emerges from Mukasonga's use of ugliness is a strong suggestion that the Hutu are ugly and that everyone is in agreement about this. Foreign journalists – considered neutral observers – found the Hutu ugly and the Hutu themselves were presented as admitting their ugliness and living with it. One important note is that Tutsi characters did not engage in any way in the Hutu-is-ugly discussion. This observation should be considered together with the construction of Tutsiness (Section 1.3) and with the discussions about the names of Tutsi characters (Section 2.3). Those discussions have shown that Tutsiness was often associated with innocence and victimhood, which implies that they could not have engaged in negative stereotyping and still claim innocence whilst still fitting in with the role of being a victim.

Sehene's (2005) *Le feu sous la soutane* also uses the contrasting technique, whereby a Tutsi character is first portrayed as beautiful before a half-Hutu character is presented as ugly. This is exactly what happened when Father Stanislas described Dafrose as having all the traits that the Rwandan beauty canon required (Sehene, 2005: 68-69), before contrasting that beauty with his own ugliness: 'Her young body with its perfect forms contrasted so much with my own, flabby and enormous for any comparison' (*Ibid.*: 74). Like Mukasonga's novel that presents Hutu characters as having the complex of ugliness, Sehene's uses Father Stanislas' self-perception to suggest that Tutsi women hate Hutu men, because of their ugliness. As he contemplated his other sexual slave Assumpta, a beautiful Tutsi girl, Father Stanislas kept reminding himself of the 'Tutsi women's arrogance and contempt towards us' (*Ibid.*: 115). He remembered what these women used to say before the conflict: 'The ugly goat – the Hutu – can never mate with a sheep' (*Ibid.*).

In a different scene, where Father Stanislas and the Mayor of Kigali discussed the burial of Tutsi victims, the narrator describes the Hutu Mayor as 'a fat fellow with red lips…limply seated in his chair…with a constant hand movement, as if he was chasing away a fly in front of his large nose' (*Ibid.*: 83). Here, the association between Hutuness and ugliness is once again emphasised. One way of doing this is to embed a complex of ugliness in a [half-] Hutu's self-perception and thinking. Another way is to make it obvious but present it side by side with Tutsi beauty. The latter approach is observed in Twagilimana's (1996) *Manifold Annihilation*, namely when Mahoro discovered for the first time both Kalinda's wife Celia and her Hutu lover, Joseph Nduru. As observed in Section 3.1., Celia was *ikibasumba*, the unequalled beauty, and 'perfection itself' (Twagilimana, 1996: 40-41). Sitting next to her that day was Nduru, 'a big black man in a dark suit and large glasses'

---

27   In her autobiography, Mukasonga (2006) refers to President Kayibanda's wife and mentions a visit to her in the presidential residence in Kigali. She realised that her being a Tutsi made her unhappy.

who was 'unspeakably ugly'. With a lot of disgust, Mahoro described Nduru as follows:

> I dislike the idea of describing him in full detail, but he was chubby, had a double chin, as I judged it, and his belly rested on his thighs as he sat. I guessed that such a breed of man couldn't easily move. This type of man was made for sitting in cars. I couldn't understand what reasons Mrs. Kalinda's heart could possibly have to be sitting beside this monster (*Ibid.*: 56-57).

Ugliness is also associated with Niko, the half-Hutu character who killed the Tutsi in Gatore's (2008) *Le passé devant soi*. Niko was born mute and so ugly that whenever he smiled everyone, including cattle, ran away from him (Gatore, 2008: 140). Even though ugliness is not a recurrent theme in Gatore's novel, it nonetheless becomes an important detail when considered side by side with Isaro's beauty. This juxtaposition of an ugly [half-] Hutu with a beautiful [half-] Tutsi amplifies and perpetuates the Hutu-is-ugly and the Tutsi-is-beautiful/handsome stereotypes.

The same is also true with Rusimbi's (2007) *The Hyena's Wedding*, where the few Hutu descriptions converge in suggesting that the Hutu are ugly. In his praise for the new Tutsi-dominated leadership in post-genocide Rwanda, local Tutsi leader Kiroko told his wife's aunt about the new approach to leadership. According to him, leadership should not mean enriching oneself, which was the case during the previous Hutu-dominated regime. Her aunt's suggestion that money usually goes hand in hand with power provoked the following reflection: 'It reminded me of the leaders I used to see driven in *beautiful cars, dressed in the best clothes – pot-bellied, ugly creatures*' (Rusimbi, 2007: 31. Emphasis added). This reflection, especially the italicised part, clearly amplifies Hutu ugliness by contrasting it with beauty. Unlike Mukasonga and Sehene who contrasted Hutu ugliness with Tutsi beauty, Rusimbi preferred to contrast Hutu ugliness with objects' beauty. Presented like this, cars and clothes seem to have more value than ugly creatures [human?]. In another instance, as Kiroko and his superior Mugabo visited the local prison crowded with genocide suspects, thus Hutu, the two leaders realised that 'the cells were congested with ugly looking people. The smell inside was so unpleasant that I constantly tried to cover my nose with my fingers' (*Ibid.*: 64). The notion of ugliness that Rusimbi used to describe the Hutu inmates seems to be related to the conditions in which those inmates were, rather than to some innate condition. It is this notion of acquired, context-related ugliness that Bahufite (2016: 46-47) used to describe the Hutu boys in the camps. Those boys had ended up becoming ugly, as their skin had hardened, their eyes turned red and their hands developed a layer of scales.

What appears in this section is that four out of the 11 novels, Rusimbi (1999), Niwese (2001), Rurangwa (2006), and Ndwaniye (2006) have not been taken into account, mainly because the notion of ugliness has not been used. However, as the previous two sections have shown, Rurangwa (2006) and Rusimbi (1999) have clearly equated beauty and handsomeness with Tutsiness. Not discussing Hutuness in relation to either implies that the reverse applies to the Hutu. As for Ndwaniye (2006), he not only kept his 'neutral' approach, but he also refrained from attributing any traits of ugliness to any character. On his side, Niwese's (2001) novel does not really discuss ugliness or beauty, except for one very brief case discussed in Section 3.1.

All in all, the analysis presented in this section leads to one major conclusion, namely that the seven novels I have investigated strongly suggest that the Hutu is ugly, whether inherently or as a result of some dire situations. The novelists used different techniques to convey this stereotype: in some cases, Hutu characters confess that they are ugly and accept it, while at the same time they strive to make themselves look beautiful; in other cases, 'neutral' foreign observers confirm that the Hutu are indeed ugly; yet in other cases, Tutsi characters label the Hutu as ugly in a straight and direct way. In rare cases, ugliness is associated with Hutu characters as a result of the extreme conditions in which they find themselves. One should also add that self-perception makes the [half-] Hutu characters show a complex of ugliness, by naturally attributing beauty to the Tutsi. One other major finding is the contrast that some novelists used to exacerbate the Hutu-is-ugly stereotype. This contrast approach consists in juxtaposing beauty and ugliness, where ugliness is associated with Hutuness and beauty with either Tutsiness or other objects.

3.4. Beauty and Ugliness in Fest'Africa Project Novels

So far, I have exclusively focused on Rwandan-authored novels of genocide, because my analysis revolves around my own strong assumption that the novels of genocide fetch substantially from cultural memory of both recent and times gone by. I want to include the Fest'Africa project novels here for two main reasons: Firstly, they are based on the testimonies of people whose memories are embedded in Rwanda's collective memories. In other words, these edited testimonies from Rwandans are likely to reflect memory-inspired stereotypes amongst Rwandans. Secondly, stereotypes are stereotypes precisely because they are repeated and reproduced both by Rwandan and foreign authors. So, this section aims to compare the use of the Tutsi-is-beautiful/handsome and the Hutu-is-ugly stereotypes discussed in Rwandan-authored novels of genocide against their use by foreign novelists.

For this comparative analysis I only discuss three of the four novels that resulted from the 'Rwanda: Writing as a Duty to Remember' project in 1998. The initiative took place in the framework of the annual African arts and literature festival known as Fest'Africa (Dauge-Roth, 2010: 90). These novels are: Boubacar Boris Diop's (2000) *Murambi: le livre des ossements* [*Murambi: The Book of Bones*], Tierno Monénembo's (2000) *L'aîné des orphelins* [*The Oldest Orphan*], and Monique Ilboudo's (2000) *Murekatete*.[28] Together with a group of other authors, whose final outputs were either travel chronicles, essays or novellas, these authors spent two months in Rwanda in 1998, mainly visiting memorial sites during guided tours. Diop, Ilboudo, Lamko [whose novel is not included here] and Monénembo 'chose the novel for its ability to create a polyvocal and intimate representation

---

28 I had wished to include Koulsy Lamko's (2000) *La Phalène des collines* but the novel proved almost impossible to find. Efforts to order it were also futile as the novel seems out of print [stock]. Also, the publisher did not respond to my multiple queries.

of victims and perpetrators' feelings and thoughts' (Dauge-Roth, 2010: 93). One important aspect is that the process that led to the authoring and publication of these novels seemed unorthodox. On the one hand, the authors' creativity was constrained within strict boundaries beyond which it could not go. According to Nocky Djedanoum and Maïmouna Coulibaly, the project initiators,

> it was imperative that African writers assert in their own words that the genocide of the Tutsis in Rwanda had occurred, that it had happened for political and historical reasons, and that its moral obligations and political responsibilities could be consigned neither to the past nor to Rwanda (*Ibid.*: 92).

This is a rather political, ideological statement that one would not expect for a literary project. In other terms, the literary authors had to demonstrate the political and historical reasons that culminated in the genocide, which means that the usual freedom that creative writers need was absent. Moreover, the project had to firstly be submitted to the Rwandan government for approval. That same government provided accommodation during the two months the authors resided in Rwanda. Worse still, 'these authors could not travel freely throughout the country because of fierce battles that were still raging, mostly in the northwest' (*Ibid.*: 93). One can borrow the 'embedded journalism' analogy and call this project 'embedded literature', as it involved prior approval and surveillance at almost all of the stages. Despite all of these weaknesses, the novels became popular amongst critics, researchers and the general public, hence the need to examine ways in which they deal with ethnic stereotypes. In what follows, I want to provide short summaries of the novels before proceeding with the analysis.

Diop's (2000) *Murambi* revolves around half-Hutu Cornélius Uvimana [sic!], who, in 1994, returned home after 26 years in a self-imposed exile, first in Burundi and then later in Djibouti, to discover that his father was the butcher of Murambi. Amongst his victims were his own Tutsi wife and two children. Cornélius spoke with survivors, who told him about how his father had organised and executed the killings before fleeing to Zaire with French troops. Caught up in a position of a son of a butcher and that of a victim, Cornélius decided to ask for forgiveness to the dead and to the survivors for his father's crimes.

Monénembo's (2000) *L'aîné des orphelins* is about Faustin Nsenghimana [sic!], a 12-year-old half-Hutu boy who witnessed and survived the genocide in the Nyamata church, where his Hutu father and Tutsi mother, together with thousands of others, were butchered. Faustin ran away but was captured by the RPF rebels, whom he later joined as a child soldier. After the war ended, Faustin lived a miserable life marked by sex, drugs and cold-blooded violence. When Faustin saw one of his friends having sex with his sister, he shot him dead. After three years in jail, with kind assistance from a Tutsi woman called Claudine Karemera, Faustin was sentenced to death at the age of 15.

Finally, Ilboudo's (2000) *Murekatete* tells the story about a half-Hutu girl named Murekatete, born into a family where her Tutsi mother was fiercely rejected by her Hutu father's relatives. Murekatete became a nun in Byumba, her place of origin, but quitted to marry a Tutsi priest, Nicodème, who was her confessor. Her father, husband and uncle all died before the genocide under mysterious circumstances.

When the genocide started, she ran away but was captured at a roadblock where her children were killed in front of her. Badly wounded, she was rescued by Venant, a passing RPF rebel, who took her to hospital and who later became her husband. Their relations became tense when they started visiting memorials and it ended with Venant raping her before vanishing to a far away place.

The question I want to address here is: How do these novels use the notion of beauty and how does that relate to ethnicity? Diop's (2000) *Murambi* contains one instance in which beauty is prominent. The novel presents an unnamed Tutsi woman, who had sought refuge at Sainte Famille church in Kigali, as exceptionally beautiful. Jessica Kamanzi, a Tutsi RPF spy, was overwhelmed when she met the woman near the church: 'Her beauty had something infernal. That type of woman who always sparks some desire amongst men …She was really dazzling' (Diop, 2000: 117). The woman was also aware of her exceptional beauty, because she would say: 'I am too beautiful to survive. I have the beauty of the sun and like the sun I can't hide anywhere' (*Ibid.*: 119). Jessica confirmed this remark that, indeed, she could not survive the genocide with that 'supernatural beauty' (*Ibid.*).

Two points are interesting here for comparative purposes. Firstly, beauty is clearly linked to Tutsiness, which was the case in the Rwandan-authored novels (Section 3.1). Secondly, beauty is presented as a burden and as something that brings bad luck rather than a blessing, which was equally the case in some Rwandan-authored novels. The nameless, beautiful woman could not escape the attention of the Sainte Famille priest [this joins Sehene's (2005) description of Father Stanislas], who kept threatening to deliver her to the Interahamwe militiamen if she refused to go to bed with him. The priest raped her and took away any zest for life that she had (*Ibid.*: 120-123). One could also add that the fact that the woman has no name, which pushes one to refer to her as the nameless Tutsi woman, turns her situation into a universal one, i.e., one that applies to all other Tutsi women. This idea of universality is further reinforced by the sun metaphor ['I have the beauty of the sun'], since the sun is a perfect symbol of universality.

Even though Monénembo's (2000) *L'Aîné des orphelin* does not engage in numerous and detailed descriptions of characters' physical appearance, it nonetheless exclusively attributes beauty to Tutsi characters. When Faustin discovered from his father that he was both Hutu [because his father was] and Tutsi [because his mother was], he was puzzled and concerned. His father tried to reassure him that Hutu and Tutsi were the same, telling him that comparing them is like comparing water with water. However, he added: 'Your mother Axelle was the most beautiful shepherdess of the entire Bimirura hamlet' (Monénembo, 2000: 138-139). The use of absolute superlative here brings to mind many other superlatives used in some Rwandan-authored novels: Father Stanislas' Tutsi mother is equally described as 'the prettiest of our [Father Stanislas'] hill' (Sehene, 2005: 123. Brackets added); Celia is presented as *ikibasumba*, the unequalled beauty (Twagilimana, 1996: 40); and Mukagatare is portrayed as 'the most beautiful girl at school' (Rusimbi: 1999: 20). The Tutsi-girl/woman-is-beautiful stereotype comes back once again when Faustin helped Rodney, a white cameraman in Kigali, find a prostitute. Faustin chose Solange for him:

> She was a beautiful Tutsi who had grown up in Nairobi. Her husband was an RPF soldier and was killed during the battle of Byumba. She smiled like an angel and she spoke English. Rodney was delighted (Monénembo, 2000: 100).

One cannot read this quote without immediately thinking about Veronica and the photocall in Mukasonga's (2012) *Notre Dame du Nil*. Like Veronica, whose beauty was unanimous both amongst her Hutu classmates and foreign journalists, Solange's beauty had absolute consensus. A neutral, foreign observer confirmed the beauty evaluation made by a Rwandan.

Ilboudo's (2000) *Murekatete* also approaches beauty from the perspective of the main character's mother. Murekatete was born from a Hutu father and a Tutsi mother and the latter, according to Murekatete herself, was pretty:

> My mother was Tutsi. Her identity card did not mention it, but her physical appearance confirmed it. She was beautiful. *But that is a pleonasm. Are all Tutsi women not beautiful?* That pretence is Tutsi. But certain Hutu men do not make any effort to dismiss that, because they marry a Tutsi woman as a necessary complement for their social success (Ilboudo, 2000: 29. Emphasis added).

This is the sole instance in which Ilboudo's novel refers to beauty, but it is certainly the most powerful and the most revealing of all cases I have identified in the 14 novels of genocide discussed so far. It is true that Father Stanislas described his mother as the prettiest on the entire hill, that Faustin's mother is portrayed as the most beautiful shepherdess, that Celia had unreachable beauty, but in none of these cases, no sweeping generalisation was suggested. Unlike the claims in all of these cases, Murekatete's claim suggests that Tutsi and beauty means the same thing and should be interchangeable. Using them simultaneously results in a pleonasm. Moreover, the blame is put on Hutu men who need social success and who can only attain it by marrying Tutsi women. The implied stereotype here is that Hutu women are ugly, which some Rwandan-authored novels have elaborated upon.

Until this point, Diop (2000), Monénembo (2000), and Ilboudo (2000) show striking similarities with five of the six Tutsi-authored novels [excluding Rusimbi (2007)], all of which discuss beauty and associate it exclusively with Tutsiness. However, one exception can be observed in Diop's (2000) *Murambi*, where Jessica Kamanzi, the Tutsi RPF spy in Kigali, is portrayed as not being beautiful. The bones of her chest could be seen and her body was 'dry and graceless' as if she had been suffering from a serious disease for a long time (Diop, 2000: 82). Even her childhood friend Cornélius, a half-Hutu, found her to be graceless. When he met her after the war, he found her unfortunate as no man was interested in her, 'simply because she was not beautiful' (*Ibid*.: 92).

Another remarkable difference worth noting here is the total absence of details about Hutu characters' physical appearance in these non-Rwandan-authored novels. Coupled with repetitive cases of the Tutsi-is-beautiful stereotype, this omission could be interpreted as meaning that the non-Tutsi are ugly. This deduction logically flows on from the reasoning that if, from a given population, one selects a small group and labels it as beautiful, one is implicitly suggesting that the ones that were not selected did not meet the selection criteria.

The conclusion here is that the three Fest'Africa novels of genocide do convey the Tutsi-is-beautiful stereotype. The exception of a not-beautiful Tutsi woman in Diop's (2000) novel seems to be an isolated case and is the only one in 14 novels [both Rwandan-authored and foreign-authored] and since it is a rare exception, it rather confirms the rule. This section has also stressed the fact that all the main characters happen to be half-Hutu, whose Tutsi mothers, at least for two of the three, were exceptionally beautiful. It should also be pointed out that, unlike many Rwandan-authored novels of genocide, non-Rwandan-authored novels do not touch upon the physical appearance of Hutu characters. At first sight, this means that Hutu characters could not be categorised as beautiful/handsome or ugly. However, this absence of description and the more or less abundant description of Tutsi characters as beautiful, lead to the following deduction: If each time a Tutsi woman is mentioned the adjective 'beautiful' and its superlative are used to the point of becoming a pleonasm, it follows that Hutu girls cannot be beautiful. In other words, putting Hutu and beautiful together would result in an antonymous situation, whereas Tutsi and beautiful together results in a pleonasm. In the last analysis, by overtly embracing the Tutsi-is-beautiful stereotype, Diop (2000), Monénembo (2000), and Ilboudo (2000), implicitly exacerbated and contributed to spreading the Hutu-is-ugly stereotype.

3.5. Summary and Discussion

This chapter has focused on the stereotypes that relate to the physical appearance of the characters. The aim was threefold: [1] finding out ways in which characters are physically described, [2] identifying the major techniques used in those descriptions and [3] establishing links between those descriptions and ethnicity. The analysis in the first section has shown that eight out of the 11 Rwandan-authored novels unambiguously associate beauty with Tutsiness. Tutsi women and girls are frequently presented as pretty and that prettiness is itself presented as a cause for [future] trouble. One technique used in this respect is placing the conviction that Tutsi girls are beautiful in the minds of the Hutu characters. Another consists in making foreigners come to the same conclusion that Tutsi girls are beautiful. Yet another technique centres on Tutsi characters' perception of their own beauty.

Similar conclusions were drawn with respect to handsomeness. As a rule, Tutsi male characters tend to always be handsome. That stereotype is conveyed either through foreigners who seem to support the idea that the Tutsi man is the most handsome of all black Africans or through Tutsi female characters. I should add here that the four novels that exacerbate this stereotype are all authored by Tutsi novelists, which might somehow explain its dominance. The findings presented in this chapter have also revealed that the Hutu-is-ugly stereotype was present in six of the 11 Rwandan-authored novels. In some cases, Hutu characters admit themselves that they are ugly, but in the majority of cases, Tutsi characters are the ones directly describing or labelling the Hutu as ugly. The novels frequently contrasted beauty with ugliness to amplify the latter in a more overt way.

The last section of this chapter took a different approach and compared the uses of the notion of beauty stereotypes in Fest'Africa project novels and in Rwandan-authored counterparts. The result was that the three Fest'Africa project novels wholly and overtly embraced the Tutsi-is-beautiful stereotype. At the same time, they completely refrained from engaging in any physical description of Hutu characters. My deduction was that describing A as indescribably beautiful and deciding to let the readers guess what non-A looks like, suggests that non-A is inevitably ugly and not worth describing.

This comparison has led to one major conclusion: There seems to be unanimity about the Tutsi being beautiful/handsome and the Hutu being ugly. This conclusion calls for some discussion, especially when one realises that there are two straight lines that divide the characters into two categories. On the one hand, there is a line connecting innocence and victimhood to positively connoted, innocence, bravery or extraordinariness evoking names and then to beauty/handsomeness. On the other hand, there is a line that connects abuse of power to land work or animal or negatively connoted names and to ugliness. Of course one finds some rare exceptions in between that confirm the rules. These lines correspond to ethnicity: The first line is obviously a Tutsi line and the second is a Hutu line.

The fact that these lines emerge from novels that convey the genocide memories makes the discussion more interesting, because the people who decide to read novels about epoch-marking events like the 1994 genocide, are not doing so to quench their thirst for entertainment. One decides to read novels of genocide because one wants to know [how other people represent] what happened in Rwanda in 1994 and the periods before and after. Rusimbi, the author of two of the novels I investigated [*By the Time She returned* (1999) and *The Hyena's Wedding* (2007)], seems to be aware that his novels have an important informative function. For that reason, prior to reading *The Hyena's Wedding*, the reader is provided with three pages of an historical and factual background that tells the reader that 'The novel *The Hyena's Wedding* reveals the untold horrors of the 1994 genocide in Rwanda' (Rusimbi, 2007: iii). As such, the novel is primarily the *revelation* or representation of what a former Tutsi refugee, who later became an RPF Member of Parliament, remembers [and forgets] about the 'the untold horrors of the 1994 genocide'. The same is true with Rurangwa, who reminds the reader that his novel is indeed fiction, but that his fictional account is grounded in an 'historical truth'. For that reason, his postface stresses that the novel should be read as a 'testimony' (Rurangwa, 2006: 197) of a former Tutsi refugee, who later became a lecturer in sociology at the National University of Rwanda, as it was called at the time.

What I am suggesting here is that these novels seem to set a deadly memory trap by stereotyping the Hutu and the Tutsi in a systematic and clear-cut, black and white, way. By demonising the Hutu and glorifying the Tutsi in all respects and without any or little nuance, these novels dangerously contribute to the normalisation and routinisation of these stereotypes in current and future generations. Current generations of researchers, critics and decision makers [especially those in the educational and cultural sectors], should play an important role in denouncing the perpetuation of these stereotypes in mass media, including novels, because, as they get repeated over and over, they end up becoming accepted by all as self-evident (Rosello, 1998: 34-35; Barthes, 1973: 69). Rosello (1998: 14) rightly warned against this process thus:

> The overall impression is that the main danger is slow petrification, gradual immobility, eventual necrosis, and the death of just about everything pleasurable: thought, originality, beauty, independence, literature. The stakes are high: stereotypes lead straight to terminal boredom, to a sort of Baudelairian ennui that you would not even wish on your nastiest colleagues.

What makes the task of challenging these stereotypes even more difficult and risky, is that they are now associated with the genocide and somehow, part of the explanation as to why it happened. Given that post-genocide, Tutsi-dominated Rwanda tightly controls the narrative around the genocide and has a law to scare critical voices away, challenging these stereotypes might expose the challenger to even greater dangers. For the time being, one has no choice but to accept that all beautiful and handsome Rwandans are [supposed to be] Tutsi, and all 'ugly creatures', to repeat the phrase often used in the novels, from Rwanda are [supposed to be] Hutu. What fate would the anti-genocide law reserve to a novelist who would reverse these stereotypes just for creative purposes? I will leave that question open.

Chapter 4

Smartness, Intelligence vs. Stupidity and Silliness

This chapter follows the same logic as the previous one and, on the one hand, attempts to identify stereotypes that are related to characters' smartness/intelligence or lack of it and, on the other hand, to eventually find out ethnic patterns in the use of these stereotypes. Here, just as in the previous chapter, I have to firstly overcome the challenge of defining smartness and intelligence in the Rwandan cultural context. It is only after having defined *ubwenge*, a term that means smartness, intelligence or cleverness depending on the circumstances under which it is used, that I engage the 11 novels of genocide to find out both the use of that concept and eventual ethnic patterns in that use.

4.1. Smartness, Intelligence & Cleverness

The question I need to answer in this section is: Whom do Rwandans consider to be smart/intelligent/clever? So far, no thorough research has been conducted into this subject to offer a comprehensive definition of *ubwenge*. For that reason, I base my definition on the use of this concept in historical tales and in popular expressions rooted in, and inspired by, age-old oral traditions and on everyday language usage combined with common sense. This section distinguishes between three types of *ubwenge*. The first type is one that I term the 'outplay-the-other' type of *ubwenge*; the second is one that could be called 'high-level-reasoning/imagination' *ubwenge*; and the third one could commonly be referred to as 'science/knowledge-based' *ubwenge*.

Ubwenge in the sense of outplaying the other refers primarily to the ability to turn difficult and complex situations around in one's favour or in favour of one's family [in the primary or the broader sense]. What makes this *ubwenge* tricky is that the 'smart person' does not necessarily bother as to whether the new situation is detrimental to someone else. *Ubwenge* in this sense might, and often does, involve a certain degree of deception and dishonest means, as long as these means contribute to reaching the situation that is favourable to one or to one's family. In this respect, one is smart or intelligent – *inyaryenge* – if one can manage to skilfully navigate between the truth and lies to achieve one's goal.[29] A good example of this type of *ubwenge* is in a short 1966 video clip that was recently [August 2016] posted on Facebook about a French speaking journalist using a Rwandan translator

---

29 The philosophy behind ubwenge in this sense is summarised by the following popular Rwandan proverbs: *Ukuri wabwije shobuja niko umuhakishwaho*, which means: 'The best truth is the one that makes one get favours from one's boss'.

to interview a Kinyarwanda speaking, coffee growing farmer about the benefits of being part of a coffee farmers' cooperative.[30] Regarding the question about why the farmer was a member of the cooperative, the farmer answered in Kinyarwanda: '[I became a member] so that I can find where to sell stuffs because they [merchants within the cooperative] don't buy from non-members'. The translator rendered the answer in French as follows:

> He became a member to be able to save money in order to pay for his children's education later. Moreover, he wanted to find a market [for coffee] because in the past he could not find it.

The Journalist went on to ask: 'Does he get any benefit from being a member of Trafipro [the cooperative in question]?' to which the farmer answered 'No, not yet'. Translating this rather short answer for the journalist, the translator said:

> There are a lot of benefits because before [being a member] he sold his coffee beans to merchants who paid a lower price compared to the official price. Now, with Trafipro, he earns money and hopes to have more benefits later.

The person who posted this video titled it *Traduction à la bwenge* [Smart translation]. The translator was most likely in the management team of the cooperative or was hired and briefed by it. What he attributed to the farmer was obviously meant to cast a very positive light on the cooperative, regardless of what the farmer had to say. Ironising, one Facebook user commented: 'Hahaha! That's what we call responsible translation…'. Another one added: '*Technicking* has been there for long!' The verb *gutekinika* [*technicking*] used in this comment comes from 'technique' and is a post-genocide neologism that is widely used in everyday language and in mass media to mean forging a story or a piece of evidence and tricking people into believing the new situation.

A more recent case of *ubwenge* in the sense of *technicking* in order to have favourable situations fitting into one's own goal is in a clip showing handcuffed Tutsi artist, Kizito Mihigo answering journalists' questions under the tight control of Rwandan police back on 15th April 2014.[31] The artist, once close to the regime the policies of which he chanted, was accused of treason and of plotting to assassinate the president. All this had happened because he had just composed a song, titled *Igisobanuro cy'urupfu* [The meaning of death], in which he openly claimed that the 1990s had seen many more other victims than the sole Tutsi and that those forgotten victims needed remembering and praying for. The sole question was in Kinyarwanda: 'Can he tell us about the allegations against him or the charges for which he will be taken to court?' Before Mihigo could answer, the senior police officer *smartly* paraphrased the question, thereby *technicking* it into a favourable question for him. He said to Mihigo before the latter could answer: 'They want to know how you decided to collaborate with groups that aim to destabilise Rwanda'.

---

30 JA Studio360 Inc., '1 juillet 1966 Trafipro (traduction à la bwenge)', posted on Facebook on 27 August 2016 [Accessed 28 August 2016].
    https://www.facebook.com/jastudio360/videos/1089861891094911/
31 Kigalihits.rw, 'Kizito Mihigo yemereye Abanyamakuru Ibyaha arengwa', posted on 15 April 2014 [Accessed 23 December 2016] https://www.youtube.com/watch?v=OA8cfZ0kl8g.

The journalist's question and its paraphrase by the police officer have nothing to do with each other. Mihigo naturally ignored the journalist's question and answered its *technicked* version. He confessed to having been in contact with ill-intentioned groups and he explained how. When the degree of deception is higher than that of the truth, such as in the two clips discussed above, the term *amayeri* is used and the smart person is called *umunyamayeri*. The term *amayeri* comes from *mayele* in Lingala, a language spoken in the two Congos where it means 'smartness', and has fully become part of the Kinyarwanda vocabulary.

Outplaying the other obviously implies the idea of competition as it supposes that the other is also trying their best to achieve their own goal. This idea of competition associated with *ubwenge* comes back in names like Kazu*bwenge*, which means 'The Smart One'. To link this to the function of Rwandan names that I discussed in *Complexities and Dangers* (Nyirubugara, 2013, see Chapter 7), this name assigns the bearer the mission to always outplay the other. This seems to be the case in Mukasonga's (2006: 40-43) autobiography, where a boy named Kazubwenge was part of the Tutsi rebels attacking Rwanda from Burundi in late 1963. The government army, supported by helicopters, stopped the attack and killed the attackers along with some Tutsi refugees in Nyamata with Kazubwenge managing to outplay them. He hid with a few friends and returned to Burundi unharmed, even though *he only had a bow* to defend himself. Also popular adages like *Utazi ubwenge ashima ubwe* [One thinks to be the smartest until one comes across smarter than oneself], *Ubwenge buza ubujiji buhise* [One realises one's own stupidity only after the initial solution thought to be smart has failed], and *Indyadya ihimwa n'indyamirizi* [The smarter one is outplayed by the smartest one], explicitly associate the idea of *ubwenge* with competition.

Rwanda's historical tales, which are an important vehicle of traditional values from one generation to the other (Vansina, 1971: 444), abound with instances of smartness in the 'outplay-the-other' sense and its opposite. One explicit example is the tale known as *Umurage n' umuvumo bya Kibaza* [The Heritage and Curse of The Questioner] (Smith, 1975: 140-145). Kibaza, The Questioner, was the first inhabitant of Rwanda when the land was still covered in wild forests. Kibaza named his first child Gatwa, his second Gahutu and his third, Gatutsi. Even though all three grew up like triplets and were close to one another, 'Gatutsi was sharper and more intelligent [than his brothers], to which he added cleverness and smartness'.[32] One day, Kibaza sent his sons to Kimenyi, the king of neighbouring Gisaka, to enquire about the start of the farming season. Gatwa, the eldest son, was responsible for the mission but his brothers should assist him if needed. Gatwa could not fulfil the mission as he had excessively eaten along the way to the point of vomiting. Gahutu, despite eating all day long, managed to put the question to Kimenyi, who promised to give an answer the next day. Gatutsi, who had eaten nothing along the way and had gently waited for Kimenyi's dinner, did not sleep but instead hid near Kimenyi's room and followed all the consultations about the first month of the farming season. Kimenyi decided to lie to the three brothers

---

32 Since this sounds like tautology, I would like to provide the original Kinyarwanda text, which also provides other terms that refer to the outplay-the-other type of ubwenge: 'Gatutsi akabarusha **ibakwe** n'*ubwenge*, ibyo akabigerekaho **ubucakuzi** n'**ubucakura**'.

so that his own kingdom could *outplay* Rwanda by letting the latter succumb to famine. Thus Gatwa reported the wrong answer to his father. However, Gatutsi privately told his father what had happened and gave him the right answer that Kimenyi had refused to give them. On that day, Kibaza appointed Gatutsi as the head of his family forever and ordered Gahutu and Gatwa and their posterity to serve him. It is clear here that *ubwenge* involves a degree of unethical behaviour [spying on one's hosts], betrayal [withholding the truth from one's brothers] and dishonesty [Kimenyi deciding to lie]. In the end, Gatutsi was the smartest of all, including Kimenyi, who could fool everybody except Gatutsi.

Besides the idea of outplaying the other by all means, one should add the notion of *ubwenge* as referring to the ability to accomplish a high deed or of thinking coherently and logically. This aspect of *ubwenge* is close to the philosophical notion of intelligence that distinguishes humans from animals. Psychologists and philosophers have defined intelligence as 'a set of cognitive aptitudes, namely the ability to perceive, remember, learn, imagine, and reason' (Lévy, 1998: 123). This ability allows human beings to structure and organise what they perceive, remember, learn and imagine through thinking and reasoning processes that can either be at an elementary level [low], a higher operational level, or somewhere in between (Piaget, [1969] 1971: 29). So one's level of intelligence is measured based on where one stands on the continuum that stretches from the elementary level to the high operational level.

This type of high-level-imagination, high-level-reasoning *ubwenge* also abounds in Rwanda's historical tales and tends to have a strong ethnic connotation. One popular historical tale presents Rugaju, son of Mutimbo, as a respected and feared dignitary who served as the right-hand man of King Yuhi IV Gahindiro back in the late 18th century (Coupez & Kamanzi, 1962: 310-317). Rugaju wanted to kill the King and to achieve that, he tricked him into going hunting with him. The King hesitated on going hunting with Rugaju when he started stumbling and sneezing awkwardly. Rugaju told him *to not reason like the Hutu* by seeing omens in snot. The King finally fell into Rugaju's trap by shooting in fetishised rests of a goat that Rugaju had sacrificed. Soon after that he became paralysed and realised that he was going to die. Without informing Rugaju, the King sent his Hutu servant named Rwatambuga, son of Mushengezi, to call back all his sons who were attending a military camp. Before going to the camp, Rwatambuga informed Rugaju about his mission and the latter asked the King why he would call back his sons. King Gahindiro denied ever assigning any such mission to Rwatambuga: 'He lies, that is usual amongst the Hutu', the King said. Before dying, the King ordered that Rwatambuga's head be split with his royal axe *Rwamukire*, which should be left in his skull until it rotted.

In this tale, like in many others, one detects the outplay-the-other type of *Ubwenge* [Rugaju outplayed the King and vice versa] side by side with the high-level-imagination, high-level-reasoning *ubwenge*. The latter, or rather the lack of it, is embodied by the Hutu in general, as Rugaju suggests that only the Hutu would take insignificant details to be omens. In addition to this, Rwatambuga shows his lack of sound judgment by reporting to Rugaju. How could he be the King's favourite servant and yet fail to realise that Rugaju was not on good terms with the

King? Only unintelligent people would report to the wrong people. Interestingly, King Gahindiro plays with Rugaju's belief that the Hutu are worthless and liars, whom no one can entrust with an important task. Rwatambuga seems to prove him right. This inability to achieve tasks, both simple and complex, comes back in popular adages like *utuma Abahutu atuma babiri*, which means that if one decides to send a Hutu on a mission, one had better send two of them. This implies that the two would put their intelligence together and as such would stand a better chance of carrying out the mission.

The last type of *ubwenge* is one that is usually associated with school-based education, whereby one's smartness [cleverness] and intelligence are associated with, and measured on the basis of, school performance. This notion of *ubwenge* is commonly referred to as *ubuhanga* and the clever person is usually called *umunyabwenge* [rather than *inyaryenge*] or *umuhanga*. Unlike the previous types of *ubwenge* that are supposed to be comprehensive and ready for use in multiple situations, the science or knowledge-based *ubwenge* is rarely comprehensive. One is clever in one discipline or two, but rarely in all disciplines and areas of knowledge. Also, unlike the previous types of *ubwenge* which are Machiavellian, as only the end counts, the knowledge-based *ubwenge* is materialised in a grade that reflects a certain process that involves some ethics. Moreover, people can be ranked from the cleverest to the least clever in a certain field of knowledge.

What emerges at this point is that *ubwenge* in the three senses is considered to be an asset and a cherished value in the Rwandan cultural context. One point that is worth raising here is one that attributes intelligence and smartness to the Tutsi and stupidity and silliness to the Hutu, as the first two senses of *ubwenge* show. One explanation comes from the origin of the historical tales that set in stone practices and perceptions in ancient and pre-colonial Rwanda and, in so doing, transmitted certain stereotypes to future [current] generations. By definition, historical tales, known in Kinyarwanda as *ibitekerezo* [reflections, thoughts] narrate events of the past and 'are told in the refined flowery language of the court, that stem from that milieu' (Vansina, 2000: 378). In the early 1700s, King Yuhi III Mazimpaka started a new form of art *Inanga*, which turned these historical tales into harp-accompanied music (Kagame, 1959: 34). So, if historical tales stem from the court, what follows is that the creation process was controlled by the court. The result obviously reflects the 'thoughts and reflections' from the Nyiginya dynasty, a Tutsi clan from which all kings of Rwanda were born until the monarchy was toppled in 1959, namely that the Tutsi were smarter and more intelligent, whereas the Hutu and the Twa were stupid and unintelligent.

The same observation can be made in relation to the genealogical poems known as *Ubucurabwenge* in Kinyarwanda. The term itself contains the notion and concept of *ubwenge* [last two syllables] and means literally *Forging Intelligence* or *Forging Science* (Kagame, 1959: 14). These poems contain the genealogy of the Nyiginya dynasty, starting with the king on the throne at the moment of composing them. They provide the king's names, those of his mother and her ancestors, those of his father, those of the latter's wife and her ancestors etc. The poems have three sections, the first of which covers the 12 fictive kings descending from the first king who landed on earth from heaven [*ibimanuka*] and was accompanied by a man called Mututsi. The second section covers ten kings known as *Abami b'Imishumi* [those who supported hardship] and starts with Gihanga, The Inventor, who is considered the founder of the Nyiginya dynasty. The last section covers 19 historical kings [*Abami b'Ibitekerezo*], that is, those in the Historical Tales, the last of whom was ousted in 1959 (*Ibid.*: 20-21). One can argue that these poems are called 'Forging Intelligence' because they provide overwhelming psychological advantage to the Nyiginya clan in particular and to the Tutsi in general. They create a myth [landing from heaven] and appoint one individual as *The Inventor* [of Rwanda], amongst others, which all confirm a certain high level of thinking and imagination that justifies a certain superiority.

The aim of this section was to pave the way for the analysis of stereotypes relating to smartness, intelligence and cleverness and their opposites in the novels of genocide. All these terms fall under the umbrella concept of *ubwenge*, which I have attempted to conceptualise as having three important meanings. It can mean the ability to outplay or outsmart the other regardless of the means one uses; it can also mean the ability to imagine, think and reason at a higher level; and finally, it can mean one's ease in learning and understanding a school subject and, by extension, in performing one's tasks later on in after-school life. The next three sections attempt to map *ubwenge*-related stereotypes and ways in which these are related to ethnicity.

4.2. The Smart and Clever Ones

This section uses the definitions of *ubwenge* provided in the previous section and identifies ways in which characters are described as possessing some form of smartness or cleverness. I want to firstly detect and then discuss illustrative instances taken from the novels before identifying eventual ethnic patterns. My working hypothesis here is that the Tutsi characters are most likely to be described as smarter, cleverer and more intelligent than the rest. This hypothesis is in line with the positive attributes assigned to the Tutsi characters as shown in previous chapters. Another explanation for this hypothesis is that, as the previous section has shown, the Tutsi have been traditionally [namely through controlled historical tales] designated as possessing innate cleverness and smartness. So in a way, this section aims to test that hypothesis in the novels of genocide I am analysing.

Mukasonga's (2012) *Notre Dame du Nil* is the most explicit in describing characters in a black and white fashion, with the main Tutsi characters showing more smartness and cleverness than their Hutu counterparts. All along the line and in all respects, Virginia and Veronica behaved and reasoned more intelligently and more smartly than their Hutu classmates. This attitude is observed both in matters relating to everyday life and to school-related performance. For instance, one day when the students, especially Modesta and Goretti, were discussing recipes that combined banana and beans, Virginia intervened to remind them of Rwandan wisdom when it comes to food and eating: one is not supposed to discuss food, the same way one is not supposed to eat in public, as one would then have to open one's mouth in front of other people (Mukasonga, 2012: 52-53). In a similar vein, Veronica, to whom the Hutu classmates had told about private discussions held between their parents and other senior government officials in their living rooms, knew that being able to keep a secret is part of what Rwandans consider as *ubwenge*. The following dialogue shows how the two Tutsi girls perceived that secret-keeping value and linked it to ethnicity at the same time:

> -VERONICA: Listen, Virginia, I have something to tell you. But don't repeat it to anyone.
>
> -VIRGINIA: You know well, Veronica, that *we, the Tutsi, can keep our secrets*. We were taught how to keep our mouths shut. We must do that if we really want to stay alive. You know what our parents keep telling us: 'Your tongue is your worst enemy'. If you think that what you're about to tell me is a secret, then you can trust me, I can keep secrets (*Ibid.*: 65. Emphasis added).

This dialogue is interesting in at least two ways. On the one hand, the ability to keep the secret is not presented as a Rwandan value but rather as a Tutsi one. On the other hand, it seems to be intimately linked to life and death. In other words, those who can keep secrets stand a higher chance of living longer, whereas those who cannot keep secrets, such as the Hutu, expose themselves to danger and death.[33] By describing the Hutu as unable to keep secrets (more in the next section), the novel suggests that they do not care about their lives. This observation takes one back to the Hutu servant, whom King Gahindiro entrusted with a secret mission only to realise that the Hutu could not keep a secret. As a result of that, his life ended brutally with a royal axe being planted in his head (see previous section).

Another good example is about Virginia, who, during breakfast time, would never help herself to sugar before her Hutu classmates had helped themselves. The latter would put so much sugar in their tea to the point of turning it into a sort of pudding. Virginia would be the last one to help herself and would take the last few grains, which she would keep in an envelope. Her aim was to collect enough sugar before the end of the term and take it to her siblings, who had never tasted sugar in their lives. Unfortunately, Dorothée, a Hutu classmate, discovered her secret and threatened to denounce her to the nuns. Virginia explained her altruistic intention to no avail. Dorothée used this situation to blackmail her:

> -DOROTHEE: Maybe we can find a solution. You are the *cleverest in French*. If you write the next assignment for me, I will keep quiet.
>
> -VIRGINIA: Please let me take this sugar to my younger sisters.
>
> -DOROTHEE: OK you will write all my assignments until the end of the year.
>
> -VIRGINIA: Promised. I swear. I will do that till the end of the year (Mukasonga, 2012: 40-41. Emphasis added).

---

33   This brings to mind a popular proverb that warns that 'an incautious animal is killed by a bush-clearing farmer [rather than a predator that sets a trap for that purpose]' [*Inyamaswa idakenga yicwa n'umututizi*].

All of a sudden, Dorothée became the cleverest student in French, with the highest grades (*Ibid.*). In this example one observes the three types of *ubwenge* interacting: Virginia had assessed the dangerous situation in which the Tutsi students were and as such had decided to never help herself to sugar, because that would bring her the fury of her Hutu classmates. In fact, the latter were so keen on sugar that their tea looked rather like pudding. So touching upon that precious commodity would worsen her situation. This is a sign of high-level thinking. However, whenever a few grains of sugar were left, she would collect them and hide them by outplaying her classmates and the nuns. In doing so, she proved to be smarter than them, even though that did not last. In this case, she used her outplay-the-other *ubwenge*, even though it was unsuccessful. One also notes that Virginia is presented as the cleverest in French, which takes us to the other type of *ubwenge*, one that is school knowledge-based. At the same time, Dorothée, whose performance in French was obviously lamentable, used her outplay-the-other *ubwenge* through blackmailing to gain artificial, fake knowledge-based cleverness. One can also add that making Dorothée look the cleverest turns Virginia into a super girl: firstly, she could write assignments for two people, one of which was the best in the entire class. Secondly, she is assumed to be a super girl because she managed to write two different assignments that could not betray any cheating or plagiarism. Thirdly, she strategically made Dorothée the best in French, thereby giving away her own position as 'the best in French'. By doing that, she manipulated Dorothée and turned her into her protector.

Similar strategic thinking is to be found in Rurangwa's (2006) *Au sortir de l' enfer*, where a Tutsi business man named Sakindi managed to secure protection from those Hutu in power, by lending them money that they would never pay back. Instead of claiming his money or taking them to court, he would lend them even more money (Rurangwa, 2006: 66-67). This means that Sakindi had a clear overview of the ethnic dynamics in Rwanda and could imagine what would happen if he claimed his money. He rather turned this situation around for his own advantage, as those whom he fed would keep him safe as long as he kept feeding them. This high level thinking intelligence should be considered together with the absence of school-based cleverness. Because of the anti-Tutsi quota system, Sakindi could not progress further than primary school. What one has here is a smart, non-educated person [in the sense of high level thinking] manipulating the highly educated Hutu who would threaten him with jail rather than paying back their debts. This case is very interesting in the sense that it shows an original interaction between various types of *ubwenge*. On the one hand, the Hutu thought they were smart because they could enrich themselves easily. Their school-based intelligence did not help them distinguish the good from the bad. On the other hand, Sakindi, despite his almost illiterate status, took advantage of that negative situation to prosper even more.

What is also interesting to note here with regards to Rurangwa's (2006) novel, is the way in which it describes the main Tutsi character Jean-Léonard. The same foreigners who declared him to be the most handsome man of all the African people (see Rurangwa, 2006: 176 & 185) also found him highly intelligent. When he was in Mauritius, visiting the family of his girlfriend Julie, Jean-Léonard impressed everyone there with his intelligence. Julie almost fainted with happiness because of the 'intelligent words that came out of his mouth at the right moment' (*Ibid.*: 173). Others, to whom he had just told the history of Rwanda, could not believe it: 'Incredible!... But this is a whizzkid. He is a true genius', one man exclaimed. Another added: 'Moreover, he speaks French without any African accent!' (*Ibid.*: 178). In his mind, Jean-Léonard despised these white people who thought they had the monopoly on intelligence whereas the black people had the monopoly on stupidity (*Ibid.*: 179). This comment regarding racism is of capital importance in this discussion because of the implied neutrality of the racist Mauritians being criticised. In their mind, all Africans were unintelligent and could not speak foreign languages properly. Obviously, this racist stereotype is used for a purpose, namely that there was an exception to this principle and that this exception was embodied by a Tutsi man.

The idea of the exceptionally intelligent Tutsi who surpasses everyone else in their surroundings is also at the heart of Rusimbi's (1999) *By the Time She Returned*. Kaitesi, the poor young Tutsi girl, embodies that intellectual superiority. She had completed her primary education with the highest grade in the entire school, which had made her start fantasising about becoming a professor at a great university one day (Rusimbi, 1999: 57):

> My attitude towards education had also changed. Having learnt from my mother that there are prospects of changing our lives, I became more serious. I was highly attentive and revised my work more regularly. I started winning good marks and better positions in class. In primary six and seven, *I was the best pupil in academic performance and discipline*. Though some boys had started tempting my discipline (*Ibid.*: 55. Emphasis added).

During high school in Kampala she faced anti-Rwandan discrimination and even sexual harassment by the teachers. Despite all of this, she kept on going to school (*Ibid.*: 98) until it became impossible, as she and other Rwandans were accused by the school administration of having a bad influence on the other pupils (*Ibid.*: 106-107).

Kaitesi's intelligence went beyond school performance, as she seemed to have a certain perception of life that even some adults did not have. For instance, a rich Ugandan businessman called Musisi, who was also a friend of Kaitesi's brother, kept harassing her and wanting to bed her despite there being almost 30 years of difference (*Ibid.*: 62-63). Comparing Musisi's reasoning and Kaitesi's reasoning side by side results in the conclusion that Kaitesi was much more intelligent than Musisi. Kaitesi wondered how someone in his 40s, married, father of many children, could think about taking a teenager from school and sleeping with her, only for her to hear the following: 'Stop that. How many girls go away with men when they are even in primary schools?' (*Ibid.*: 63). Taking advantage of her poverty, Musisi tried to lure her by using a different but more stupid argument: 'Will you eat education? I have money to cater for all your needs if only you can decide now. I will build a good house and even give you a car' (*Ibid.*: 64). It goes without saying that Musisi's arguments were unintelligent whereas Kaitesi's reaction was highly intelligent.

One finds a similar case of a young girl showing more intelligence than an adult man in Bahufite's (2016) novel. After dropping out of school to sustain her family by working in the farm of a Zairean family, 15-year-old Nadine found herself in a situation where she was arguing with 27-year-old Martin, her boss' son, over getting married. The very first time they met, Martin immediately asked her to marry him (Bahufite, 2016: 80). Nadine rejected his request, because she could not marry a foreigner whose culture was strange to her:

> -MARTIN: You will learn about my culture and you will realise that it's not different from your own…I told you that I would like to marry you. That would be good for you. That way you won't be a refugee anymore, he argued.
>
> -NADINE: But I have no feelings for you. How do you want me to live with someone who only inspires me friendship? I responded.
>
> -MARTIN: Love will come later, I am sure. Moreover, in your case, you don't need to love someone to live with him. I offer you shelter, food and new cloths. If you become my wife, you won't be repatriated by force, because you will have become Zairean.
>
> So for him that marriage was a way for me to find a shelter in case the situation would worsen. What about my family? Has he thought about them or that was not his business? (*Ibid.*: 81-82).

Like Kaitesi, Nadine rejected the unusual proposal which was supported with unintelligent arguments. However, the intelligence of the two adolescents was nothing compared to the determination of the two non-Rwandan characters (Bahufite, 2016: 85-89; Rusimbi, 1999: 116-130). Both Musisi and Martin managed to outsmart the two girls and raped and impregnated them, forcing them to be their *de facto* wives, whether they wanted it or not. After raping Nadine, Martin triumphantly told her: 'I have told you that you will be my wife. You are mine now, even if you don't want to live with me'(Bahufite, 2016: 88).

Even though *Sheridan* does not dedicate long descriptions to Kenya's intelligence, it nonetheless uses some superlative formulations to show her 'extraordinary intelligence' (Mbabazi, 2007: 85). Kenya was a professor at a Paris-based university and was happy about her intellectual and personal blossoming (*Ibid.*: 7 & 9). Shortly after falling in love with her, Hutu army officer Miko told her, face to face, that he admired 'your intelligence and your independent thinking' (*Ibid.*: 94).

One could be tempted to add Twagilimana's (1996) novel in this analysis, but that novel poses a major challenge in this respect. As already noted, this novel puts the Tutsi and the Hutu from the south in the same basket, namely that of the victims of the Hutu from the north. Amongst thousands of people who were jailed when the war broken out in October 1990, only Victor Kalinda was identified as Tutsi. In this respect, the many university professors who were arrested cannot be included here, since nothing pushes one to assume that they belonged to either ethnicity. What can be asserted here though, is that Jean Mahoro, for whom the author did not provide any background, seemed to be a very clever man. He worked as an accountant for a car parts company, but his knowledge of world affairs, of philosophy, linguistics, semiotics, literary theory, etc., and his informed discussions with university professors, made him stand out. His knowledge distinguished him from the common mortals.

Intelligence also plays a role in Niwese's (2001) *Celui qui sut vaincre* and is associated with the Tutsi, though in a different way. After listening to the recording of the evaluation meeting of the RPF's insiders, the meeting in which they put together ideas about how to keep killing and humiliating the Hutu, whilst at the same time doing everything to escape international justice, Ngenda was surprised by the level of organisation and planning the Tutsi had reached. To his friend he said: 'Despite all, these people are intelligent. Unlike them, we sleep quietly as if we were on a conquered island!' (Niwese, 2001: 39). This type of intelligence combines the first two forms of *ubwenge* that I discussed in the previous section, namely doing whatever it takes to turn the situation into one's advantage and outplaying the international justice system. At the same time, Ngenda's remark recognises Tutsi superiority in this type of intelligence.

Beside this Machiavellian intelligence, Niwese's (2001) novel attributes school-based intelligence to Ngenda, who was the best student at Saint André Secondary School in the early 1970s (*Ibid.*: 79). His unequalled performance was rewarded with a scholarship to a European university, where he equally impressed his professors. According to his former professors, he was 'a brilliant and diligent student' (*Ibid.*: 49). However, when he returned to Rwanda with a degree in International Relations to become the country's Minister of Foreign Affairs, he changed. His idealism gave way to a belly-guided doctrine, *le ventriotisme*, consisting in enriching oneself before everything else (*Ibid.*: 49). The portrait one has here is one of an intelligent man who could not manage public affairs intelligently, which boils down to being stupid, as the school intelligence is supposed to boost intelligence in everyday life and in public affairs. At the same time, Ngenda displayed the outplay-the-other intelligence when he was caught on a bus without a ticket. He tricked the controller and police into thinking that he was a lost immigrant who was looking for the Immigration Office. Police showed him the way, but when they were out of sight, he boarded the next bus and proceeded on with his journey (*Ibid.*: 15-16).

Unlike Ngenda who receives an 'intelligent but...' description, Hutu army officer Miko is portrayed as being a highly cultivated man, with sound reasoning and a brilliant academic background. In this respect, the narrator introduced him as 'a brilliant officer' from Rwanda (Mbabazi, 2007: 36). His Tutsi lover Kenya would also ask him how he managed to not be as short-sighted as most men (*Ibid.*: 91). Indeed, his way of challenging received ideas and rejecting simplistic answers to complex questions, demonstrated his high level of reasoning. For instance, Linda, his French instructor and short-time lover, once asked him why the Hutu and the Tutsi were killing each other, even though they had everything in common, except small, insignificant details. Miko, who refused to provide a cliché, simplistic answer, made an analogy with the war in Northern Ireland, where people who spoke the same language, worshipped the same God, read the same Bible, etc., killed each other because of commas and periods here and there in the same Bible (*Ibid.*: 64-65). I am labelling this answer as intelligent because it invites the reader to not hasten to the 'good guys vs. bad guys' conclusions that usually simplify conflicts. As an army officer, it would have been easier for him to blacken the Tutsi and their rebellion and whitewash the Hutu and their army.

The novels discussed in the previous paragraphs confirm, to some extent, the hypothesis with which I started this section, namely that Tutsi characters are endowed with a high level of thinking, an advanced ability to outsmart the other and exceptional knowledge-based intelligence. This pattern emerges in an explicit way in five novels, whereas one, namely Niwese (2001), stresses Tutsi intelligence in a Machiavellian sense. This does not imply that this pattern is absent in the four remaining novels. It rather means that in some of the other novels, the pattern is implicit or implied. For instance, Rusimbi's (2007) *The Hyena's Wedding* presents the main [Tutsi] character Kiroko, a high school dropout, as an intelligent local leader compared to seasoned and much better educated Hutu leaders. Yet in other novels, such as Gatore's (2008) *Le passé devant soi* and Sehene's (2005) *Le feu sous la soutane*, the emphasis seems to be on half-Hutu and half-Tutsi characters, whom I discuss in Section 4.4. Ndwaniye's (2006) *La promesse faite à ma soeur* is the sole novel that resists any analysis that attempts to associate levels of intelligence with ethnicity, which is in line with the remarks made about this novel in previous sections. In the seven novels I analysed in this section, only two, notably Mbabazi (2007) and Bahufite (2016), explicitly label a Hutu character as intelligent and brilliant the whole way through. In another – Niwese's (2001) – a Hutu character is only endowed with school-based intelligence but deprived of the capability to intelligently manage public affairs.

4.3. The Stupid Ones

Many of the examples mentioned in the previous section imply some stupidity, simply because detecting intelligent reasoning or a smart action often makes more sense when considered side by side with the reverse. For instance, Musisi's argument to take Kaitesi out of school makes more sense when it is opposed to Kaitesi's sound reasoning (Rusimbi, 1999). Similarly, Nadine's intelligent reasoning becomes obvious when it is opposed to Martin's stupid view of what love means (Bahufite, 2016). My task in this section is to find out ways in which the notion of stupidity or lack of intelligence is used and how that use is associated with ethnicity. Since this section discusses the opposite of what the previous section discussed, it follows that my hypothesis follows suit. So, in this section I hypothesise that Hutu characters have mostly been cast as unintelligent, holding illogical and ridiculous reasoning and unable to accomplish complex tasks.

Amongst the novelists in whom I am interested, Mukasonga is certainly the one who extensively discusses the theme of stupidity the most [and its opposite as shown in Section 4.2]. As it slightly appears in the previous section, Tutsi characters' intelligence and smartness were often portrayed as being the opposite to Hutu characters' stupidity and lack of intelligent judgment. As a general rule, Hutu characters seemed to think artificially and engaged in empty discussions or in illogical reasoning. For instance, when Virginia evoked the basic Rwandan wisdom that food should never be a subject of discussion and that one should be ashamed to open one's mouth in front of other people [hence the idea to not eat in public],

Gloriosa, the main Hutu character who was following the discussions, brutally told her the following on their way to the refectory: '…you, Virginia, you will be forced to open your mouth in front of us to eat the leftovers of true Rwandan girls' (Mukasonga, 2012: 53). This reaction reflects a significant lack of intelligence on the part of Gloriosa. Firstly, she ignored what seemed to be a popular wisdom and logic in Rwanda and, instead of learning it or showing inquisitiveness about why Rwandans had such principles, she decided to force someone to violate those principles. Secondly, Gloriosa was keen on punishing someone simply because that person was reminding her classmates of something so basic. Such a reaction cannot emanate from an intelligent person. Finally, looking at classmates in terms of true Rwandans [Hutu] and others [false Rwandans?], seems ridiculous especially when the reasoning comes from someone previously presented as a future leader.

Hutu characters' stupidity becomes more flagrant when Godelive engaged in a discussion with Immaculée about makeup and hairstyles. Godelive wanted to look beautiful [thus she was ugly. See section 3.3] and she had some ideas about what she could do. One professor, Mrs de Decker, used red varnish for her finger and toe nails and Godelive wondered whether or not that varnish could be used on her own lips (*Ibid.*: 167-168). Two aspects make this part stand out: Firstly, one's ugliness is used to show one's stupidity. In other words, the external look and internal thinking processes are both below the average. Secondly, Godelive's father was a rich man, a banker, who was very close to the president and who certainly lived in an environment where people wore makeup. Presenting this young Hutu girl as willing to use nail varnish for her lips suggests that one can live in an environment without realising how that environment works, which is, indeed, a sign of stupidity.

This approach is also used for Gloriosa, the ugliest of all as Section 3.3 has shown. At some point, Gloriosa started wondering why the statue of the Virgin Mary, the *Our Lady of the Nile*, looked like a Tutsi girl (*Ibid.*: 198-199). One day, she and a few classmates decided to break the small Tutsi nose of the statue so that a larger Hutu nose could be put in its place. As they attempted to hit the nose with a hammer, the entire head fell off. The next day, an emergency gathering took place and, surprisingly, the school administration was not furious about the crime. Gloriosa stood up and spoke to the assembly. According to her, the Tutsi, the *Inyenzi* [cockroaches], had decapitated the Virgin and had to pay for their crime. However, she went on to say that it was a good opportunity for there to be a better statue with a Hutu-looking Virgin:

> …we will soon have a new *Our Lady of the Nile* statue that will reflect a true Rwandan woman, with the face of the majority people, a Hutu Virgin of whom we will be proud. I am going to write to my father. He knows a sculptor (*Ibid.*).

When Gloriosa went back to her seat, she told Modesta that 'I am already a minister'. The most ridiculous aspect of Gloriosa's reasoning and action resides certainly in her obsession about the look of the statue of the Virgin Mary and its nose. The obsession was so extreme that she saw a Tutsi woman in that statue. To her, she should look like a Hutu [true Rwandan woman or majority people]. The last comment that Gloriosa made, that she was already a minister, is perhaps the most strategic of all the comments in the novel, because the generation that was in school in the early 1970s was the one that was in charge in 1994. Thus Gloriosa, the future minister, announced that the Tutsi cockroaches would pay and they paid in 1994.

In addition to this, unlike the Tutsi characters who prided themselves for having grown up with a sense of secrecy (See previous section), Hutu characters seemed to pride themselves on failing to keep secrets. Most of the discussions at school revolved around highly sensitive subjects about which the students had heard at home, when their fathers, all senior politicians and officials, had been talking in private. For example, Godelive, whose father was a banker and a close friend of President Kayibanda, told her classmates that the president had asked her to accompany his own daughter, who was travelling with King Baudouin and Queen Fabiola of Belgium. As already noted in the previous section, this discussion ended with Gloriosa commenting that Godelive's low grades and ugliness should not be an obstacle since Hutuness did not need any of them (Mukasonga, 2012: 165). Here again a Hutu character, Godelive, is portrayed not only as being unable to keep a state secret, but also as being mediocre at school, to which one should add that she was ugly to the point that Gloriosa, the ugliest of all, pointed it out. Other cases of indiscretion included Gloriosa's mother saying in public that she was going to have an official dinner at the Belgian embassy (*Ibid.*: 27- 29), Goretti revealing that her father [Army Chief of Staff] was very busy receiving many senior people in the Ruhengeri military barrack (*Ibid.*: 99) and immaculée saying that she once heard her father say that King Baudouin was the one who was sterile, not Queen Fabiola (*Ibid.*: 165 – 166), amongst other cases.

Regarding school performance, it emerges from some novels that Hutu characters are portrayed as mediocre whenever their educational background is mentioned. In the previous section I touched upon Dorothée, who suddenly became the best student in French because a Tutsi classmate was writing her assignments. The assumption here is that Dorothée was not clever in French and probably not in other disciplines. Like Dorothée, Damascène, the head of the militia that killed refugees at the Sainte Famille church, is described as intellectually mediocre (Sehene, 2005: 46). Damascène was three years older than Father Stanislas, but because he was repeating classes over and over, the latter overtook him in school. Father Stanislas thought that Damascène became an anti-Tutsi extremist in order to compensate for his failure in school. It is worth comparing Dorothée and Damascène, as both appeared to be mediocre students, who compensated that mediocrity with anti-Tutsi behaviour. Dorothée turned her mediocrity into fake intelligence through blackmailing or psychological violence [remember the outplay-the-other type of *ubwenge* and its Machiavellian aspect], whereas Damascène turned his mediocrity into physical violence against the Tutsi. One can also assume that Gloriosa's anti Tutsi violence was probably motivated by her poor school performance, for which she needed some compensation. Anyway, she was the one who vehemently defended the idea that high grades and beauty were not essential to true Rwandanness.

In addition to poor performance and mediocrity, Hutu characters seemed to have an awkward understanding of concepts like love. As noted in the previous section, Tutsi students like Kaitesi (Rusimbi, 1999) resisted pre-mature sexual intercourse and marriage that would interfere with their education. For Hutu characters, things were different. For instance, Frida, a daughter of a senior Rwandan diplomat in Kinshasa attending the Lycée Notre Dame du Nil, along with her father, had a weird idea of love and how to combine it with education. In her father's eyes, she became an 'ornament for the receptions and dinners at the embassy' each time she went on holiday to Kinshasa (Mukasonga, 2012: 109). To foster his diplomatic career, her father pushed her to date Balima, a man who was close to President Mobutu and who was later appointed as Ambassador to Kigali, to be near his fiancée. Frida kept attending school but would have intimate moments with her fiancée on school premises. Following pregnancy complications, Frida died before completing her education (*Ibid.*: 120). This perception of calculated, interest-driven, love also guided Hutu character Hogoza's decision to marry Ngenda who was, at the time, a minister. When Hogoza realised that the minister was interested in her, she agreed to marry him to fulfil her dream of becoming a minister's wife. She thought that 'even without love, it was worthwhile marrying the position [of minister] to be called Mrs. so-and-so' (Niwese, 2001: 64. Brackets added). This obviously stupid woman later left her husband after he had lost his position and wealth and was living on charity in Europe.

Another aspect of unintelligent judgment or reasoning that is worth mentioning here is one of being unable to foresee consequences. The Hutu mayor, whom Father Stanislas approached to request the authorisation to bury the bodies of the Tutsi killed at Sainte Famille church, is a good illustration of unintelligent thinking (Sehene, 2005: 83-84). The mayor argued that Father Stanislas could not have the bodies buried unless he provided death certificates for each one of them. He knew very well that he was asking the impossible, which is another sign of stupidity. However, the most shocking sign of stupidity is that someone in the public office thought it would be a good idea to let bodies rot out there. It was as if he ignored the public health hazards they would pose. The conclusion that Father Stanislas drew after this unintelligent refusal is equally interesting: 'Like Damascène, this duty-blinded mayor is Hutu before being human' (*Ibid.*: 84). This conclusion suggests that the mayor's reasoning was typically Hutu and, by extension, that Hutu reasoning was intrinsically not human.[34]

---

34 Many other writings, both fiction and non-fiction, have repeated this generalisation about the Hutu by presenting those who happen to escape this rule as exceptions. For instance, Philip Gourevitch's (1999) *We Wish to Inform You That Tomorrow We Will Be Killed with our Families*, presents a testimony in which a Tutsi survivor refers to a Hutu priest as follows: 'He was a Hutu, this priest, but he was kind' (Gourevitch, 1999: 125). The logical deduction here is that all Hutu are generally unkind. Only a few, like the priest, are kind. The same generalisation is in Thierry Dushimirimana's (2006) short film titled *A love letter to my Country* that features a Tutsi girl, Martha, and a Hutu young man, Rukundo, who fall in love and plan to marry each other despite the opposition of their respective families. Martha and her uncle were the sole survivors of the genocide, whereas Rukundo's family had participated in that genocide. To convince her uncle, Martha says: 'Father [sic!], he is Hutu but he is very nice'.

Taking the wrong, unintelligent decision is also observed in Rusimbi's (2007) *The Hyena's Wedding* and is attributed to a Hutu character, Rucagu, who joined the new Tutsi-dominated regime and repeatedly showed unintelligent thinking when he had to make crucial decisions that affected many people. One of them was about determining where the housing area for the returnees and survivors should be, so that the solidarity camp could be settled and organised (Rusimbi, 2007: 82). Rucagu suggested 'a vast dry area', pushing Kiroko, the young Tutsi local leader, to ask him how bricks could be made in an area that had no water:

> I told them that it was almost impossible to organise the camp in a dry place. The youths needed water to drink, wash and make bricks. Mr. Rucagu defended his choice by pointing out that it was the only land available for the construction of new houses for returnees and survivors of Mayanje. And the water was to be provided by a charitable organisation in the area (*Ibid.*).

What one has here is a Hutu leader who was putting a project together without taking essential elements such as water into account. Rucagu preferred to leave the water issue in the hands of some charities. This reasoning is opposed to intelligent reasoning coming from a Tutsi, namely Kiroko, who thought that it would be a better idea to shift the site to the nearby stream, rather than depending on charities for water. Rucagu rejected this idea as the preparations had already begun. Indeed, water did become an issue when the activities began and Kiroko kept reiterating his point about the stupid idea of selecting a dry site. Instead of blaming himself, Rucagu put the blame on the charities. Rucagu is presented as a naïve leader, who believed that foreign charities were there to help reconstruct the country, whereas they had a hidden agenda. At some point, Kiroko found it useless to continue arguing with someone like Rucagu and started suspecting that his wrong and unintelligent judgments might be deliberate:

> I deliberately stopped arguing with someone who had ignored my advice earlier on, a leader who was very unpopular among survivors in Mayanje. If all the talk about his dishonesty was true, it wouldn't surprise me if he had made the mistake deliberately (*Ibid.*: 86-87).

To top it off, Rucagu took the decision to keep the activities going within the solidarity camp despite a raging meningitis epidemic. Kiroko, Mugabo and all the other leaders thought it would be wiser to shut the camp, but Rucagu wanted to keep it open until the end of the month. His argument was that 'people can die anywhere' (*Ibid.*: 99). This time, Mugabo, the Tutsi chief and all the other leaders did not give up. They decided to shut the camp.

The case of Rucagu is important to comment upon, especially by linking it to Dorothée's case that I have already mentioned. Like Dorothée, who could not pass her French classes without the help of Virginia [a Tutsi character], all Rucagu's decisions would lead to failure and catastrophes if Mugabo and Kiroko [both Tutsi characters] would not intervene. The suggestion made in both cases is that a Hutu could not achieve anything important unless a Tutsi helped him/her or completed the task in his or her place. Rusimbi's (1999) *By the Time She Returned* rarely discusses Hutuness but when it does, it suggests that whatever the Hutu politicians are said to have completed in the late 1950s, when they toppled the Tutsi monarchy and instituted the Republic, should never be credited to them. As Kaitesi took oath before joining the refugee organisation that would later turn into a rebel group, she heard from a senior member that 'the Hutu were only used as tools to advance colonial interests' (Rusimbi, 1999: 144). What this implies is that since the tool cannot achieve anything on its own, there needs to be someone intelligent enough to operate the tool.

The analysis I have conducted so far with regards to intelligence vs. stupidity stereotypes has resulted in a black and white table, with one column consisting of characters who are portrayed as smart, clever and intelligent, and the other column showing those presented as unintelligent and stupid. The situation would indeed be completely black and white in the first column where no single Tutsi character has so far been portrayed as unintelligent if it wasn't for Niwese's (2001) novel breaking this rule. *Celui qui sut vaincre* is the only novel amongst the 11 that overtly ridicules Tutsi characters. The novel stresses the idea that the new Tutsi leaders were mere herdsmen who were only good at keeping cattle (Niwese, 2001: 13). The arguments provided by former rebel soldiers during a meeting that discussed their promotions is illustrative. One man stood up to argue in favour of more stripes on his shoulders and said:

> Before joining the guerrilla, I took care of about one hundred cows. All my life of shepherd, my herd never damaged anyone's farms. How can I not deserve the sergeant stripes to head only 60 men? I had full control over 100 cows, why should 60 people be more difficult to manage? (*Ibid*.: 13).

The suggestion made here is twofold: Firstly, the soldier could not distinguish between animals and human beings. In his eyes, animals and people are the same, hence the emphasis on numbers rather than on what the numbers represent. If one can manage 100, one can easily manage 60, regardless of what one puts after these figures. Secondly, it is suggested here that the Tutsi rebels' behaviour was close to that of animals' behaviour, marked by no logical, human thinking. This is linked to the construction of Tutsiness as revolving around killing the Hutu or making them suffer in a Machiavellian way (see Section 1.3).

In a case similar to Dorothée asking if she could use nail varnish on her lips (Mukasonga, 2012), an old Tutsi man, whose son was a senior rebel officer, made very interesting comments after settling in one of Ngenda's villas in Kigali. The old man had moved in with his cattle, which he had brought all the way from Uganda where he lived. In those comments, the old man congratulated the intelligent Hutu who had built the house, because he had laid a trough for cattle within the house. He was referring to the bath. This particular Hutu had also laid a lake in his compound so to be able to eat fish (*Ibid*.: 14). In this case, he was referring to the swimming pool. What is unintelligent here is not that the man ignored what a bath or a swimming pool was. It is rather the fact that no one in his entourage corrected him, which leaves the reader with the idea that none of them knew what they were. Taking the reasoning further, one could wonder how such people could run public affairs in a modern state that has little to do with cattle affairs.

One could also add Célia to the list of the rare unintelligent Tutsi characters, but this would be debatable. It could be argued that living a double life with two men and having four children outside marriage cannot be labelled as intelligent. However, the general context that Twagilimana's (1996) novel sketches implies that Tutsi women were at the mercy of powerful Hutu men from the north. A counterargument could be that Célia had no choice but to do what Nduru, the powerful Hutu man, wanted her to do to save her life and the life of Kalinda, her husband.

In the second column showing Hutu characters, one can also detect rare exceptions to the rule that Hutu characters are generally stupid and unintelligent. One Hutu character who showed a few signs of intelligence is Immaculée Mukagatare who, despite her indiscretion discussed above, openly challenged the powerful Gloriosa's unintelligent perception of education, family and marriage:

> -IMMACULEE: …If we are here [at school], at least for most of us, it is because we have to promote our family, not for our future but for the future of the clan. We are already good merchandises since most of us are from rich and powerful parents who will find a way to negotiate the highest price for us. The diploma will just add some more value. I know that many of us are so pleased by that game, since that's the only game on which they base their pride. On my part, I don't want to be part of that market any more.
>
> -GLORIOSA: Listen to her… she speaks like a white woman in a film or in the textbooks that our French teacher makes us read! What would you become, Immaculée, without your father and his money? Do you think a Rwandan woman can survive without her family, her father's first and then her husband's? (Mukasonga, 2012: 123. Brackets added).

Immaculée displayed her capacity to analyse and evaluate a societal issue before drawing a logical conclusion. She seemed upset by the idea that she had no say in her own future, and that her education was important only because it increased her commercial value on the marriage market. Gloriosa was wholeheartedly of the opinion that what Frida and her father did [marrying her to a diplomat whilst still at school], was the right thing to do for a true Rwandan woman, whereas Immaculée rightly revolted against that.

Like Immaculée, Juma, the Hutu Moslem houseboy at the Benimanas', did display his intelligent reasoning and judgment by refraining from directly confronting the Hutu extremist who was trying to recruit him (Rurangwa, 2006: 16-17). When Butihoro told him that time would come for him to rape his boss Mathilde and her daughters, Juma refused, arguing that Mathilde was like his mother and her daughters were like his sisters (*Ibid*.: 16). Indeed, Mathilde and her husband somehow adopted Juma at the age of ten when his father died. Butihoro went on to tell him that if he did not rape and kill them, they [Mathilde and her daughters], in turn, would kill him. God-fearing Juma replied with Allah's prescription to not hate one's neighbour, pushing Butihoro to remind him that the Tutsi were not his neighbours, but rather his enemies. Juma promised to attend the next CDR [Hutu extremist party] meeting, but only to ensure that Butihoro left him alone. The reasoning that followed Butihoro's departure shows that Juma was not only capable of asking intelligent questions but also of finding logical and reasonable answers to them:

> Why this hatred against the Tutsi? Why do they want to exterminate them? I would have understood if they had attempted to fight Islam. But I've never seen any Tutsi throw a stone at Moslems. I've never seen any of them setting fire on the Biryogo or Nyamirambo mosques. Why do they want to exterminate them? And myself, a Moslem, I am well treated by the Benimanas, who, unlike me, are Catholics and who nonetheless consider me like their child! (*Ibid.*: 18).

Even though this reasoning is too simplistic [e.g., the entire aspect of war is left out], Juma's conclusion stands and is to some extent logical, given all the premises he used as the basis of his reasoning. If one has never harmed you, your interests or your religion, why would one be hated?

In addition to intelligent thinking, Juma also seemed smarter than the Hutu extremists led by Sembagare, who wanted to get him involved in the killings. When Sembagare brought Jean-Léonard to his father's home to show him the bodies of the members of his family, he found Juma there holding a machete and covered with blood (Rurangwa, 2006: 86). To survive, Juma had taken a machete and smeared blood over his body to make the killers believe he was one of them. When Butihoro came to check if the Benimanas were dead, he found Juma there proudly holding his machete. Juma hastened to tell him that he had had the chance to rape one of Mathilde's daughter (*Ibid.*: 88). All these tricks helped Juma outplay the killers by creating a false impression. Juma used his smartness again to outplay the killers when Sembagare asked him to finish Jean-Léonard off with his machete. Jean-Léonard also urged him to shorten his agony. Instead of doing this, he escorted him through Kigali, perfectly mimicking a victim-killer situation. In other words, whoever saw them walking thought that Juma was taking Jean-Léonard to his final destination. It is with this stratagem that Juma managed to rescue Jean-Léonard by taking him to a safer part of Kigali that was later to be captured by the RPF Tutsi rebels (*Ibid.*: 90-91).

This section has attempted to identify and discuss cases of stupidity and unintelligent thinking and has proven the initial hypothesis to be correct. In almost all cases, Hutu characters are described as lacking in smartness and as holding unintelligent thinking. In addition to this, whenever educational background is provided, Hutu characters are portrayed as mediocre students. To compensate for that mediocrity, they mostly embrace anti-Tutsi ideology, which they either turn into psychological or physical violence. Only a few Hutu characters, i.e., Ngenda (Niwese, 2001), Mukagatare (Mukasonga, 2012), Juma (Rurangwa, 2006) and Nadine (Bahufite, 2016), could be said to have displayed a certain level of smartness and intelligent judgment, which leaves one with no other conclusion other than that the Hutu are generally stupid, mediocre and unintelligent. Only in one Hutu-authored novel were Tutsi characters shown as demonstrating unintelligent thinking, which seems to be the exception that confirms the rule that the Tutsi are generally smart and intelligent. The next section takes this discussion further, this time with a focus on half-Hutu and half-Tutsi characters.

4.4. Mixture

The previous two sections have pointed out quasi black and white situations, where smartness and intelligence were explicitly attributed to one ethnic group, whereas their opposites were associated with the other. In this section, I want to explore the grey areas which happen to coincide with characters with mixed ethnicity. Characters with blood connections amongst the Hutu and the Tutsi seem to think and behave differently, maybe because of the identity crisis through which most of them go. Schematically speaking, Section 4.3 has provided the left end of the intelligence/smartness continuum, whereas Section 4.2 has provided the right end of the same continuum. Hutu characters tend to be near the left end and Tutsi counterparts near the right end. The space between the right and left is the one that hybrid characters seem to occupy. However, as already discussed, the term 'hybrid' is not helpful for my analysis because a half-Hutu character behaves and thinks very differently from a half-Tutsi character. My hypothesis here is that the half-Hutu characters are expected to be at some distance from the left end and more towards the middle point of the continuum, whereas the sole half-Tutsi character is likely to be some distance from the right end and nearer to the middle point.

Gatore's (2008) *Le passé devant soi* is the only novel that revolves around half-Tutsi and half-Hutu main characters and, for that reason, it offers an ideal start to this section. The question is: Where on the intelligence/smartness continuum can one place Isaro [half-Tutsi] and Niko [half-Hutu]? Their thinking and behaviour are a mixture of stupidity and intelligence but at different degrees. Isaro is presented as an intelligent girl right from the start. If she suddenly started feeling the urge to discover herself and whom she really was, it is because 'she could no longer accept just being that brilliant girl of whom they [her adoptive parents] were proud' (Gatore, 2008: 53. Brackets added). However, this brilliance is repeatedly coupled with a stupid attitude, one that consisted in deliberately 'destroying her successes', giving up the lead she had accumulated during her studies and stopping all extra-curricular activities that had given her 'exceptional elegance' (*Ibid.*). At first sight, these remarks should place Isaro at the far right end of the intelligence continuum just like the Tutsi characters discussed in Section 4.2. However, unlike the Tutsi characters for whom intelligence was an asset, her own brilliance seemed to have become a burden. For that reason, she engaged in unintelligent behaviour by destroying all that made her brilliant and had given her an advantage over the rest.

Isaro also adopted an unreasonable conduct by dropping out of school and ending all contact with her adoptive family resulting in her isolating herself. Her family's wrong-doing, which they ignored until very late, was that they had prevented her from being an orphan. They had prevented her from mourning her dead parents. By saving her, they made the mistake of not allowing her to lament what had happened to her:

> She had to stick to that silence and oversight as a way of expressing her gratitude, of displaying her happiness so that they can feel no regret, and of giving the false impression that what she had thanks to them compensated for what she had lost (*Ibid.*: 52).

This attitude and behaviour are part of what I termed outplay-the-other *ubwenge*, because she skilfully played a double game and cheated her adoptive parents. They thought they were doing the right thing to make her happy and she did everything to make them believe that she was happy, even though she was in a deep crisis. In a way, she managed to outplay her parents by succeeding in keeping her crisis under the radar for a long time, until she began a less intelligent, self-destructive process. At some point, however, when she had broken all contact with her parents, she realised that 'that attitude towards them [her parents] had been stupid' and she regretted it (*Ibid*.: 44-45. Brackets added), which took her back to a more intelligent mood.

Despite her regrets, Isaro did not return to her previous life nor did she resume her studies. Instead, she put together a memory project that would take her to Rwanda, where she collected genocide life stories. Her aim was to capture and understand people's subjectivities in relation to the genocide, including their lies and omissions as well as their exaggerations (*Ibid*.: 77). The project itself, the idea behind it and its intent and scope, are signs that Isaro was intelligent enough to design and then complete this achievement. Nonetheless, in the process of doing this, she committed suicide, the most unintelligent achievement one can think of (*Ibid*.: 183-184).

Like Isaro, Niko had a life that is marked by a mixture of intelligent and unintelligent thinking and actions. His life itself started off with a [Hutu] father who did not realise that his [Tutsi] wife was in her final stage of pregnancy. He left her to give birth without any assistance (Gatore, 2008: 79- 80). His father's stupidity caused a wrongful start to his life and would mark all of its stages until Niko's death. It might also explain why stupidity would outweigh intelligence in his thinking, attitudes and behaviour. A few rare moments of intelligent thinking on the part of Niko include his trick to divert the killers' attention away from their victim. When Niko saw Hyancithe, a Tutsi girl, running for her life and being followed by Hutu killers, he let one jug loudly fall, pushing the killers to stop their pursuit and instead come to his workshop. In the meantime, Hyancithe was already out of their reach (*Ibid*.: 124). This way, Niko managed to tactfully outplay the killers, whose stupidity made them forget what their initial goal was.

Niko also seemed more intelligent than the people around him when his uncle Gaspard died after excessively drinking alcohol together with his friends. When Gaspard fainted, his [stupid] friends continued drinking as if nothing had happened. Only Niko 'put his drink and food aside to come near him' and realised that he was dead before taking his body away (Gatore, 2008: 133-134). A similar attitude appears in one of his frequent dreamlike reflections during which Niko seemed to ask himself reasonable questions and to almost draw intelligent conclusions. As he was observing the killers under his command burying the dead, Niko wondered why people would bury their own victims so quickly. Unlike the Kigali mayor who cynically required death certificates before burying the victims (Sehene, 2005), Niko realised that these people needed to be buried, not only because of the unbearable smell of rotting bodies, but also to enable the killers and their accomplices to forget what they had done (Gatore, 2008: 135-136). At some point, he even engaged in quasi philosophical reflections about why victims obeyed their killers, even though they knew that they had no chance of surviving. He wondered: Is it a matter of dying in politeness and obedience? Or perhaps a way of leaving all responsibilities and guilt on the killers' conscience? He tried to imagine what the last thought of the victims might be: 'You [the killer] have no single reason to kill me and I don't want to give you any possibility to use the pretext that I disobeyed or struggled against you...' (*Ibid.*: 131. Brackets added).

Niko's intelligence was observed more in his daydream reflections than in real-life actions and behaviour. The sympathy he seemed to have in his dreams vanished as soon as he recovered consciousness and resumed playing his role as a militia commander once again. In his dreams he would come to the conclusion that those who were being killed had no reason to die. Yet, he would proceed and kill them as soon as the daydream ended. Except for the jug he let fall to delay Hyacinthe's murder, there was no other single instance whereby he devised a strategy to rescue anyone. Unlike Juma (Rurangwa, 2006) who would pretend to be a militiaman and use that cover to rescue a targeted person, Niko completely and enthusiastically drowned into the killings. One can argue that his stupidity resided in the lack of coordination between his dreamlike reflections and his actions, which places him much closer to the left end of the continuum.

Niko's intelligence pattern is to a great extent similar to Father Stanislas's (Sehene, 2005), except that the latter had had a more or less normal upbringing and had received the best education there was in the country. Unlike Niko, who was rejected by his father and by society at large, Father Stanislas did not have to suffer any rejection in society, even though his classmates would sometimes remind him that half of his blood was Tutsi. However, contrary to Niko who was forced into the killings, Father Stanislas seemed to take the initiative himself and to justify why killing the Tutsi was needed. Looking back at his actions from his cell in France, Father Stanislas expressed no regret, as what he did was part of his duty. He was a small piece in a larger system that was fighting a war to defend the nation and 'my people'. The duty to which he was referring to is, 'the collective work aimed to counter the Tutsi invasion' (Sehene, 2005: 140). The reasoning here seems unintelligent for one who had completed higher education and is supposed to be able to distinguish between the refugees seeking protection and the fighters on the battlefield. Similar unintelligent actions and reasoning are abundant in the novel, including one argument in which Father Stanislas had with a government officer, whose soldiers were shelling the rebel positions from the church's yard. The officer used the predominantly Tutsi refugees in the church as a human shield to ensure that the rebels would not shell back.

>-OFFICER: Don't worry *Padiri* [Father]...you only have *inyenzi* [cockroaches] inside the church.
>
>-FATHER STANISLAS: It's my church!
>
>-OFFICER: They are all traitors. They are RPF accomplices. And they hate you the same way they hate all of us because you are a Hutu.
>
>-FATHER STANISLAS: Possible. But they [rebels shelling back] are going to damage my church! (*Ibid.*: 21-22. Brackets added).

One has the notion of *ubwenge* at two levels in this dialogue. The first level is one that includes the idea of outplaying the other or pushing the other to take an action that would put them in a disadvantaged position. The army officer and his soldiers were shelling the RPF positions from Sainte Famille and, in doing so, they wanted the RPF to shell back and kill the predominantly Tutsi refugees in the church. Indeed, the RPF shelled the church and damaged it (*Ibid*: 26-27). This is what Rwandans mean when they use the expression *guhenda ubwenge* which means, tricking the other into a situation that gives one advantage. The second level is one at which Father Stanislas reasoned. The officer assumed that he would worry about the Tutsi in the church, but Father Stanislas' preoccupation was somewhere else, i.e., the building that was exposed to the shelling. This is low-level intelligence in the sense that, given the overview he had of the situation, Father Stanislas found the building to be the most important thing that deserved protection and preservation whereas, high-level intelligence would set human casualties as an absolute priority.

Nonetheless, Father Stanislas showed a few signs of intelligent thinking especially when faced with dilemmas. One such dilemma was when Damascène, his former classmate now leading a group of militiamen, came and asked him to give him the list of all the Tutsi refugees who had registered so that they could join the RPF-controlled area with the help of the UN peace keepers. The following reasoning shows that Father Stanislas could still consider all the elements in place and assess the gravity of the implications that his decision would have:

> I am caught in a deadlock. If I refuse, I will be exposing the lives of all refugees to danger. If I comply, I will doubtless be condemning the Tutsi to death. Given the circumstances, the latter solution seems the lesser evil, because, I can still convince Damascène to spare women and children (Sehene, 2005: 58).

Father Stanislas handed the list over to Damascène, urging him to spare women and children but to no avail (*Ibid*.: 59). The questions here could be: Was Father Stanislas' reasoning stupid here? What would a smart, intelligent person have done in this case? This time, unlike the previous instance when the building counted more than the Tutsi, he realised that the lives of many innocent people were at stake, which was not the case when he was defending his church. So there is a change to his reasoning here. He also seemed to realise that he had to choose between exposing *all* the refugees and sending *some* of the refugees to death. The most difficult part here was to determine what he meant by '*all* the refugees': Does *all* mean including the Hutu refugees? Does it mean including Tutsi women and children whose lives he attempted to spare? If the latter was the case, was his intention to spare women's lives motivated by his empathy or rather by the concern that the pool of women to rape would shrink or dry up? Being unable to answer these questions pushes one to place Father Stanislas at some distance from the left end of the intelligence/smartness continuum. In any case, he is far from the middle point as his reasoning showed more unintelligent, stupid thinking than intelligent thinking. At one point he pretended to care for the lives of the Tutsi, but at the other point, he would show a completely opposite behaviour. For instance, he knew that transferring the Tutsi to the RPF-controlled area would save their lives, yet he would consider those who registered for the transfer as being ungrateful to him (*Ibid*.: 50-51).

In Mukasonga's (2012) *Notre Dame du Nil*, Modesta seemed to be in a similar, though much less dramatic, situation. As a half-Hutu, she had to constantly watch out and please Gloriosa by, for instance, ostensibly approving whatever negative comments she made about the Tutsi (Mukasonga, 2012: 34). In a way, she was smart because she knew what to do to survive in a hostile environment. Gloriosa kept telling her that despite her effort to stay away from her 'half-sisters', she still resembled the 'snakes' (*Ibid.*). Managing to find her way through such a situation was quite an achievement that places Modesta somewhere in the right half of the intelligence/smartness continuum.

However, Modesta's overall attitude offers a mixed picture of her intelligence. Since she knew all too well that her Hutu classmates were not, and could not be, her friends, she turned to the two Tutsi classmates, Virginia and Veronica, and built a close friendship with them. As a sign of friendship, Modesta started telling her secrets to Virginia and Veronica (*Ibid.*: 87). One of the secrets was about the tense situation at home, where her Hutu father openly regretted having married her Tutsi mother (*Ibid.*: 93-94). From the Rwandan cultural perspective, Modesta was a stupid girl, because family issues and secrets are not meant to be shared with strangers. In addition to this, Modesta kept repeating her secrets to her 'friends' who did not tell her about their own secrets. A smart, intelligent person usually understands that friendship brings around reciprocity. Instead of sharing their own home secrets, Virginia and Veronica refused to trust her. For instance, the two girls did not want to let her know that they frequently and secretly paid a visit to Mr. de Fontenaille [a white man who lived near the school]. Virginia commented on their relationship as follows:

> ...I sometimes have doubts: Why is she [Modesta] keen on talking to us, Tutsi, hiding herself from her famous friend [Gloriosa]? Is it because she is half-Hutu or because she wants to spy on us? Poor her! Why does she complicate her life? (*Ibid.*: 206. Brackets added).

The two Tutsi girls seemed much smarter by keeping their own secrets for themselves and by assuming that Modesta might be ill-intentioned. What this comes down to is the observation that Modesta displayed a sense of smartness when handling her relationships with Gloriosa and her Hutu classmates and a great deal of stupidity when dealing with her Tutsi classmates. Unlike Father Stanislas who had some power and choices to make, Modesta looked like a victim and her thinking took place in that framework. In this sense, her reflection to Virginia seemed intelligent as her conclusions were both logical and coherent: She would prefer to become a nun rather than suffering what her mother had suffered. Instead of having children who were Hutu, Tutsi or half-Hutu or half-Tutsi, she simply wouldn't have children (*Ibid.*: 93-94). I am labelling this reasoning as intelligent because Modesta did not try to engage in violent behaviour to deserve trust. She was thinking deeply about a serious issue and she came to a conclusion that made sense: instead of beginning a family in a society where ethnicity comes before humanity, one had better limit the number of potential future victims by becoming a nun.

The patterns I have sketched above do not apply to Fortunata Uwera's case (Twagilimana, 1996). This half-Hutu character behaved and thought reasonably the whole way through. She also seemed to have a high-level of intellect that enabled her to discuss world news and current affairs with Mahoro. Unlike her mother, who had turned her father's life into a nightmare, she stayed close to her weak father, taking care of him when he was hospitalised. The only controversial behaviour that could raise heated discussions was her decision to accept to have sex with, and get pregnant from, her official but not biological father (*Ibid*.: 248-249). Was this incestuous behaviour smart or stupid? One argument would not call this relationship incestuous because Fortunata was not Kalinda's biological daughter. So what happened was between two consenting adults, regardless of what they had been calling each other all those years. From this perspective, Fortunata was more intelligent than her own Tutsi mother and Hutu father, who had ruined a Tutsi man's life. She seemed highly altruistic by sacrificing her own reputation to give a glimpse of satisfaction to a man whose sole wish was to have a child before dying. Also, managing to persuade Mahoro that her pregnancy was a Good Samaritan action rather than a cheating one, is quite an achievement. She won his sympathy and finally, they both got married.

The main conclusion from this section is that the same character who suffered from an identity crisis (see Section 1.5) thinks and acts in a way that includes both stupidity and intelligence/smartness. Half-Hutu characters have been described as showing more signs of stupidity and unintelligent thinking than signs of smartness and intelligence, whereas the sole half-Tutsi character, Isaro, seems to have more features of intelligence than signs of stupidity. The case of Fortunata Uwera seems to contradict this conclusion, as that half-Hutu character displayed a rather intelligent behaviour. This could be explained by the fact that Fortunata was culturally Tutsi, for she had grown up in a 100% Tutsi family and had considered her mother's Tutsi husband to be her father. This conclusion is consistent with the hypothesis with which I opened this section. It is also in line with the observation made earlier that half-Hutu characters tended to behave more or less like Hutu characters, whereas the sole half-Tutsi character tended to behave like the other Tutsi characters. This section did not take into account Rusimbi (1999 & 2007), Niwese (2001), Rurangwa (2006), Mbabazi (2007) and Bahufite (2016), because none of these novels included characters with mixed ethnicity. Ndwaniye's (2006) novel was also left out because the author abstained from including ethnicity amongst his themes.

4.5. Summary and Discussion

This chapter has discussed the concept of *ubwenge* in the 11 novels of genocide. Based on Rwanda's historical tales, proverbs and everyday use of language, the first section identified three types of intelligence. The first one referred to the ability to outplay the other in order to be in an advantaged position or situation; the second one was identified as the one with the capability to imagine, think and reason at a higher level; the last type referred to school-based performance, which can also be extended to outside school environments such as the workplace.

The analysis of the novels of genocide in the light of these three types of *ubwenge* resulted in the conclusion that Tutsi characters are systematically portrayed as intelligent and smart. They are superior in all senses of *ubwenge* compared to Hutu characters, who are predominantly stupid, mediocre and unintelligent. In some cases, suggestions are made that when Hutu characters perform well or above the average, it is because they have cheated or received help from Tutsi characters. The cases of unintelligent Tutsi characters seem rare and limited to one Hutu-authored novel. Similarly, very rare cases are presented showing intelligent Hutu characters. These two situations [unintelligent Tutsi and intelligent Hutu] appear as rare exceptions in the 11 novels I am analysing.

Unlike Tutsi characters who are intelligent, brilliant and smart all the way through and in all respects, and contrary to Hutu characters who are the opposite of their Tutsi counterparts, characters with mixed ethnicity seem to navigate in between. They are neither completely stupid nor completely smart and intelligent. In line with some conclusions in the previous chapters, the sole half-Tutsi character seems very close to the Tutsi characters in the way she thinks and performs at school. The sole difference is that, every now and then, she engages in stupid self-destructive behaviour and actions. The same is true when it comes to half-Hutu characters who show little signs of intelligence and smartness, whilst displaying more signs of stupidity and unintelligent judgment. One half-Hutu character who grew up believing that she was born from a Tutsi father, showed intelligent behaviour similar to one of the other Tutsi characters.

The analysis presented in this chapter raises one important point that needs more discussion, namely the petrification and spread of the stereotypes that Hutu are stupid and unintelligent, that the Tutsi are intelligent and smart, and that the rest are somewhere in between. Since there is almost unanimity about these stereotypes amongst most novelists, it would follow that they would be easy to assimilate for the readers in the current and future generations of Rwandans. What makes the situation worrying is the trap that this situation sets by repeating and refining the stereotypes that historical tales and myths have been conveying for centuries. The difference between the stereotypes in historical tales and those in the novels of genocide is that the former tend to be dismissed as reflecting the thinking that prevailed in those times gone by, whereas the latter are fresh. What they have in common, however, is that they draw a clear line between the Hutu and the Tutsi, presenting the former as mainly stupid and unintelligent and the latter as mainly smarter and more intelligent. In a way, the novels that used these stereotypes have given a new lease of life to old stereotypes which, as already observed, were deliberately created by the royal circles over centuries and were used to install the idea of Tutsi superiority in popular culture.

One might wonder what the consequences of this recycling of ethnic stereotypes might be in the future, when these novels have become old memory texts, those that people tend to canonise. Let's take an example of an imaginary Rwandan whom I will name Mbyariyehe, a name that means *In which type of society is my child born?* By the time Mbyariyehe starts introducing himself, his educational background and his professional achievements, his ethnic profile will gradually emerge in the minds of the listener or of the reader. If he goes into detail, e.g., how good he was in Mathematics, how he was the best amongst his classmates, how he obtained advanced university degrees, etc., the chance is high that the listener or the reader will start concluding that Mbyariyehe is a Tutsi, or at least someone with some Tutsi blood in his veins. Let's make another assumption that the listener or the reader is a foreigner or is a Rwandan living abroad, who meets Mbyariyehe outside Rwanda where he can freely ask about his ethnicity. The interlocutor would most likely observe: 'So you must be a Tutsi'. If Mbyariyehe says: 'No, I am a Hutu', then the interlocutor would have to deal with three possibilities: [1] Mbyariyehe is one of those rare Hutu people who are genuinely brilliant; or [2] he is a half-Hutu and his Tutsi blood explains his intelligence; or else [3] he must have received help from a Tutsi who wrote his thesis or dissertation. The stereotypes discussed in this chapter and in the previous echo Du Bois' (1926) remark in relation to the stereotypes of the Negro that white artists had spread:

> Suppose the only Negro who survived some centuries hence was the Negro painted by white Americans in the novels and essays they have written. What would people in a hundred years say of black Americans?

This question is more than relevant in the Rwandan context. The example I want to give here might seem far-fetched, but I still believe it has a close link with the images of the typical Hutu and the typical Tutsi that emerge from most novels. In a press conference on 28th June 2010, a journalist asked President Paul Kagame why the hygiene inspection programme in hotels and restaurants had stopped. He wondered whether that had to do with the fact that Dr. Jean Damascène Ntawukuriryayo was no longer the health minister [he was then speaker of the Senate, and was to run for president in that year's election]. Responding, President Kagame said in Kinyarwanda:

> That has to do with bad execution of policies in many sectors. Even Ntawukuriryayo himself, when he was still minister, *needed to be reminded of his duties, as he often forgot them. He is not the one who initiated the plan*. Policies relating to hygiene, be it corporal, domestic, or food hygiene etc., were set up by *us* long ago. The execution was not good as those in charge of it showed *little commitment*. Even the one you're talking about [Dr. Ntawukuriryayo] would go on the field and complain to hotel owners saying: '*It's not our policy. It's the president's policy*'.[35]

Opinions, views and interpretations might diverge about this answer. But reading this response, especially the italicised parts, after going through this chapter on stereotypes, one does not need a magnifying glass to see intelligence-related stereotypes at work in the real world. The journalist implied that Dr. Ntawukuriryayo had booked an important achievement [thus was intelligent as he was capable to book success], but the president dismissed that idea, suggesting that Dr. Ntawukuriryayo often forgot his basic duties of ensuring that hotels and restaurants lived up to hygiene standards. Even when the president awakened him,

---

35 'Monthly press conference – Kigali 28th June 2010', download 28th May 2013 from http://www.paulkagame.tv/podcast/?p=episode&name=2010-06-29_monthly_press_conference_kigali_28_june_2010_.mp3. [the website is now offline].

he would complain to the hotel owners rather than do his work [how can he be intelligent in that case?]. Firstly, the president said he is the one to be credited: It was *his* idea in the first place [so he is more intelligent!]. Secondly, he was the one to realise that the minister was sleeping and decided to awaken him. I leave it to the reader to guess the ethnicity of the President and of Dr. Ntawukuriryayo and to find similarities, both in the tales I used as examples and in the novels of genocide I have analysed.

Part Three

Propaganda

Chapter 5

Promoting a Certain Narrative

Writing a novel about events as tragic as the genocide and a war that ended with one of the warring parties claiming victory, can hardly escape the propaganda trap. This trap implies that at some point, the novelists consciously or unconsciously engage in promoting one perspective of the past rather than the other, depending on their own memories, i.e., their own experience, sympathy and connections with one of the former parties at war or, with the different actors during the genocide. In this respect, one author might be a Tutsi, who sympathised with the RPF rebels, whose relatives fought amongst those rebels and who survived the genocide or whose family was targeted. Another author could be a Hutu, who grew up in the Hutu Republics and developed sympathy with the system, whose family was targeted or even killed by the RPF rebels and who ran away from the rebels into exile. One can imagine many possible profiles between these two and can draw some hypotheses about what possible propaganda lines are likely to emerge from their novels.

Three working hypotheses can be advanced here, partly inspired by my previous analysis about parallel remembering amongst the Hutu and the Tutsi (Nyirubugara, 2013). The first hypothesis is that Tutsi novelists are most likely to be inclined towards the current dominant narrative that casts the 1990 to 1994 period as one of a liberation struggle, the aim of which was stopping the genocide against the Tutsi. The second hypothesis is that some Hutu authors are likely to stay 'neutral' and 'colourless' about the past or simply to tell the 'safest' story possible, by including a few aspects from the officially promoted narrative. This is close to what I called 'self-imposed' amnesia discussed in *Complexities and Dangers* (*Ibid.*). The third hypothesis is that some other Hutu novelists are likely to challenge the government-sponsored narrative and focus on the repressed part of the memories of the 1990 to 1994 period and thereafter. Their novels link the RPF rebels to the pre-independence Tutsi monarchy, stressing the killings of the Hutu civilians by the RPF and paying little attention to the genocide against the Tutsi.

This chapter aims to analyse the use of propaganda in the novels of genocide. It opens with a theoretical discussion about propaganda that aims to define the sense in which I use the concept, its meanings and workings and ways in which the novels serve as channels through which propaganda is conveyed to the public. I then move onto one potential subject that is likely to generate a lot of propaganda in the novels, namely the choice of focus between war, war and genocide, and genocide.

5.1. Understanding Propaganda

Discussions about propaganda in Rwanda have exclusively focused on the role of *Radio Télévision Libre des Mille Collines* [RTLM] and its hate broadcasts during the genocide. Scholars in various disciplines (e.g., Chrétien, Dupaquier, Kabanda, & Ngarambe, 1995; Kirschke, 1996; Fujii, 2004; Frère, 2005; Chrétien, 2007; Des Forges, 2007; Straus, 2007; Mironko, 2007; Yanagizawa-Drott, 2013) have all offered a rich body of literature about ways in which hate propaganda contributed to mass violence in 1994. Some authors empirically measured the correlation between RTLM propaganda reception and participation in violence. For instance, Yanagizawa-Drott (2013: 378) estimated that 10% of the participation to genocidal violence could be attributed to the RTLM propaganda. This exclusive focus on RTLM and, to some extent, on the *Kangura* newspaper, might suggest that no political propaganda is taking place or has taken place outside of these two defunct outlets. It might also lead to the wrong conclusion that propaganda is always associated with extreme cases of violence.

In this section, I am attempting to take propaganda away from RTLM and *Kangura* and will focus on fiction, specifically novels, as other powerful vehicles for propaganda. To do so, I first need to address the following preliminary questions: What is propaganda? What roles does memory play in propaganda? How does propaganda permeate fiction in general and novels in particular? By answering these questions based on existing literature, I want to pave the way for more focused discussions about concrete cases of propaganda in the novels of genocide.

The concept of propaganda is much more complex than the popular perception that equates it with lies and deceitful manipulation. Propaganda might have many different forms, but all of them have at least three central elements: an opinion, [mass] media, and persuasion (Ellul, 1972). Propaganda is thus defined as

> an attempt to spread an ideology through the mass media of communication in order to lead the public to accept some political or economic structure or to participate in some action (*Ibid.*: 63).

Presented like this, propaganda seems to be a normal and inevitable aspect of communication used not only by politicians but also by activists, advertisement professionals and religious preachers, amongst other types of communicators. One could easily add novelists to the list if they have a point or a version of the past or, of an event they want to promote. All of these categories of people come with clearly defined opinions and views and they want to persuade the public to embrace them. They do so by using newspapers, radio, television, the internet, social media, pamphlets, novels and many other types of mass media.

Mass media are a key element for propaganda to exist and function efficiently. Without adopting a techno-determinist stance, it could be argued that if the printing press had not been invented halfway through the 15th century, the spread of the Reformation movement would not have been successful. The swift development of Protestantism in 16th century Germany and Europe is, to a great extent, attributed to the new-born mass medium, namely the book (Fèbvre & Martin, [1958] 1984: 288). The book has even been credited for allowing the very first mass-media-driven propaganda campaign, i.e., the Reformation propagandists' campaign

(*Ibid.*). Reformation propagandists took great advantage of the new mass medium to produce and circulate biblical texts in everyday language which was accessible to ordinary people and to get rid of a number of established traditions and practices within the Church (Soulié, 1980: 168-169).

Reacting to this Reformation propaganda, the Catholic Church leadership put in place an unprecedented and institutionalised propaganda apparatus, the *Congregatione de Propaganda Fide* [The Congregation for the Propagation of Faith] in 1622, to win back the believers who had joined Protestantism (Prendergast & Prendergast, 2013; Jowett & O'Donnell, 2012: 2). Setting up the Congregation, Pope Gregory XV gave it almost absolute powers, mobilised substantial financial means and asked its members to do all in their power to bring the lost sheep back to 'the pasture of true Faith' (Prendergast & Prendergast, 2013: 20). This historical moment is perceived by many authors as the invention or birth of propaganda in its modern sense. It ceased referring to its initial and etymological meanings revolving around *spreading, expanding, multiplication, enlarging, generating*, etc., (Auerbach & Castronovo, 2013: 1-2; Prendergast & Prendergast, 2013: 24), to mean 'actively spreading one's ideological truths to those who are either ignorant of these truths or allied to other, quite opposed, truths' (Prendergast & Prendergast, 2013: 23).

As such, propaganda gradually integrated the manipulation of the public through mass media in order to have them adopt one's views and opinions. The notion of manipulation adds a negative connotation as it might include straight lies and falsehoods, in which case it is referred to as *black propaganda* (Ellul, 1972: 15; Jowett & O'Donnell, 2012: 18). It might also use covert, subtle, imperceptible and psychological manipulation that leaves no apparent sign of deceit, in which case it is labelled as *white propaganda* (Ellul, 1972: 15; Jowett & O'Donnell, 2012: 17). Finally, it might be somewhere between *black* and *white* propaganda, in which case it is called *grey propaganda* (Jowett & O'Donnell, 2012: 20). Propagandists usually use all three types of propaganda simultaneously, as they play a complementary role: black propaganda is meant to weaken the enemy or the adversary, whereas white propaganda aims to softly push people in a certain direction without them noticing it (Ellul, 1972: 15-16).

Whatever colour it has, propaganda has to be overwhelming to be successful since its aim is to create individuals whose reactions and behaviour are precisely predictable when certain words are pronounced or certain symbols and signs are used (*Ibid.*: 31). For propaganda to be omnipresent, it must:

> surround man by all possible routes, in the realm of feelings as well as ideas, by playing on his will or on his deeds, through his conscious and his unconscious, assailing him in both his private and his public life (Ellul, 1972: 11; see also Buitenhuis, 1976: 280).

Surrounding man by all possible routes includes feeding him with content through all imaginable mass media that is filled with propaganda, so that he can hear no dissonant voice. Newspapers, magazines, television, films, radio, novels, posters, speeches, textbooks, plays, etc., all tell a similar story, albeit in different ways (Ellul, 1972: 10; Auerbach & Castronovo, 2013: 7). Obviously, propaganda is successful because it rejects and excludes any form of contradiction and the idea of any dialogue that could bring dissonant voices to people's minds (Ellul, 1972: 11; Buitenhuis, 1976: 280 & 290-291).

It is at this point that memory enters into play, especially in places like Rwanda, where it is fiercely contested. To have a dominant narrative that casts a certain light on pre-colonial Rwanda as a paradise lost, on colonial Rwanda as the beginning of ethnic tensions fuelled by colonialists, on the late 1950s and early 1960s as the beginning of the genocide against the Tutsi and, on the 1990 to 1994 war as a liberation struggle to end the genocide, requires a sophisticated, all-encompassing propaganda system. Besides all traditional tools and instruments such as mass media, education, calendrical celebrations and commemorations, courts of justice, political speeches, etc., the Tutsi-dominated government has also put in place laws that prevent any dissonant opinions about the memories around the 1990 to 1994 war and the 1994 genocide. The most known and most repressive is the 2008 *Law Relating to the Punishment of the Crime of Genocide Ideology*, which defines the genocide ideology as

> an aggregate of *thoughts* characterised by conduct, *speeches*, documents and other acts aiming at exterminating or inciting others to exterminate people based on ethnic group, origin, nationality, region, colour, physical appearance, sex, language, religion or political opinion, committed in normal periods or during war (Republic of Rwanda, 2008. Emphases added).

From the propaganda perspective outlined above, this definition simply tells everyone the following: Make sure you *think* the way the system wants you to think; make sure what you *say* is in conformity with the official narrative. Since mass media are the main vehicles, the same law prescribes heavy penalties [20 to 25 years in jail and a fine of 2 to 5 million Rwandan francs or €2,300 to €5,900] for whoever is thought to be spreading the genocide ideology 'in public, through documents, speeches, pictures, media or via any other means [thus including novels?]' (*Ibid.*). This law, as it appears here, ensures a *de facto* unanimity about the past, because any counter-narrative that would suggest that the RPF rebels were far from being liberators and that the genocide was much more complex than currently suggested, etc., would immediately fall into the law's claws for

> marginalising, laughing at one's misfortune, defaming, mocking, boasting, despising, degrading, *creating confusion aiming at negating the genocide* which occurred, stirring up ill feelings, taking revenge, altering testimony or evidence for the genocide which occurred (*Ibid*. Emphasis added).

It goes without saying here that all doors seem closed to any dissonant look at the past. This is most likely the explanation of the palpable caution and prudence on the part of Hutu novelists such as Gatore (2008), Ndwaniye (2006), and Bahufite (2016), who obviously avoided getting into troubled waters by leaving ethnicity in the background. Gatore opted for not naming Rwanda and not mentioning the genocide and ethnicity in any way. That way, he avoided running the risk of marginalising or laughing at anyone's misfortune. Whoever would accuse him of creating confusion around the genocide, for instance not mentioning the ethnicity of the victims and of the killers, would have to prove that he wrote about the genocide in the first place. On his part, Ndwaniye (2006) named Rwanda and the genocide, but rarely engaged in ethnicity-related discussions. He also tactfully referred to the contested past, the 1950s to the 1970s, the war, the genocide, etc., and focused on his main character's early life in a rural area in western Rwanda, rather than on any political aspects. As for Bahufite (2016), she never mentioned 'Hutu' in her novel and she only mentioned 'Tutsi' once in passing as well as quickly touching upon the fact that they were hiding 'during the events that had cost the lives of thousands of Rwandans' (Bahufite, 2016: 172).

What the above-mentioned law mainly does, is encouraging cultural artefacts that support and reinforce the dominant memory narrative. In this way, the genocide memory constitutes a source for propaganda in the sense that it is used by the government propagandists, backed by the law, to create a unidirectional, polished and cleansed set of beliefs and values about Rwanda's recent past (Misztal 2003: 15). Repeated over and over in all types of mass media and through all sorts of channels, without any possibility of being challenged, and regardless of whether or not they belong to black propaganda or white propaganda, those tightly controlled beliefs and views about the genocide will ultimately be accepted as absolute truth (Stebbing, [1939] 1952: 83).

At this stage, one could wonder how propaganda permeates novels and turns them into one of those mass media that surround and wholly encircle man. Du Bois (1926) once made a sweeping statement that 'all Art is propaganda and ever must be', which, despite its generalisation, contains a great deal of truth in it. Du Bois made this statement in a period during which black artists were still rejected by the white-dominated cultural industry that refused black artists' works, especially those portraying black people in a positive light. The statement holds not only in this extreme case of discrimination, but also in less extreme or less dramatic situations where certain truths, ideological or not, are conveyed through creative works. In addition to this, novels and other creative works come into being in a certain historical, social and political context from which they cannot escape.

What I am suggesting here is that the prevailing socio-political environment in a given place, at a given moment in history transpires in the novels written during that period. For the case of post-genocide Rwanda, where memory is a sensitive and divisive issue and part of the government's all-encompassing propaganda, it would follow that the novels would reflect the state of affairs in one way or another. As Landsberg (2004: 4) nicely put it, no matter in which form they are expressed, memories are always about negotiating one's relationship to the past. In this respect, all the novelists discussed in this book negotiated their own relationships to that past marked by the genocide and its aftermath. Writing at a specific moment, those authors shaped their memories of the genocide by taking into account their experiences but also the political reality of that moment, namely the official narrative and the 2008 law that protects it. Some novelists would opt for self-imposed amnesia (see more about this in Nyirubugara, 2013) and adopt either a version close to the official narrative or avoid hot themes altogether, whereas others would overtly challenge the official narrative and promote their own memories. One could say that propaganda takes great advantage of novels and their creative, inventive power in the sense that they provide contexts, explanations and justifications of what is taking place in the present (Ellul, 1972: 14).

The 20th century witnessed many cases in which propagandists integrated novels into their campaigns. During World War I, for instance, British officials in charge of propaganda secretly brought creative writers together and urged them to write propaganda creative works, including novels, to promote Britain's views and values whilst downplaying Germany's (Buitenhuis, 1976: 277). The government made all of the financial arrangements for the publication and distribution of these works, which massively ended up on the market without anyone suspecting that they contained government-sponsored propaganda. In 1917 alone, 8,500,000 works were published and distributed throughout Britain (*Ibid.*: 278 & 280). Most of these works blackened Germans as a nation, using statements such as: they are 'sinister, ugly' people (*Ibid.*: 278), they are barbarians who chop children's heads off (*Ibid.*: 280), they have a poor, unworthy culture (*Ibid.*: 283) and they deserve to cease existing as a nation (*ibid.*), etc. At the same time, they whitewashed everything relating to Britain and its allies. Similar practices were observed during World War II (Foulkes, 1983: 2-3) and during the Cold War (Romeo, 2014).

The strategy to recruit creative writers outlined in the previous paragraph brings to mind the 1998 Fest'Africa project. This project brought a few African creative writers together and took them to Rwanda to write about the genocide. In his acknowledgement, one of the authors, Senegalese novelist Diop (2000) thanked the Rwandan government for co-sponsoring the project together with Fondation de France. Another one, Djiboutian Waberi (2000), wrote fictional essays which he described on the back cover as echoing a *historical truth* of the genocide. Taking into account the government sponsorship, the guided and tightly controlled tours the authors had during their stay in Rwanda (Dauge-Roth, 2010: 93) as well as the *historical truth* that emerged from the project, Rwandan novelist Rurangwa (2006: 196), who also participated in the project, rightly concluded that the dozen Fest'Africa project authors had become 'ambassadors of the Rwandan People in their respective countries and in the world'. The use of the term *ambassadors* is very important here, because it implies a mission and the duty to defend certain interests, no matter what. In this case, one might think that the one who sponsored the project, controlled and approved it, is the one whose interests are defended by these *ambassadors*. Since propaganda is about spreading and promoting a certain ideological truth in as much mass media as possible, Sections 5.4 and 6.3 focus on cases from the Fest'Africa project novels.

In a nutshell, this section has briefly fleshed out the concept of propaganda and its relation to both memory and novels. What has emerged from this discussion is that propaganda comes from those in a position of power, who have a certain control of mass media and the power to decide which opinions and views can be safely promoted and propagated. Memory and novels are close allies of propaganda in the sense that memory provides a ready-made reservoir from which propagandists select materials that fit their purpose, whereas novels inescapably reflect the prevailing environment, i.e., the one controlled by the system that produces propaganda. Since my focus is on memories of the genocide and ways in which they permeate novels, my propaganda analysis is limited only to those attempts, both explicit and implicit, by novelists to persuade the reader about what is worth remembering about the 1990 to 1994 war and the 1994 genocide, about who is to be blamed or praised and for what, about who is to be considered the victim or the killer, etc. I am including here *implicit* attempts because, to use Foulkes' (1983: 3) words, 'Propaganda does not often come marching towards us waving swastikas and chanting "Sieg heil"'. The fact that it is operating in an imagined, fictional world increases its capacity to conceal itself and calls for analysis beneath the surface. So the next three sections focus on the novels of genocide that display propagandistic features in one way or another, explicitly or implicitly. By propagandistic features, I mean those cues that lead one to think that either the dominant, official narrative or the repressed, banned narrative about the contested past is being pushed forward in the novel.

5.2. War and/or Genocide in Hutu-Authored Novels

The first memory aspect that causes divergent interpretations of the memories of the 1990s amongst Rwandans is where the emphasis should be placed between the 1990 to 1994 war and the April to July 1994 genocide. My previous analysis of autobiographical accounts showed that the Hutu tended to put more emphasis on, and prioritised, the war that victimised hundreds of thousands of Hutu long before and after the 1994 genocide, whereas the Tutsi tended to focus on the genocide and excluded everything relating to the war (Nyirubugara, 2013). Also, research has shown that when they are asked to tell about what happened in the 1990s, Hutu respondents tend 'to refer to *intambara*, the war, *ubwicanyi*, the killings or more vaguely, *ibyabaye*, the happenings or *amahano*, horror or tragedy', which the Tutsi respondents would so rarely do (Longman & Rutagengwa, 2004: 170). To ensure that there is no dissonance about what happened between 1990 and 1994, the government inserted the French term [written in Kinyarwanda] *jenoside* in the Constitution and specified that it started on 1st October 1990, the date on which RPF rebels launched their attack from Uganda, and that it was *exclusively* against the Tutsi (Nyirubugara, 2013: 58).

The first question that helps understand the main orientation of the novel is: Who is the victim and who is the killer or villain in the novel? If the novel emphasises that the victim is Tutsi and the killer or rapist a Hutu, then the novel has a genocide-centred approach. But if the victim is a Hutu and the killer or rapist is an RPF Tutsi rebel, then the novel has a war-centred approach. Of course, the situation might be somewhere in between, e.g., with Hutu victims and Hutu killers, usually falling under the genocide-centred approach, as the victims' wrongdoing is usually helping or being sympathetic to the Tutsi. My hypothesis in this section is that the Hutu novelists are expected to offer either a mixed approach – war-and-genocide – or an exclusively war-centred view. For the sake of structure, I will discuss Hutu-authored novels in this section and Tutsi-authored counterparts in the next.

Where do Hutu-authored novels place the emphasis between the war and the genocide? Three of the five Hutu-authored novels, namely Niwese (2001), Mbabazi (2007), and Bahufite (2016), clearly adopt the war-centred approach that challenges the official narrative, whereas the other two, i.e., Ndwaniye (2006) and Gatore (2008), stay more or less within the genocide-centred framework. Niwese's (2001) *Celui qui sut vaincre* does focus on the war but not *per se* the 1990 to 1994 war. Situated in post-genocide Rwanda, the novel rather stresses the warlike attitude and the love of war amongst the RPF strategists and leaders. A very important part of the novel is the recording of an evaluation meeting amongst RPF insiders, in which all agreed upon the love of war, especially when the victim was a Hutu. The RPF expert and insider who analysed the situation observed that the system was in the crosshairs of international justice because of 'charges of war and genocide crimes against both the civil and military leaders of our society' (Niwese, 2001: 22). More specifically, the RPF expert evoked the case of the prosecutor of the International Criminal Tribunal for Rwanda, the lady from the ICTR, who kept reminding about 'the large-scale massacres committed during our army's offensive' and after the former government was defeated (*Ibid.*). What is interesting here and throughout the entire expert analysis, is that the crimes were not denied or minimised. Instead of that, the expert stated what seemed to be obvious to everyone who attended the meeting:

> Nobody ignores that before 1994, that is, since October 1990, we eliminated hundreds of people in north-eastern regions. And what to say about post-1994? Thousands of internally displaced people died in Kibeho in 1995. Our army is responsible for that and the plan of attack was elaborated here. In this same place. The NGOs and the UN blue helmets who were there saw it all. They have irrefutable evidence they can throw in our face at any time (*Ibid.*: 22-23).

This passage and many others in the novel clearly shows that the reader is being persuaded that the RPF war was not a liberation war, but rather a dirty war, during which 'war and genocide crimes' were committed against the Hutu. Most of the factual details such as the start of the war, the location where it took place, the massacre of the Kibeho displaced people, are historically correct but used in a way that contradicts their use in the official narrative. Given that the novel does not even once touch upon the genocide against the Tutsi, perhaps because it is situated in the period after 1994, one could confidently conclude that it openly adopted the exclusively war-centred approach to memory, whereby the Hutu is the victim of the Tutsi-dominated RPF.

Bahufite's (2016) *Une vie qui n'est pas mienne*, whose acknowledgements include a word of thanks to Niwese for his 'relevant corrections and remarks', focuses on the post-genocide war by the new RPF-led leadership in Zaire, which is presented as an extension of the 1990 to 1994 war in Rwanda. The novel dedicates a chapter to 'war' (Bahufite, 2016: 21-24) but does not specify who was fighting and why until later in the novel. The main points in there are that it ended Nadine's dreams of studying Journalism or Law in Rwanda or in Europe (*Ibid.*: 21 & 23), caused the death of thousands of people (*Ibid.*: 23) and directly or indirectly affected everyone (*Ibid.*: 24). Throughout the novel Nadine kept blaming that war and those who were provoking it and at some point, as she was in the refugee camp, she made a promise to herself to make them pay:

> Inside myself I revolted, cursing all those who had pushed us into exile. I swore to avenge myself one day, even though I ignored the form that vengeance would take. I felt hatred mounting in me and I was often frightened to experience such a destructive feeling (*Ibid.*: 34; see also *Ibid.*: 121 & 138).

Even though the ethnicity of the fighters and the victims is not mentioned, it is very easy to imagine who the Tutsi and who the Hutu are in this novel. The camps obviously sheltered Hutu refugees, whereas the RPF army, which is later mentioned (see *Ibid.*: 170) as the one hunting down and slaughtering the refugees, were predominantly Tutsi. It is clear here that *Une vie qui n'est pas mienne* is a war-centred novel, because in no single case are the Tutsi presented as victims of the Hutu killers, whereas it abounds with cases of the Tutsi killing the Hutu.

In a similar vein, Mbabazi's (2007) *Sheridan* emphasises the crimes committed by the RPF rebels against the Hutu, but does so in parallel with massacres – the term genocide is not used – against the Tutsi by Hutu militiamen. What *Sheridan* and *Celui qui sut vaincre* have in common is that the crimes committed by the RPF were witnessed or reported on by an RPF insider, rather than by a Hutu victim. Unlike the RPF expert who said 'yes we massively killed the Hutu and we should do our best to escape justice', Mihigo, a young Tutsi boy recruited by, and serving under, his uncle and uncompromising Hutu killer Colonel Karekezi, was disgusted by what he saw. When the war resumed after the shooting of President Habyarimana's plane, Mihigo witnessed over and over again the 'unnameable' committed by the RPF against the Hutu (Mbabazi, 2007: 229, 283, 289, amongst other cases). One day, he was 'confronted with the killing of around twenty defenceless and tied-up civilians, whose sole wrong was that they were Hutu' (*Ibid.*: 159).

During those days, Mihigo had a feeling that his co-fighters felt pleasure in making Hutu blood flow, as if it streamed from a 'natural inexhaustible, non-human, source' (*Ibid.*: 199). He was also disgusted by the rapes of Hutu women by RPF soldiers, who did not hesitate to kill the husbands who attempted to protect their wives (*Ibid.*: 199-202). These women had become 'appetisers', *amuse-gueule*, for RPF soldiers (*Ibid.*: 200) and would often volunteer to protect their families (*Ibid.*). The crimes were so violent that the mental health of both Mihigo and his uncle started ailing. Mihigo was haunted by what he had seen (*Ibid.*: 290), whereas his uncle could not get rid of recurrent nightmares during which his Hutu victims would torment him: if there is one thing he feared the most, 'that was the night', because 'the blood of thousands of innocent people that he had willingly shed would frightfully spoil his sleep' (*Ibid.*: 287). The sole ally he had during the day was alcohol, which would make him forget or manage the previous night's nightmares (*Ibid.*: 288).

Regarding this dominant war-focused perspective of the 1990 to 1994 memories, Mbabazi's (2007) *Sheridan* adds another dimension whereby the killer and rapist was a Hutu and the victim a Tutsi. The novel does not refer to this situation as *genocide*, although it calls it *the unnamable* once (*Ibid.*: 304).[36]

---

36 The qualifier 'unnamable' was used three times in reference to the RPF killings against the Hutu (Mbabazi, 2007: 229, 283, 289) and once in reference to the massacre of Burundian Hutu by the Tutsi-dominated army (*Ibid.*: 292-293).

Unlike the *unnamable* against the Hutu, which was officially sanctioned by the RPF leadership, the *unnamable* against the Tutsi seemed to be the work of Hutu militiamen and very few soldiers. The army leadership, including army chief General Amato and special forces commander Miko, seemed busy fighting the RPF and preventing it from taking over the country.

The novel as a whole does not contain any classic scenes of genocide killing with all the visual descriptions that make them more appealing. For instance, when Kenya and her step-sisters run away from the militiamen near the Nyanza hill, where a dozen grenades had just exploded amongst the Tutsi refugees, no description of the dead and the dying is provided. A comment similar to 'their sole wrong was being Hutu' used for the Hutu victims, is not provided (*Ibid*.: 167-168). Thus instead of the detailed, emotional description of the scene, one reads that 'the deafening explosions directly caused ravages, leaving nothing but the screaming of those who were badly wounded by shrapnel' (*Ibid*.). The novel handles the scenes of the Hutu killings by the RPF rebels differently and produces what Barthes (1968: 85-88) called *effet du réel*. One such visual description is when the Hutu refugees from the areas occupied by the RPF reached Gisenyi and told other Hutu refugees about what they had seen:

> They were frightened and traumatised. Their stories were always the same: the reconnaissance units of commander Salim invaded villages at dusk and generally killed, to serve as example, all Hutu dignitaries after assembling them in front of a petrified public. …Their favourite technique, *Akandoya*, consisted in solidly tying the arms behind the back in a *chicken-wings* position, the elbows and ankles together with a solid rope, leaving the rib cage completely stretched; this method is seemingly harmless, except that the victim died later and little by little in atrocious suffering, spewing blood following internal bleeding caused by debunked shoulders and a broken sternum (*Ibid*.: 228-229).

This meticulous description is, in my view, a cue that the novelist wants the reader to be moved by that part of Rwandans' memory that has received little attention. It has simply been pushed to the margins and declared not worth remembering. Remembering it means denying the genocide. In the light of the 2008 *Law Relating to the Punishment of the Crime of Genocide Ideology* discussed in the previous section, this novel could easily fall under the genocide ideology, as it questions – thus creates confusion – the official narrative about 1990 to 1994.

Rape is also part of the *unnamable* against the Tutsi and it is worthwhile comparing its significance when it is committed against Tutsi women and when it is committed against Hutu women. The novel contains two cases of rape against Tutsi women. The first one took place when Kami, Yuhi and Orange had just sought refuge in a church after the explosion of grenades near the Nyanza hill. Militiamen were about to kill them when Matamata, a militia leader rescued them and took them to his place, where they served as sex slaves for him and his men until the end of the war (Mbabazi, 2007: 170-171). The second case was again against Kami, whom Matamata had left home in Gisenyi to handle another case. During his absence, Giovanni, an army commander born from an Italian father and a Rwandan woman whose ethnicity was not revealed, entered the compound in search of 'sex to calm his nerves' (*Ibid.*: 248), and sodomised her (*Ibid.*: 253-254). A comparison between these two instances and the cases mentioned in relation to Hutu women shows that rapes of Tutsi women by the Hutu were not only limited, but also incidental, whereas rapes of Hutu women by Tutsi rebels were systematic and part of the military strategy. Moreover, the sole army leader involved in the rape of a Tutsi woman was not a Hutu, he was Italian with a Rwandan mother, which could be interpreted as suggesting that the Hutu army leadership did not sanction rape.

Unlike Niwese's (2001) *Celui qui sut vaincre*, Mbabazi's (2007) *Sheridan*, and Bahufite's (2016) *Une vie qui n'est pas mienne* that openly challenge the official memory line, Ndwaniye's (2006) *La promesse faite à ma soeur* and Gatore's (2008) *Le passé devant soi*, chose a more cautious, less confrontational approach. Most of the two novels' contents perfectly fits the official narrative or at least refrains from raising any major doubt about it, let alone challenging it. As repeatedly pointed out in previous chapters, Gatore (2008) concealed his reference to Rwanda, whilst at the same time providing enough clues about which country and society he was referring to. The deduction that Niko was half-Hutu and Isaro half-Tutsi is debatable, because nowhere in the novel can one find the words Hutu and Tutsi. So the question about whether Gatore (2008) invited the reader to think more about the war rather than, or in addition to, the genocide is a challenging one, as it takes one to a different level of interpretation, involving even more deductions. However, the exercise is worth doing and the huge challenge it poses makes it even more interesting.

One can argue that Gatore's novel is mostly about the genocide at a village level. Throughout the novel, one sees innocent victims being hunted down because of who they were (e.g., Gatore, 2008: 124-125). In a way, the novel reinforces the dominant narrative of the genocide by adding some more complexities to it. For instance, Niko found himself in a dilemma because of his mixed ethnicity. He was a Hutu because his father was, but he had some Tutsi blood coming from his late mother. He had to choose where he stood and choosing meant killing his own father, a Hutu, who had betrayed his ethnicity by marrying a Tutsi (*Ibid.*: 129-131). No Tutsi was killed in this particular case but, the death of the Hutu father implies the systematic killing of the Tutsi and all those considered to be their accomplices. Moreover, unlike Mbabazi (2007) who did not make the killing of the Tutsi visual, Gatore (2008) deployed all of his talent in doing so. As he was being taken to a small field where he used to play and where a lot of movement could be observed, Niko saw the following:

> As he got nearer and nearer, he realised that the crowd was not as disorganised as it appeared at first sight. In the middle of the ground sat people tied up, like himself. Disfigured corpses were piled up further in the corner. Around and between these two groups walked people diversely armed. Most of them carried machetes. Some also had cudgels, spears, bows, sickles, forks, scissors; anything that allows one to hit, pierce or cut. A few men, generally those who give orders, have fire arms (*Ibid.*: 126).

It would not require an exceptional painter to put this scene onto a canvas or a piece of paper. It is so detailed that it provides a clear message to the reader: here is a scene of genocide; here are the arms the killers used; here is the hopeless situation in which those who are going to die find themselves; there, in the corner, are those who have been killed after torture, etc. Another clear point here is that the killing is presented as systematic and as having the approval of the entire village, as they all seemed to be comfortable with the scene.

Even though Gatore's novel embraces to a great extent the official narrative of the genocide, it does create some dissonance. The killings seemed systematic, but the planner was missing. In the quote presented above, those who gave the orders are not presented as army officers and it is not clear from whom they received their fire arms. More importantly, when Niko finally proved his loyalty by killing his father, he emerged as a champion in killing, raising a suggestion that the killers were like him. In other words, if someone who could not speak and who was rejected from school was the one commanding the killers, it would follow that those under him were worse. The suggestion made here is that the killers were not the normal, ordinary Hutu, which the official narrative suggests, but those in the margins of society.

In addition to the above, Gatore's novel omits an important aspect of the official narrative, namely the role of the *liberator*. The killings stopped, not because the RPF Tutsi rebels intervened, but because 'there was no one to kill anymore' (Gatore, 2008: 135) and if Niko ran away to the *Iwacu* Island, it is not because someone was trying to arrest him, but rather because he was haunted by the memory of his killings. Like Colonel Karekezi's nightmares (Mbabazi, 2007), Niko's daydreams did not give him any respite. After one such dream,

> he did not need to reflect upon it before deciding to go. Being the furthest and loneliest possible was urgent and vital to him. The world would but fill his mind with unbearable memories. He therefore needed to vanish from it (Gatore, 2008: 143).

In short, Gatore's novel does embrace the official narrative to some extent, but does not include all key aspects that constitute the core of the message. What is for certain throughout, is that the war and its implications in terms of who was the killer and who was the victim is missing altogether in the novel. In no case does Gatore (2008) suggest that a Hutu died outside the killings conducted by the Hutu themselves.

Although the adjective *neutral* might seem inappropriate when one is analysing a novel or any other work of arts, one might have good reasons to describe Ndwaniye's (2006) *La promesse faite à ma soeur* as the most neutral of all the 11 novels of genocide at the centre of this analysis. One reason for this *cautious* approach could be the fact that the novel is situated long after the end of the war and the genocide. Another one could be that the author willingly avoided controversial discussions probably because he, as the autobiographical novel suggests, might be caught up in between. Ndwaniye must have struggled to find a way to tell the story of Jean's relatives, including his sister and her family, without engaging into controversial matters. One solution appears to be the daydream, which offered a suitable framework in which part of the story was told. As he was watching television alone, a few days after his arrival in Kigali, Jean suddenly heard the voice of his late father calling him. Then, in a vision, Jean saw his father surrounded by all the members of the family who had died.

> At that moment, I saw almost all family members whom I had known and who had passed away. They sat in the reversed order of their death. There was my sister Antoinette, killed during the genocide, then my father who had passed away a few weeks before her. Then came my maternal and paternal grandmothers. My paternal grandfather whom I could vaguely remember as I was too young when he died, closed the row. Each of them wore the best cloths… (Ndwaniye, 2006: 53).

It is important to note here that the word genocide is used in a daydream and in relation to a half-Hutu woman who had married a Tutsi man. It is also interesting to note here and in many other instances that Ndwaniye does not use the *genocide against the Tutsi* formula (e.g., Ndwaniye, 2006: 43, 45-46, 67, 71-72). This might seem to be an insignificant detail but when one looks at the other words used in the novel to describe the 1990 to 1994 period, one realises that the novel looks at that period from a rather all-inclusive approach. The use of the term *évènements* [events, happenings] stands out and suggests that the genocide is one amongst many other important events that took place in that period. For instance, as he discussed with Ignace, the director of Sinai Guest House in Kibuye, Jean explained to him the reason why he had been unable to visit his country much earlier, adding that he had powerlessly followed 'the 1994 events' (*Ibid.*: 88). Also, before paying a visit to his brother in jail, he went to visit the house in which the latter's family lived 'before the events' (*Ibid.*: 90). Later on, while drinking beer at Edelweiss Hotel, Jean refrained from asking the bartender about 'the fate the events had reserved to them [hotel's staff]' (*Ibid.*: 106. Brackets added). Finally, speaking of his friends from his youth with whom he had played football, Jean said: 'Only Mateso has survived all the storms until today. Samuel and Juma went into exile whereas Benjamin, Saidi and Innocent were killed during the 1994 events. …' (*Ibid.*: 127). The frequent use of the *1994 events* and similar terms like the *drama* (*Ibid.*: 106-107 & 169) or *tragedies* (*Ibid.*: 84) suggests that the novel is implicitly trying to persuade the reader that there have been many more *storms* and *tragedies* during that particular period and that the genocide was one of them.

My initial working hypothesis was that the Hutu-authored novels would most likely tell a story that features both the war and the genocide or one that would exclusively focus on the war. The assumption was that the Hutu victim, who is excluded from the official narrative, would be presented as such and the RPF rebels would be the villains. This hypothesis holds in three of the five novels, as Niwese (2001), Mbabazi (2007) and Bahufite (2016) overtly point towards the RPF as the Hutu mass killers and the Hutu as the innocent victims. However, unlike Niwese (2001) and Bahufite (2016), who adopted the exclusively war-centred approach, Mbabazi (2007) slightly included the killings of the Tutsi by the Hutu without necessarily calling them genocide. Ndwaniye's (2006) novel also confirms the hypothesis in the sense that it seems to suggest that the genocide was one amongst many tragedies of the 1990s in Rwanda. It is in Gatore's (2008) novel that the hypothesis seems not to hold. The novel has a clear focus on the genocide and has Hutu killers on one hand and Tutsi victims together with those Hutu who were associated with them, on the other hand. In the next section I undertake a similar analysis, but this time with a focus on Tutsi-authored novels.

5.3. War and/or Genocide in Tutsi-Authored Novels

Four of the six Tutsi-authored novels revolve around 1994 in a direct way, whereas the other two, Mukasonga's (2012) *Notre Dame du Nil* and Rusimbi's (1999) *By the Time She Returned*, somehow provide an historical context, with a suggestion that the 1994 genocide was a culmination of what the novels discuss. Even though Rusimbi (1999) ends the novel with RPF rebels heading towards the border to start the October 1990 war against the Rwandan government army, it does not describe the war at all. The same is true for Mukasonga (2012), whose novel sketches a mini-genocide at the school level back in the early 1970s, with support of the officials and the complicity of members of the Catholic clergy. It would be incorrect and inappropriate to include these two novels in the analysis that aims to find out whether the novelists opted for the war-centred, the genocide-centred, or the mixed approach, since they both took 1994 as the future which was already known to the authors at the time of writing. In this respect, a better analysis would look at these two novels as embracing a historical approach, as they pave the way for a certain understanding of events to come. For the remaining four novels, I want to test the hypothesis that the Tutsi-authored novels would most likely offer an exclusive genocide-centred approach, which is in accordance with the official memory narrative.

A close look at Sehene's (2005) *Le feu sous la soutane* shows that this novel is mainly about the killing of Tutsi refugees at the Sainte Famille church by Hutu militiamen and about rapes by a [half-]Hutu priest. Both the killings and the rapes are presented as being part of a plan to annihilate the Tutsi, the enemies of the Hutu majority power. Instead of going through a few cases whereby the victim was Tutsi and the killer Hutu, I want to rather zoom in on one or two of them, to show ways in which the novel takes a persuasive turn by emphasising that the killing was more than mere killing and rape more than mere rape. In one case, when Father Stanislas had become a regular killer, the novel portrays a situation that sums up the genocide- centred approach of the novel. At some point, when the killings had reached their climax at the Sainte Famille church, corpses were piled up all over the courtyard, where one could see a disordered mixture of body parts and blood tainted cloths. Father Stanislas seemed to have some pleasure watching the scene:

> I am no longer alone doing this job, everybody is now busy with the task. The slaughter is actively underway. And these heaps of bodies spread all over – isolated legs, arms still folded with bleeding elbows thrown in one corner, headless torsos – bloody parts of a broken-up human puzzle, have lost all humanness (Sehene, 2005: 104-105).

This scene is so visually described that the reader cannot help but pause to digest all the horror it describes. One wonders the wrongdoing the victims had committed to deserve such a cruel death that ended with the dismembering of their bodies. And when the reader comes back to continue reading, he or she gets confronted with the following:

> Militiamen are laughing and loudly boasting their achievements during the 'work'. Then those crime soldiers engage in a sort of horror competition. They kill row by row. With a methodical diligence that seems far from any desire, one militiaman rapes a woman in front of everyone. Behind him, other militiamen fight pending their own turn and some, in a hurry, turn to the corpses…The spectacle becomes torture for me [Father Stanislas], when the man, after quenching his desire [raping a pregnant woman], snatches the foetus from the woman's womb and crushes it against a wall (Sehene, 2005: 105. Brackets added).

This is what one would call a typical genocide scene that not only shows that the victim was innocent – how on earth could a foetus have committed any wrong?- but also that the killer went far, far beyond any imaginable limit and took pleasure in doing so. It is worth noting the resemblance between this scene and the one in Mbabazi's (2007) novel, when he visually describes tied-up Hutu in a chicken-wings position, who died slowly from internal bleeding (see previous section). These two scenes share their visual details but also their intention to persuade the reader about what they should keep in mind when they have finished reading and have put the novels back onto the shelves.

Although Sehene's (2005) novel is dominated by the killings and raping of Tutsi refugees at the Sainte Famille church, it also includes the war. Unlike Mbabazi (2007) and Niwese (2001) who emphasised the Hutu victims of that war, Sehene (2005) framed the war as an attempt to end the genocide. For instance, one of the rare cases in which the author mentions RPF rebels is when a commando made an incursion in the church to deliver some Tutsi refugees. The only person who died in relation to that was a Hutu called Mugabo, who had opened the door to the rebels so that his Tutsi wife and their children could be rescued. Mugabo was killed by militiamen the next day (Sehene, 2005: 87-88). Another case is when the government army decided to use the Tutsi refugees at the Sainte Famille church as a human shield by positioning their heavy artillery in front of the church. The thinking was that the army would shell the RPF positions but the RPF rebels would not dare shell back because, in doing so, they would be killing fellow Tutsi (*Ibid.*: 21-22). Contrary to that expectation, the RPF rebels shelled back and hit the church:

> All refugees try to run away from the main gate, swarming the other end of the nave, crouching between benches or behind the altar. The central aisle is tainted with blood, littered with dismantled bodies, trampled on to death during the panic (*Ibid.*: 23).

This is a scene of war. An army shells the positions of the enemy and the enemy shells back, causing human and material casualty. However, this scene is special in the sense that it is the only one in which the RPF rebels were indirectly involved in the death of innocent people. The sole culprit here was the government army, even though they did not shell into the church themselves. Their Machiavellian plan was to push their enemies to do that, which comes down to the same thing as shooting them themselves. It is also important to note here that even when the RPF rebels shelled back, their bombs did not directly kill. At least the novel does not suggest this. They created panic within the church, and panic created a stampede and the stampede resulted in the death of Tutsi refugees. So one has some kind of war-centred approach in this novel, but this approach frames the warring parties differently from what my hypothesis has suggested. The war is framed as part of the genocide, as both had the same killers who targeted the same victims.

In one instance, Sehene's (2005) novel slightly mentions killings allegedly committed by RPF rebels, attributing them to rumours. Unlike Mbabazi (2007) and Niwese (2001) whose novels tell us about those killings from the perspectives of the Tutsi killers themselves, *Le feu sous la soutane* takes the Hutu killer's [Father Stanislas'] perspective and turns it into a rumour:

> According the *rumour* circulating amongst militiamen, the guerrillas *would* now be only five kilometres away from the city centre. *People talk* about gouged eyes, of systematic assassinations of Hutu intellectuals. No one *would* survive, *it seems* (*Ibid.*: 124. Emphases added).

Telling a story with a caveat that it is a rumour and then filling it with the conditional before closing it with 'it seems', is a clear invitation to the reader to really not take the 'rumour' seriously. What one should take seriously with regards to RPF rebels, is the portrait that Father Stanislas made of them when he met them at the Hotel des Mille Collines:

> Tall and slim, …[they] check [identity] papers at the entrance. They also search vehicles. Fortunately, I have already gotten rid of my arm before coming! To my amazement, the rebels politely talk to those they search and control. They are kids, aged hardly around fifteen for most of them. What! Would these children defeat the all-mighty Rwanda army? I can't believe it (*Ibid.*: 135. Brackets added).

The message is clear here. On the one hand the reader has a rumour packed with a lot of conditionals and on the other hand, the same reader is served with a first-hand witness account. The choice is quickly made about which image of the RPF rebels to keep in mind. They are polite kids! They cannot possibly do what the rumours claim about them.

Rurangwa's (2006) *Au sortir de l' enfer* follows more or less a similar pattern with a clear focus on the genocide against the Tutsi. Unlike Sehene (2005), whose novel starts with refugees in the church, Rurangwa's (2006) novel takes time to build up a context for the genocide, before confronting the reader with scenes of horror. On many occasions one reads about the Hutu extremists announcing the final solution months before the genocide. *Kangura* Hutu journalist Célestin Sembagare, who was also a member of the CDR party that championed the Rwanda-is-for-the-Hutu ideology, is presented as the prophet and preacher of the genocide to come.

His articles in *Kangura*, which were signed by Hassan Ngeze,[37] contended that true Hutuness started with the size of one's nose. If one's nostrils could accommodate three fingers, then that person was Hutu and part of those who deserved to live (Rurangwa, 2006: 70-71). One day, as he was having a glass of beer in the Tutsi-owned Hotel Chez Martin, he observed the female Tutsi bartenders there and told himself:

> 'I will have Tutsi she-dogs[38] at my mercy on the D-day! He said to himself. It seems you've said that you can never go to bed with Hutu men. Well, that day, we will be twenty. We will f**k you in turns. And when we're tired, we will use bayonets, bottles or sharp wooden sticks'.
>
> Célestin Sembagare impatiently waited for the day when the genocide would kick off to commit these erotic atrocities and quench his monstrous sexual phantasms (*Ibid.*: 70. Asterisks added).

A similar scene suggesting a genocide-in-the-making with clear details of what will happen when it kicks off, is when the CDR militant Butihoro came to recruit Juma, the Hutu houseboy at the Benimana's, a Tutsi family.

> -Juma, he asked, have you ever gone to bed with a Tutsi girl?
>
> -Never!
>
> -The CDR is going to give you the opportunity to do so. Juma, you will shortly have the pleasure of raping Tutsi girls and women. You will rape Jeanne, Marie and their mother at your ease if you want (*Ibid.*: 16).

These two scenes, together with others, have an obvious aim to persuade the reader that all the Hutu, even down to the houseboy, not only knew that the genocide was coming, but also had a list of tasks to be accomplished when it started. I want to emphasise the fact that the houseboy is informed about the coming genocide and its details, because at that time [perhaps today, too] in Rwanda, the houseboy, *umuboyi*, had the lowest social status in society. Usually, *umuboyi* lives in his boss' house, eats there and does all kinds of work for the family for a meagre salary. The assumption in the novel is that, if people at the lowest step of the social ladder knew about the coming genocide in detail, then everybody else would have known about it too.

---

37 Hassan Ngeze is part of those who were convicted by the International Criminal Tribunal for Rwanda [ICTR] set up in 1994 to judge genocide crimes and crimes against humanity committed in Rwanda in 1994. He is currently serving a 35-year sentence in Mali. In the early 1990s Ngeze founded Kangura, a paper that spread anti-Tutsi propaganda before the genocide.

38 It is not easy to translate this insult as it has a peculiar meaning in the Rwandan culture. Dog, *imbwa*, usually refers to men [not women], and is the opposite of Man, *umugabo*. As observed in Section 2.3 when discussing the name Mugabo, *umugabo* is a catch-all noun that includes virtues and values like bravery, courage, honesty, trustworthiness and the like. *Imbwa* means just the opposite. However, the female dog, *imbwakazi*, is something else. It can be argued that it is the worst insult one can address to a Rwandan woman/girl, and I think that the use of *chiennes de Tutsi* [Tutsi she-dogs] is used in this sense in Rurangwa's novel.

When the D-day came, Sembagare was at the same Hotel Chez Martin, where he urged the Tutsi who were there to get ready for what was going to follow: '*Inyenzi-Inkotanyi!* he said, drink your last glass of beer and say your last prayer! You have killed the Father of the Nation, you're going to pay a high price!' (Rurangwa, 2006: 76). So when the reader reaches these classic scenes of horror, he or she already knows what is going to happen: the victims are the Tutsi who are paying for not having large nostrils. Tutsi women and girls are going to be gang-raped, because they allegedly said that they could never go to bed with Hutu men, the assumption here being that the latter are collectively and inherently ugly. One of the scenes that sums up the genocide-centred approach of the novel in a detailed and visual way, is when Hutu CDR militant Casimir Kayiru came with a group of militiamen to kill his own brother, Anastase Benimana and his Tutsi wife together with their children: 'here am I, dog traitor!'[39] (*Ibid.*: 79), Kayiru said to his brother. After a brief exchange about his brother's complicity in the death of President Habyarimana, Kayiru told his brother that what was the most essential for the latter was not the understanding of his [Kayiru's] behaviour, but seeing his actions. This is what he showed him:

> …he grabbed a studded club from one of the militiamen escorting him and, using all his strength, smashed his brother Anastase Benimana's skull. He fell on the floor and died without saying anything. …Using a machete, he cut his head off and with his iron knife, he cut off his genitals before the eyes of Irène [his Tutsi wife], of his two daughters and of his son. Then, by means of a bayonet, Casimir Kayiru took Alain-Pierre's [his nephew] viscera out… (*Ibid.*: 79-80. Brackets added).

Obviously, this scene that was meant for Anastase Benimana to see is an invitation for the reader to come into Benimana's living room and visualise the horror. As Benimana died first he could not see what came after his death. The fact that the victims in the above-mentioned quote are Hutu does not disqualify the scene as a genocide scene. On the contrary, it reinforces it in the sense that it pushes the reader to conclude that if a Hutu suffered to the extent Benimana suffered, then the Tutsi would have suffered even more. And, indeed, the fate of Irène, Benimana's Tutsi wife, proves this observation to be right. When Kayiru ordered his escort to start avenging President Habyarimana, they rushed to Benimana's two daughters and gang-raped them, forcing their mother Irène to watch as the two girls screamed, in pain (*Ibid.*: 80). Then suddenly, Kayiru ordered them to stop: 'It's now the turn of their dog mother [*chienne de mère*]' (*Ibid.*). Petrified by the rape of her daughters, Irène did not resist the militiamen when they tore her skirt and underwear. When she was completely naked, Kayiru invited everyone to come and see 'what the vagina of Tutsi women looks like!' (*Ibid.*), before touching its lips with his bayonet. At that point, the militiamen started playing with her intimate parts, measuring them. Irène just shut her eyes, refusing to be a witness of her own

---

39 Once again, *chien de traître* [dog traitor] here poses a problem of translation. In Kinyarwanda it would be *imbwa y'umugambanyi* [the dog that betrayed his community/family/country etc.]. Betraying implies that a Man is no longer a trustworthy fellow, thus imbwa in the eyes of those who see betrayal in his actions or behaviour.

torture, but this gesture of hers pushed Kayiru to tell his men to see how Tutsi women reach orgasm [by shutting their eyes] (*Ibid.*: 81). One of the militiamen said that they rather wept, because Irène had already burst into tears. Helped by his men, who immobilised her arms and legs, Kayiru raped his sister-in-law:

> When he was about to ejaculate, he looked into Irène's eyes to realise that she had stopped breathing. He had just raped a dead woman. Neither the militiamen nor he had realised that. He turned his eyes to Diane and Denise [Irène's daughters] to take his revenge on them but they, too, had stopped breathing. …
>
> -You should not have died before my pleasure, dog Tutsi woman! You got me, dog Tutsi woman! I am going to kill you. And I am going to kill your f**king girls. (*Ibid.*: 81. Brackets & asterisks added).

This is arguably [one of] the most powerful and emotional passages of Rurangwa's (2006) novel. It combines many elements in one and leaves the reader no choice but to pause a bit and meditate. In this beyond-comprehension situation, one notes different things that are relevant for this analysis. There seem to be levels in types of death: The Hutu father suffered the least, as he did not see the scene of horror that his brother had promised him. His half-Hutu son suffered more, because he had to first witness the father's brutal death and to see him naked being mutilated. Diane and Denise, the two daughters, endured even more suffering because, in addition to seeing what their brother saw, they also saw their uncle take his viscera out before being gang-raped to death. Until here, the situation is already unbearable, beyond any human comprehension. Yet, there is a Tutsi woman who had been watching all of this and who had to still go through a humiliating, dehumanising experience of militiamen playing with her private parts. By the time his brother-in-law raped her, she had already psychologically died, which explains the absence of any resistance. Her physical death becomes a formality, a relief, compared to all the stages she went through to reach it. Interestingly, instead of celebrating her death, which would have been logical for a zealous killer like Kayiru, the latter was frustrated by it. For him, it should have waited until his pleasure was satisfied. Irène's death becomes the sole punishment for all the crimes that took place in Benimana's house that day. In Kayiru's mind, everything boiled down to raping a dead woman, which seemed to be a disturbing reality for him.

What all the above comes down to is that when the novel starts discussing the war, the latter inevitably emerges as an effort to end what Kayiru, Sembagare, and Butihoro were doing to the Tutsi and to those that were sympathising with them. In this respect, when Jean-Léonard came back to Rwanda three years later and saw people celebrating *Liberation Day* on the 4th of July, one immediately associates that day with the genocide rather than with the war. The implied idea is that if the war killed someone, it killed Kayiru, Sembagare and the like. In the last analysis, thus, Rurangwa's (2006) novel has an unequivocal genocide-centred approach with the war, far in the background, associated with the genocide rather than the fight against the government army that made casualties amongst innocent Hutu.

Compared to Sehene's (2005) and Rurangwa's (2006) novels, Rusimbi's (2007) looks at the genocide from a distance. Whereas Rurangwa's (2006) novel announced its preparation and coming, its execution and its aftermath, Rusimbi's (2007) *The Hyena's Wedding* refers to it as a past event that the new RPF leaders had to deal with. In this perspective, the novel presents the genocide and the war as two sides of the same coin. A genocide was being committed against the Tutsi and the RPF waged the war to stop it. To put it simply, the two main characters, Kiroko and Mugabo, represent those two sides of the coin, as the former was a survivor whose family was wiped out before the latter and his men intervened.

The novel reminds us that tens of thousands of Tutsi had sought refuge in the Nyamata church, where militiamen would attack them every now and then with machetes and grenades (Rusimbi, 2007: 1). Many other Tutsi refugees had preferred to hide in the nearby swamps, hoping to have more safety there rather than in the church (*Ibid.*: 5). This way of looking at the genocide from a distance, as a past happening, does not yield any visual scene of horror. Compared to Sehene (2005) and Rurangwa (2006), Rusimbi (2007) somehow failed to let the reader see the reality of the genocide. The only time an attempt is made to let the reader visualise a scene relating to the genocide, is when an official delegation came from Kigali to visit the church turned genocide memorial:

> Displayed in the shelves were skeletal remains of the dead; men, women and children who were butchered by Interahamwe. Also on display was a human skeleton with arms and legs still tied together with a strong rope. Mugabo explained that it was once a woman who was raped. Interahamwe militias had seen a beautiful lady with her husband in their house. The Interahamwe macheted the husband immediately, tied the woman and stripped her naked. They raped her in turn and finally pushed through her body a thick, long sharpened stick to complete the job. Tears ran down people's cheeks as they listened to the sad story and burst out crying to the almighty God (Rusimbi, 2007: 60).

The idea behind this description is clear: The Interahamwe committed a genocide and raped Tutsi women in a humiliating way. Considered side by side with the scene of Kayiru spectacularly and humiliatingly killing his brother's family (Rurangwa, 2006: 79-81), this passage does not succeed in winning the reader's sympathy. However, my point is not about the artistic or aesthetic merits of the novel, but rather about what the novel wants the reader to remember after reading it. This passage, as well as a few others in the novel, definitely tells the same story as the scene of Kayiru killing his brother's family, namely that Hutu killers massively killed the Tutsi and raped Tutsi women. In this sense, the novel wholly embraces the genocide-centred approach.

What Rusimbi (2007) explicitly adds that Sehene (2005) and Rurangwa (2007) only imply, is that the RPF rebels are unambiguously presented as the rescuers of the trapped Tutsi. Mugabo, the RPF officer who became a local leader after RPF's victory, was a living incarnation of that rescue. From his position behind the hills, Mugabo could hear the Tutsi screaming in the church. During the attack to rescue the refugees, Mugabo lost one leg following enemy fire (Rusimbi, 2007: 1). He even managed to rescue those who were hiding in the swamp:

> The swamp had saved many Tutsi who had hidden there during the massacres. Government soldiers and Interahamwe militias were well informed but could do little to force out their intended victims. Whenever they attacked with their guns, they couldn't hit those who cautiously lay flat in the water. The difficulties with the militias' struggle to hunt them out of the swamp meant that the Tutsi could survive in large numbers until the time Mugabo's rescue team took over the area. They were luckier than those who had hidden in the church (*Ibid.*: 5).

This quote perfectly shows the way in which the genocide and the war were merged into one. Hutu government soldiers, using war weapons, were obviously not fighting the RPF rebels behind the hills. Instead, they were shooting at the innocent Tutsi, whose sole defence strategy was making themselves invisible by 'lay[ing] flat in the water'. Mugabo came in as a rescuer but nothing is said about his fight before that particular moment. By omitting what he and his men were doing between 1990 and 1994, the novel pushes the reader to never think of the war outside the genocide. The latter called for the former. The war stopped the genocide and the rest was a liberation war that aimed at preventing that genocide.

I have reserved Twagilimana's (1996) *Manifold Annihilation* for the end of this section, because it offers a different perspective on the 1990 to 1992 period. The three Tutsi-authored novels discussed above converge in merging the war and the genocide, whereas Twagilimana's novel obviously focuses on war, even though some genocidal violence can be implied in a few instances. One explanation for this is that the novel is mostly situated in 1992 and perhaps even early 1993, a period that falls outside the April to July 1994 genocide. Also, even though the official publication time of the novel is 1996, the author signed off with 'Buffalo, New York December 1993' (Twagilimana, 1996: 256), which suggests that the manuscript was ready six months before the genocide. With these observations in the back of the mind, it makes sense that the war would dominate the novel.

Twagilimana's (1996) novel is the sole Tutsi-authored novel that explicitly mentions the suffering of innocent civilians in the war that opposed Hutu-dominated government forces and the Tutsi-dominated Intrepid Fighters. Throughout the novel, one reads that 'The war continued to victimise many of the citizens of the country of the thousand hills' (Twagilimana, 1996: 82; see also 85, 130). Unlike Mbabazi (2007) and Niwese (2001), who explicitly identified those innocent civilians as Hutu, Twagilimana never once mentions what the ethnicity of those 'many [of] displaced persons living miserably and plagued by war, hunger and illness' (Twagilimana, 1996: 130. Brackets added) were. Even so, the novel repeatedly suggests that the Hutu government soldiers were the source of civilians' suffering, whereas the Tutsi Intrepid Fighters are portrayed as representing relief and liberation for them. For instance, when the rebels captured the city of Ruhengeri and freed all the prisoners in the high-security prison there, they only killed government soldiers and celebrated their victory with the population:

> …the rebels captured the city, killed forty-five unprepared soldiers, occupied the city and liberated all the prisoners, including all those who had sinned against the Guide … Some went with the rebels back to the mountains. Those who didn't were shot by the military who came to liberate the city.

> ... Many people were arrested after this attack, especially those who spent the day drinking beer with the invaders. The rebels had opened grocery stores and found cases of beer and invited everyone to celebrate. They drank until they forgot that they were soldiers. Some were surprised drank and, unable to fight or run, they were killed with bottles of Primus or Miitzig beer in their hands. People who fled the severe fighting came to Kigali and told us the atrocities they had seen (*Ibid.*: 133).

As it appears here, the battle of Ruhengeri involved 'good guys' and 'bad guys'. The good guys redeemed the sinners, gave food to the hungry and killed the unprepared villains. However, the powerful villain got the upper hand and killed drunk rebels and innocent civilians. Like Mbabazi (2007), who uses survivors to tell the story of the massacres committed by Tutsi rebels, Twagilimana (1996) puts the Hutu army's atrocities, including systematic rapes (e.g., Twagilimana, 1996: 135-136), in the mouth of the survivors.

What is more, all the destructions that were reported during this battle were blamed on the Tutsi rebels by the corrupt Hutu regime, for propaganda purposes. The true culprits were the Hutu army soldiers who, instead of chasing the Intrepid Fighters, robbed banks after blowing up their safes (*Ibid.*: 134). The Hutu government soldiers obviously did this because they ignored the reason why they were fighting. One of them, who had lost both eyes during the war, told Mahoro the following in a military clinic in Ruhengeri:

> Most of us didn't know why we were fighting against people who spoke our language, called us by our names, and had so much in common with us. To begin with, I didn't even know why they attacked us. I wish the war would stop (*Ibid.*: 161).

The war that dominates Twagilimana's (1996) novel is one that is fought by a Hutu-dominated army, which was both unprepared and undisciplined and targeted civilians rather than the military. On the other side was a motivated, well organised Tutsi rebellion that committed no crime against the Hutu.

In short, this section confirms my hypothesis to a great extent. The Tutsi-authored novels overwhelmingly focus on the genocide, with only one focusing on the war. What has appeared is that two of the four [Sehene, (2005) and Rurangwa (2006)] used powerful, visual descriptions to bring the genocide reality in front of the reader's eyes, in what appears to be an effort to minimise other realities or other aspects that do not fit in with the official narrative. Although the descriptions are less intense and visual, the third one, Rusimbi (2007), does in fact promote the same view about the genocide. Another interesting point is that the war, which opposed the Hutu government forces and the Tutsi RPF rebels, permeates the novels in different ways. Unlike some of the Hutu-authored novels that promote the idea that the war was a Hutu exterminating machine in the first place, the Tutsi-authored novels implicitly or explicitly present it as having rescued the Tutsi. In one novel, Twagilimana's (1996), the war emerges as a struggle without any goal amongst the Hutu soldiers, who used their power to kill and rape innocent civilians. In no case do Tutsi-authored novels suggest or imply that innocent Hutu casualties were amongst RPF rebels' victims.

5.4. War and/or Genocide in Fest'Africa Project Novels

Since propaganda revolves around the idea of surrounding man with messages to persuade him to embrace a certain ideological truth, it makes sense here to once again include Fest'Africa project novels, to find out where they put their emphasis on between war and genocide. From the observations I made in Section 5.1., that the Fest'Africa project authors were co-sponsored by the Rwandan government, that the same government supervised all their tours and that some of the participants concluded that the foreign authors had become ambassadors of Rwandan people, it follows on that one would expect these novels to embrace the official narrative. This narrative, as observed in previous sections, places the genocide against the Tutsi in the centre and minimises the 1990 to 1994 war during which hundreds of thousands of Hutu are either put between brackets or considered as killers who were killed whilst killing.

To start with, Diop's (2000) *Murambi* does reflect the official account of the 1990 to 1994 period, with the entire novel revolving around the genocide with the war being framed as an effort to stop the genocide. The clear emphasis on the genocide resides in the fact that most of the novel tells us about the tours that Cornélius had at the genocide memorials throughout the country. When he reached the Murambi memorial, where his Tutsi mother and siblings had been killed by his Hutu father's militiamen, the novel shows how the genocide was prepared and supervised from above and executed by ordinary people and militiamen. Dr. Karekezi, Cornélius' father, represents the Hutu elite, as he is presented as a political rival of President Habyarimana (Diop, 2000: 154). He encouraged the Tutsi refugees and his own wife and two children to go to the Murambi vocational school, where they would be protected. In the meantime, he mobilised militiamen and the military, took time to go and say goodbye to his family and headed an attack that killed between 50,000 and 60,000 Tutsi (*Ibid.*: 103, 132, 137-139). While thinking about the moment Colonel Musoni and he were marching to the vocational school to finalise the preparations, Dr. Karekezi remembered what had gone on in his mind:

> The colonel [Musoni] knew that Nathalie and my two children, Julienne and François, were amongst the refugees. However, we did not say a word about it.

> On the way to the vocational school, I thought about Julienne and François, and about their mother. It's nobody's fault. When the end nears, she will curse me thinking that I never loved her. That's not true. It's just history that wants blood. Why should I only shed other people's blood? Theirs [wife's and children's] is equally rotten (*Ibid.*: 137-138. Brackets added).

What is being described here is obviously a genocide, which is systematic, pre-mediated, well prepared and with an empty justification that only history should be blamed for it. The above passage sums up Diop's (2000) approach, one that consists of describing a horror scene whilst letting a witness tell us about the involvement of Hutu authorities, army officers, and militiamen.

It is in this context that the RPF war is introduced to the reader in a way that turns it into a liberation struggle that aims to end the genocide. Diop (2000) invites the reader to discover and follow the war through the eyes of Jessica

Kamanzi, a Tutsi RPF spy in Kigali. During the 1990 to 1994 war, Jessica was in charge of RPF's cultural activities, and when the Arusha negotiations began, she was the RPF typist. She told Cornélius, a former classmate before entering into exile together, that she had 'never carried a rifle or participated in any military actions of the guerrilla war' (*Ibid*.: 46). In other words, the account of the war comes from a woman who had no military background, who was interested in culture and in doing normal work like typing. The profile of the witness is so peaceful that the war story that came from her has a more attractive and persuasive potential. However, Jessica admitted having a double life: a secret life and a public life (*Ibid*.: 37). Her public life consisted of posing as a Hutu woman carrying a fake Hutu identity card (*Ibid*.: 41), which helped her gather intelligence for the RPF fighters. At some point, when the genocide kicked off, she knew that

> Time for liberation has come. Since this morning, our troops have been progressing towards Kigali. But will they be in all places in time? No, unfortunately. In some places, butchery has already started (*Ibid*.: 46).

As it appears here, the RPF rebels are saviours. The only thing that could be reproached to them was being late. Their struggle was noble to the point of pushing Cornélius to feel ashamed of not having been a part of it (*Ibid*.: 62). However, the war aspect that seems more interesting here is the secret war that Jessica and other 'comrades' fought within the country. This war implied that they did not engage in any rescue operation that would hinder their secret mission by removing their public life cover. For instance, when her friend Theresa told her that she was going to hide in the Nyamata church, she let her go and refused to warn her about the dangers of going there. Theresa, who ignored Jessica's other life, insisted that she should follow her into the church, but Jessica refused and wished her good luck:

> I thought exactly the opposite [of the idea that the church offered protection]. The fighters with whom I entered Kigali have learnt that future victims will be encouraged to hide in churches where they will be exterminated. But, personally, I have nothing else to suggest to Theresa (*Ibid*.: 40. Brackets added).

Jessica's attitude here might reduce the reader's sympathy but in the last analysis, the death of Theresa is perceived as an unavoidable sacrifice for the sake of the larger struggle. Anyway, Jessica had to keep her cover in order to coordinate other secret fighters like herself scattered all over the country. One of these was Stéphane Nkubito, who was in the western region of Bisesero, where unprecedented killings took place during the genocide. Despite the chaos prevailing in the country, Nkubito managed to send a letter to Jessica on the 8th of April:

> Stéphane Nkubito, our comrade in that sector, wrote it a few hours before being discovered and killed. It seems they did not take time to interrogate him. They did not suspect that he was part of the agents of the Rwandese Patriotic Front operating in Bisesero. Our comrade's letter shows the extent to which the killers are organised and determined. They are ready for everything, this time (*Ibid*.: 38).

One realises here that Diop's (2000) novel is literally in line with the dominant narrative of the 1990 to 1994 period. However, the novel does indirectly question that same narrative by making suggestions that contradict some key assertions. One of them is that the RPF rebels had agents all over the country, which leads to the deduction that some of those who were killed, like Nkubito, were RPF fighters, rather than innocent Tutsi. This comes down to unintentionally denying the genocide one is trying to demonstrate, a phenomenon I would call *affirmationism* (See Section 5.5 for more discussion).

Monénembo's (2000) *L'aîné des orphelins* does follow a similar approach, except that it dedicates less time to genocide scenes. It focuses more on life in the RPF controlled zones and on post-RPF victory Rwanda. Despite this limited space for the genocide, the latter serves as the starting point and as the background for the entire novel. 12-year-old Faustin, a Hutu born from a Tutsi mother, witnessed the massacre of those who had sought refuge in Nyamata church. This scene of genocide is so visually painted that it shows on one side people who were going to die because of their ethnicity and, on the other side, those who were determined to wipe out the Tutsi:

> At dusk on 13 [April], for the first time, jeeps and trucks packed with Interahamwe militiamen, drugged and drunk, crossed the bridge on the Nyabarongo. They broke into the streets of Nyamata in a steady stream of howls and klaxons. The men jumped out of the cars and started shooting in the air…After that, they rushed to the church, pissed on the tomb of the Italian nun [who had spoken of a genocide in the making on the radio and had been killed because of that] and threatened to set the building ablaze.
>
> -What are we going to do? Screamed their senior chief.
>
> -We're going to burn the Tutsi and their friends!
>
> -Why shall we do that?
>
> -Because they are cockroaches (Monénembo, 2000: 143-144. Brackets added).

One can imagine what Faustin witnessed after that: Houses belonging to the Tutsi and marked with a red cross beforehand were burnt; women who attempted to run away with their children were caught and their tendons were cut; toddlers' heads were smashed against the wall (*Ibid.*: 151-152). At some point, the sub-governor, *sous préfet*, who had been there all that time, used a megaphone to call everyone into the church, where the army would protect them (*Ibid.*: 153). Once in the church, the Hutu were invited to leave the church, but Faustin's father refused to do so if his wife and child were not allowed to go with him (*Ibid.*: 154-155). Faustin saw the militiamen open fire and throw grenades into the church. He survived thanks to a dead woman who had fallen above him and who 'had had the strength to smile at me amidst swarms of flies and pieces of decaying corpses' (*Ibid.*: 157).

This scene of genocide horror pushed Faustin to run away to Byumba, a region that was already under RPF control and this is where the war aspect of the novel comes in. As he proceeded to Byumba, Faustin came across an RPF soldier who arrested him, suspecting him of being a genocidaire (*Ibid.*: 36-37). Talking to his superior through a walkie-talkie, the rebel described Faustin as follows: 'All signs show that he is a genocidaire. Otherwise, why would he run away? I found him under a tree in the bushes of Bugesera, probably after a refugee column has abandoned him' (*Ibid.*: 40). Despite this conviction that Faustin had something to do with genocide, the young rebel treated him humanely. He shared his food with him until they reached a rebel base in Rutongo. Even in Rutongo, Faustin found a military base where war prisoners were well treated, as they were registered, given food, interrogated without any violence and given leisure time. One night, an RPF captain who was interrogating him invited him to come and follow football with him on the radio (*Ibid.*: 46). Faustin became a member of the RPF family in Rutongo, as he took care of their cattle until Kigali fell into RPF's hands. He marched to Kigali behind RPF tanks, as part of the RPF fighters (*Ibid.*: 46-47).

Unlike Diop (2000) who stresses the secret dimension of the RPF war, Monénembo (2000) seems to emphasise the kindness, fairness and humanness of the RPF troops. The Tutsi rebels were so disciplined that they even spared the lives of those who showed all signs of being genocidaires. Not only did they refrain from killing them, but also they treated them humanely. Keeping in mind that the other side, the government army and militiamen were slaughtering the Tutsi in a systematic way, the reader has no other alternative but to conclude that the kind, humane soldiers were just there to stop the barbaric adversary who were attacking defenceless Tutsi. However, Monénembo (2000), like Diop (2000), seems to have fallen in the affirmationist trap by presenting some of the Tutsi victims as RPF militants. A few days before the Nyamata killings, militiamen had killed the Gisamanas, a Tutsi family near Faustin's home. Faustin's father thought that nothing would happen to his own family because, unlike the Gisamanas who were RPF sympathisers, 'we've never mixed with anything. Nothing will happen to us. We need just to stay here' (*Ibid.*: 152-153). This part seems to suggest that there were those who were not innocent amongst the victims.

Following a similar path, Ilboudo's (2000) *Murekatete* brings together the genocide and the war, inviting the reader to consider the RPF rebels as liberators. The entire novel revolves around Murekatete, a half-Hutu woman who married a Tutsi man. Her husband, uncle and father had died a few months before the genocide, which means that when the time came to run for safety, she had to do that alone with her two children. The attempt to sneak them out of the country together with a Zairean diplomatic family, arranged by a Hutu soldier, failed when Murekatete was discovered at a roadblock. Her children were killed there and then she was badly wounded and ill-treated before being thrown into the bush, along the pathway. Up until here, this has to do with the genocide, even though the victims were both Hutu [Murekatete] and Tutsi [her children]. Anyone considered Tutsi or close to them was obviously being hunted down. Then came the good Samaritan:

> My killers thought I was dead. They ignored my regeneration capacity…But that day, the battalion of which Venant was a part, marching towards the liberation of my tortured people, passed along that way. I moaned a great deal and Venant's commander came to me and realised that there was still some

breath in that dislocated body. I did everything to keep that breath, and the commander decided to give it a chance. Venant was designated to carry me to the hospital, fifteen kilometres away. Alone, afoot, without a stretcher. The order was a military one, which he had no choice but carry out. Its execution required a lot of altruism, a lot of generosity. Since that moment, I witnessed Venant's great heart…Even today, I look at my saviour without ever finding a rational explanation (Ilboudo, 2000: 15-16).

What is presented in this quote is a eulogy to the RPF soldiers, who seemed to have a profound humanitarian sense towards people faced with suffering. The commander decided to stop, took a look at Murekatete and, as such, decided to weaken his battalion by detaching Venant to a task that had no military objective. When one reaches the part where the RPF rebels are described as altruists, generous and kind-hearted, one perceives it as a repetition, because all the actions described here point to that conclusion. However, repeating this helped Ilboudo persuade the reader that the RPF rebels were saviours and good Samaritans, before anything else. A bracket could be opened here to point out the resemblance between Venant's action and the one played by the former government Hutu soldier who carried Nadine on his back when she fell sick in the Zairean forests (Bahufite, 2016: 186-188). The similarity is that the two innocent women were dying when the rescuer took action. Another one is that both had to use their physical strength in extreme conditions to rescue the two women. Yet another is that the two women were unknown to the good Samaritans and were not of any strategic interest to them. The sole difference, apart from ethnicity, is that the Tutsi soldier was on the conquering side, thus running no danger as such, whereas the Hutu soldier was running for his own life. In other words, the Hutu soldier took more risks as he voluntarily delayed his own progress and therefore exposed himself to being killed by the RPF soldiers.

The only time that the Tutsi good Samaritans did something wrong was when they engaged in reprisals after their victory. Venant, who had married Murekatete, once told the latter about a comrade who had 'exterminated with a machine gun all the inhabitants of the opposite hill whom he suspected of killing his own family' (*Ibid.*: 67). That rebel had left Rwanda under President Habyarimana's regime and had left all of his family behind. During the genocide, this family was wiped out. When Venant and his colleagues went to arrest him, he preferred to commit suicide (*Ibid.*). What appears here is that for the first time in this novel, the death of innocent Hutu people is mentioned. However, this mention is connected with, and justified by, the death of innocent Tutsi. One finds a similar instance in Faye's (2016) *Petit Pays*, where Pacifique, a former refugee in Burundi who joined the RPF, shot dead a group of Hutu reported to have killed his own family-in-law. He was arrested right away, court-martialled and shot by his own comrades (Faye, 2016: 177). The suggestion here is that if some innocent Hutu died, it is because a lot of innocent Tutsi died before them. The death of the latter triggered the death of the former. Moreover, the suggestion is made that where reprisals took place, attempts to render justice were made. In the above-mentioned cases, the comrade who committed suicide and the rebel who was executed are presented to the reader as people who were under unbearable psychological pressure, which pushes the reader to sympathise with them.

The main conclusion from this section is that the three Fest'Africa novels confirm all my hypothesis in that they stress the genocide against the Tutsi and do cast a heroic, law-abiding, good Samaritan-like light on the Tutsi rebels' actions during and after the genocide. In these novels, the genocide seems well organised, systematic and supervised from above. When and if the RPF rebels are mentioned, they are introduced as rescuers and liberators, who even tolerate the Hutu genocide suspects, whom they treat humanely. The only time that Hutu innocents were killed, was when they were suspected to have killed the Tutsi. Even in that case, the RPF system took action to punish the culprit. However, when analysed closely, the three novels reveal some interesting details that could push an attentive reader to the conclusion that some *affirmationism* is taking place in the novels. I have coined the term *affirmationism* – existing theory does not offer a better alternative – to refer to the efforts the novelists made to affirm that the genocide took place and that the RPF did all it could to stop it, whereby they used aspects that would rather deny it or give some justification for it. In one novel, the RPF is said to have a network of secret operatives throughout the country, some of whom were killed. In another, the massacre of ordinary Tutsi people is linked to their open sympathy with the rebels in a time of war. Yet in another, a Tutsi family is said to have been exterminated because one of its members had left the country to join those who were fighting the official army.

5.5. Summary and Discussion

The aim of this chapter was to engage the novels and question them about the narrative they push forward. This questioning took me to propaganda, which I discussed from a theoretical perspective, defining it as using a persuasive approach to promote a certain narrative rather than another through mass media. Since Rwandans have conflicting views about their past, and since the government actively promotes one view and criminalises all others, my idea was to find out ways in which the novelists oriented their inspiration through their selection and packaging of material relating to the 1990 to 1994 period. I narrowed down the scope to focus on the war and its Hutu victims, on the war and the genocide with their victims amongst both the Hutu and the Tutsi, and on the genocide with its Tutsi victims.

The main conclusion from the analysis of the five Hutu-authored novels is that four of them promote, in different ways, the view that the 1990s have witnessed more than just the genocide against the Tutsi. Three of them even placed a clear emphasis on the systematic mass killings of the Hutu civilians by the Tutsi rebels who later became the government army. When the genocide was mentioned, it was in more or less timid terms. In one novel, namely Gatore's (2008), it appeared that the inclusion of the war and the Hutu victims was absent, as it entirely embraced the genocide-centred approach, though with some nuances.

As for the four out of the six Tutsi-authored novels that directly discuss the 1990 to 1994 period and beyond, the hypothesis that they would put the genocide with its Tutsi victims at the centre was largely verified. In the rare cases when the war was mentioned, it was framed as an effort to end the genocide. Moreover, no Hutu casualties are mentioned except those attributed to the Hutu government army. In other cases, those casualties are attributed to mere rumours. At the end, the image of the RPF rebels that is promoted is one of kind, young, disciplined, rescuers of Tutsi civilians facing extermination.

I have also included three Fest'Africa novels which, given the circumstances under which they saw the light of the day, appear to be embedded novels or propaganda novels. The aim was to find out ways in which they cast the light on the genocide and the war. My hypothesis that they follow the official narrative was verified, since they all emphasise the systematic killings of the Tutsi by the Hutu and the intervention of Tutsi RPF rebels to stop the genocide. In doing so, they portray a rebel army that is altruistic, generous and respectful of human values. Those novels do not mention any innocent Hutu casualties except once when the last member of a Tutsi family decided to kill all the inhabitants of a hill to avenge his own family.

The findings presented in this chapter call for some reflection about the contribution of novels of genocide to the discussions about post-genocide Rwandan society. The Rwandan-authored novels discussed in this chapter present a cracked picture of Rwandan society, which confirms the observation that arts and artistic production reflect what is going on within society. It is most likely that, as I was paraphrasing or illustrating my points with quotations, some readers were saying to themselves: 'Yes! That's what really happened' or 'No way! This is blatant negationism'. In my view, hastening to label a novel as negationist is not the right way to approach the issues at hand. A better labelling would be 'counter-memory', which refers to the memories excluded from the official narrative (Rigney, 2012: 19). 'What really happened' is never a given but rather the result of interpretation. There are many things that happened that none of the novels discussed. There are many other things that happened which most novels touched upon while interpreting them in conflicting ways, and there are still many other things that only one or a few of the novels decided to focus on. Whatever the case, novels in general and novels of memory in particular, cannot escape selection. More specifically, novels of memory, under which novels of genocide fall,

> configure memory representations because they *select* and *edit* elements of culturally given discourse: They combine the real and the imaginary, *the remembered and the forgotten*, and, by means of narrative devices, imaginatively explore the workings of memory, thus offering new perspectives on the past. Such imaginative explorations can influence readers' understanding of the past and thus *refigure culturally prevailing versions of memory* (Neumann, 2008: 334-335; see also Mead, 1990: 98; Hutto, 2007: 1; Schmid, 2010: 65. Emphases added).

In this respect, then, the novels at the heart of this analysis reflect a selection of what the novelists remembered and wanted remembered by the readers. This implies that a lot was left out of the selection as they were deemed not worth remembering. Also, evoking negationism in the case of some of these novels presupposes an unquestionable version of memory, the challenging of which only stems from foolishness. If one were to take into account the provisions of the 2008 *Law Relating to the Punishment of the Crime of Genocide Ideology* in Rwanda, the novels by Niwese (2001), Mbabazi (2007), and Bahufite (2016) would be good candidates for negationism. The version of the past that inspired these novels takes the focus away from the genocide and the sole Tutsi victims. The three novels go even further to portray the official liberators and genocide stoppers as ruthless killers who devised a Hutu-killing machine throughout the 1990s. Judged from the 2008 Law perspective, these novels 'create confusion' by presenting the liberator as a killer and by reminding that there are hundreds of thousands of Hutu victims who still have to make it into the official narrative.

Another point worth discussing at this level is one relating to *affirmationism*, which consists in unwittingly providing evidence that contradicts or weakens the point that one wants to make. I have pointed out some *affirmationist* cases in relation to Fest'Africa novels, but many other cases can be detected especially in Tutsi-authored novels. One such case is in Rusimbi's (1999) *By the Time She Returned*, which does not even touch upon the genocide since it ends in October 1990. However, as RPF's commander-in-chief Mugabo addressed his troops before crossing into Rwanda, he told them:

> A lot of blood is going to be shed. We shall lose our lives and property. We shall lose friendship. *They will be hunting us like wild pigs. But that will only take place for some time and the trend will reverse thereafter…* We are going for a tough war. It will be decisive and losing it means *the end of our race* (Rusimbi, 1999: 162. Emphases added).

One can easily detect a few elements here that weaken the point that the novel wants to make, namely that the war was aimed to end the killings of the Tutsi that had been taking place since the late 1950s. The italicised parts announce a genocide-to-come and intimately link it to the war. The war is presented as the cause for the genocide-to-come. The war is a possible cause for 'the end of our race'. In this respect, the notion of a pre-meditated, planned genocide becomes superfluous, because the war waged by a Tutsi rebellion – not visceral hatred against the Tutsi preached amongst the Hutu – is presented as its sole cause. In his second novel, Rusimbi (2007) becomes even more *affirmationist* by suggesting that there were RPF local contacts within Rwanda before the genocide. One of them was Kiroko, who proudly said: 'I had been one of the local contacts for the freedom fighters. They would come and sleep in our homes, tell us what they thought was right' (Rusimbi, 2007: 20-21). This fragment nullifies one of the novel's main points that Kiroko's family was targeted by Hutu militiamen simply because they were born Tutsi. The novel offers another reason, namely that infiltrated RPF fighters spent nights there, turning that family into a military target. The same is true with Mama Cama, a local pub owner who 'was well known for her contribution during the struggle to overthrow the previous regime'. Mama Cama 'had offered moral and material assistance to Mugabo's forces during the long war' (*Ibid.*: 78).

Affirmationism is also present in Faye's (2016) *Petit Pays*, which leaves the reader with the idea that all the Tutsi victims of the 1994 genocide were killed simply because they were born Tutsi. However, the novel provides other possible reasons as to why certain Tutsi families were targeted. For instance, Gabriel's uncle, Pacifique, joined the RPF rebels and walked around armed in Kigali in civil cloths. He would clandestinely visit his own sister Eusébie and warn her about imminent massacres. One day in February 1994, he told his two sisters, Eusébie and Gabriel's mother Yvonne, that 'the Hutu extremists don't want to share power with *us, the RPF*' (Faye, 2016: 138. Emphasis added). Before leaving the house, he told his sisters to not wait for him to travel to Gitarama the next day:

> Watch out while on the way. I won't be travelling with you to Gitarama, as I am on the secret services' radar and I don't want them to make a link between you and me. RPF soldiers' families top the list of the people to be killed (Faye, 2016: 140-141).

So when one reaches the heart-breaking scene of the killings of Eusébie's family (*Ibid*.: 176), one might come to the conclusion that the secret agents who had been tracking Pacifique had a justification to kill the family that Pacifique had turned into a military target.

Even though I have dedicated a few paragraphs to negationism and affirmationism, I still believe that these two concepts are not helpful when one wants to analyse and understand ways in which Rwandans fictionalise their past. Both concepts refer to narratives that contradict what one holds to be *the* unchallengeable narrative. Both concepts imply a central, reference narrative from which all other stories are supposed to stem. The one that challenges it becomes a negationist, whereas the one that unwittingly weakens it becomes an affirmationist. On one hand, expecting everyone to tell the same story in the same way comes down to killing the creative spirit that keeps memory alive through works of fiction. On the other hand, labelling one novel as a negationist and the other as an affirmationist means nothing but forcing the authors to compare their stories with some official narrative and engage in some kind of cultural conformism.

Chapter 6

Historical Contexts

The heading of this chapter might be misleading as one could wonder about the relevance of historical background or history, within fiction. As discussed in the introduction, novels are inspired by, and look closely like, reality but cannot be equated with it. Even when real names of places, e.g., Rwanda, Kigali, the Sainte Famille parish and of people who really existed, e.g., President Habyarimana, Captain Mbaye Diagne, are used in a context similar to the historical context, the reader is expected to consider them separately from the real people and the real context. The same way that tales start with 'once upon a time…' and use other cues to warn the listener or reader that the story that is going to be told is not real, novels use paratextual marks such as the mention of 'novel' on the cover or a note that explicitly invites readers to consider any coincidence as fortuitous and other narratological indices to avoid the reader becoming mistaken (Genette, 1991: 89).

So, a legitimate question here is: Historical context for which happening? Here one is immediately stuck in a philosophical contradiction, because nothing really happens in a novel, as a happening presupposes a physical environment or space, physical objects and often real people and time. All these are artificially present in the novel and, because of that, any historical context to any artificial happening would be artificial itself. Despite this artificiality, it is still worth analysing the ways in which the novelists who fictionalised the genocide, which was a real historical happening, embedded it in a certain historical context within the fictional world they created. In other words, which version of pre-colonial Rwandan history, of colonial Rwandan history, of the First and Second Republics' history, do the novels provide to try and win the reader into embracing a certain view of the genocide? All of the novels, except three, namely Niwese (2001), Gatore (2008), and Bahufite's (2016), use some form of historical context in one way or another, to establish a link between the past that is long gone and the genocide.

In this chapter, I will firstly engage Tutsi-authored novels to map the patterns that emerge from their use of historical contexts. Then, I will explore ways in which the historical contexts are provided in Hutu-authored novels, before doing the same in relation to the Fest'Africa project novels.

6.1. Historical Background in Tutsi-Authored Novels

In this section I want to test the following hypothesis: Tutsi-authored novels are likely to offer an historical context that is in line with the official narrative, i.e., pre-colonial Rwanda is paradise lost, European colonialists and missionaries were agents of division, etc. Given that Rusimbi's (1999) *By the Time She Returned* tells the story of Tutsi refugees in Uganda between the time the monarchy was toppled in the early 1960s and the time those refugees waged war against the Rwandan government troops in October 1990, it makes sense to start with this novel. It contains a lot of references to the past and the function of these references seems to be to explain why those refugees were in exile. They also justify why an armed struggle was the sole option for them. Rusimbi's (1999) novel unequivocally portrays pre-colonial Rwanda as a paradise lost that ended when the Europeans came in. For instance, Kaitesi's mother told her children, whilst drinking *Waragi* [locally brewed liquor in Uganda], that King Kigeri IV Rwabugiri [1853-1897] was the last king of that heroic and harmonious Rwanda:

> This drink [Waragi] is good for tough men. Men who have survived fire, drinking and talking about their past. The *heroic past* of ancestral kings and chiefs who refused to sell our people to the slave dealers. *Our kingdom was powerful and beautiful*. Kings like Rwabugiri were supermen. He had enlarged our kingdom to the size of Africa. When he died, Belgians took advantage. They divided, ruled and massacred our people. Those who survived ran to strange lands. So, let them drink as they think about themselves – their bravery, stupidity and cowardice as well (Rusimbi, 1999: 52. Brackets & emphasis added).

The historical context in which the novel is set is obvious here. It goes from pre-colonial Rwanda – heroic, powerful, and beautiful – to independent Rwanda passing via colonisation. All but pre-colonial Rwanda is bad, marked by divisions, massacres and exile. Kaitesi's mother, Mukakigeri, whose father was not only a chief under the Tutsi monarchy but also the brother of the last king of Rwanda (*Ibid.*: 19), was the one telling her inquisitive daughter about both the Rwanda of those times gone by and about contemporary Rwanda. For instance, when Kaitesi naively asked why the Hutu killed the Tutsi in the late 1950s and early 1960s, and whether it was true that the Tutsi had previously mistreated the Hutu, Mukakigeri confidently replied: 'No, my daughter. It was propaganda. The fact is the Tutsi had been administrators since time immemorial. The Belgians came, took over power from us and gave it to the Hutu' (*Ibid.*: 25). Intrigued by this answer, Kaitesi drew the conclusion that the Tutsi must have been unfair to the Hutu by monopolising power: 'You should have shared with the Hutu' (*Ibid.*), she remarked. This remark infuriated her mother who made a distinction between the Tutsi who ruled and the rest of the Tutsi:

> Not all Tutsi were rulers. It was only the Bahindiro to offer kings while the Bega offered queens. The rest of Tutsi were either chiefs or common men. The Hutu were essentially common peasants. When a Hutu miraculously became wealthy, he was given the *honour of becoming a Tutsi*. A *poor Tutsi was looked at as a Hutu* (*Ibid.*: 25-26. Emphases added).

This dialogue between Kaitesi and her mother literally conveys the official historical narrative of pre-colonial Rwanda and the relationships amongst the Hutu and Tutsi. However, this narrative contains one obvious contradiction about the paradise-lost idea, because it suggests that the Hutu were essentially peasants and poor by default, unless a miracle occurred, in which case they had the honour of becoming a Tutsi. This means that in that paradise-lost Rwanda, being a Tutsi was an honour, whereas being a Hutu was a disgrace. Becoming a Tutsi was a promotion whereas becoming a Hutu was a demotion.

Rusimbi's (2007) *The Hyena's Wedding* seems to follow a similar approach, this time by trying to link post-genocide leadership to pre-colonial leadership. In fact, pre-colonial Rwanda implicitly appears as a model for post-genocide Rwanda. A good illustration of this is when Mugabo, the RPF rescuer of the Tutsi in Nyamata, was looking for someone to lead the Kayumba village. At some point, an old man named Kamali suggested that Kiroko should be the one because he spoke like his father, who once governed the area under the Tutsi monarchy. Justifying why Kiroko should lead the village, Kamali said:

> You survived the genocide and perhaps saved many people. You resemble your father, who was once a local leader in this area. We worked together, while he lived, and developed the area. He worked day and night and ensured stability and prosperity in Kayumba village. That was before the colonialists renamed it a sector. He used to be very stubborn in response to the Belgian colonialists by rejecting their names. That is why he was overthrown in the so-called 1959 revolution. A segregative Hutu regime was instituted. They could not allow your father or any other Tutsi to participate in leadership. They never allowed Tutsi children to compete favourably in schools, business or any other field. We were persecuted long before the recent genocide (Rusimbi, 2007: 22-23).

Pre-colonial, paradise-lost Rwanda is not explicitly mentioned here, but everything points to the fact that all that came after it was wrong. The colonialists spoilt what was there and overthrew Kiroko's father who had actively resisted them. The pseudo-event they call the 1959 revolution resulted in a segregation-based Hutu system. The Tutsi were persecuted all this time. After such an historical context, the genocide becomes an inevitable culmination of the process in the reader's mind.

The idea of pseudo-revolution comes back in Twagilimana's (1996) *Manifold Annihilation*, where the 1959 change of power is rather labelled as a mere coup d'Etat. In fact, there have been many similar coups before: One took place in 1896, when two Tutsi families fought amongst themselves, which ended with one winning; another took place in 1959 when the Belgian colonialists killed King Rudahigwa, which paved the way to the contested succession by his half-brother; yet another coup took place two years later when the Hutu leaders took over from the last Tutsi monarch and established the 'republican monarchy'; the last coup was in 1973, when Major General Habyarimana ousted President Kayibanda and proclaimed the 'second republican monarchy' (Twagilimana, 1996: 94-95). The novel puts all these changes of power in the same basket in a dismissive way:

> Each was heralded as a revolution in a remarkable ideologization of language. Maybe another revolution will come that will proclaim a true republican republic in which the people will be the center of government (*Ibid.*: 95).

The political history of Rwanda provided here reveals a lot of aspects that show where the novel is coming from and where it is heading. The most important message is that nothing special happened between 1959 and 1961, which is the period usually associated with the Hutu Revolution. The change from a Tutsi monarchy to a Hutu regime is reduced to the same status as the fight between two clans or to a classical military coup. The only thing that happened in that period was the assassination of King Rudahigwa by the Belgians, the same who would advise the new King and his entourage to flee the country. In short, the Revolution that the Hutu claimed to have accomplished was a non-event, as they received power from the Belgians, without making any effort.

Mukasonga's (2012) *Notre Dame du Nil* also provides some references to the past where some nostalgia is perceptible. Kalinga [or Karinga], the dynastic drum that symbolised the monarchy, is praised and portrayed as a symbol of paradise-lost, pre-colonial Rwanda. The hope that Karinga will be reinstated as a symbol of Rwanda appears in the dialogue that Virginia had with Rubanga, the disgraced royal secret keeper. Rubanga told Virginia that those who had attempted to destroy the drum whilst ending the monarchy had failed, as the drum had made its way to the Nyabarongo valley and had sunk so deep in the ground that nobody could reach it:

> That's Karinga, the Drum of the Kings, the Drum of Rwanda, the Root of Rwanda, the Drum that contains all Rwanda in its womb…Its enemies hunted it down, wanted to burn it, that's why it sank in the depth of the earth. Its enemies sought for it to no avail. Perhaps will Karinga one day resurface from the earth. No one knows when. But from the depth of the earth, it watches over Rwanda… (Mukasonga, 2012: 144).

Considered within the framework of what I called 'The Drum Impasse' (Nyirubugara, 2013: 89), the deadlock in the late 1950s amongst the Hutu and the Tutsi leaders about whether the Drum, with its adornments of the Hutu Kings' genitals, should be maintained or not as a symbol of Rwanda, this idolisation of Kalinga suggests that the Drum had nothing wrong with it. The statement that it is 'the Root of Rwanda' echoes the discussions of the late 1950s that the infamous adornments the Drum wore, indeed embodied the blood-tainted process that had cost the lives of many Hutu (*Ibid.*: 91). The context in which the Drum is placed suggests to the reader that the era of Kalinga was a paradise lost, which Rwandans should strive to recover. It is also interesting to note here the similarity between Mukasonga's (2012) novel and Twagilimana's (1999), especially where both announce a possible resurfacing of Kalinga or a more genuine revolution. This might be interpreted as linking post-genocide Tutsi leaders to the paradise-lost, pre-colonial Rwanda.

Unlike Mukasonga's (2012) novel which focuses on the Kalinga-centred context, Sehene's (2005) offers the reader a certain historical context of the events and process that caused the removal of Kalinga, namely the 1959 Hutu revolution and its aftermath. Damascène, the Hutu militia leader who killed the Tutsi at the Sainte Famille church, is presented as a product of the Hutu revolution and its totalitarian doctrine. What is very interesting here, in my view, is the reflection that Father Stanislas made about Damascène and his hatred against the Tutsi. A suggestion is made in this reflection that

> Damascène, *like most of the Hutu*, is a victim of the totalitarian 'majority people' doctrine, because the 1959 'social revolution' has locked us in the absolute, radical rejection of the Tutsi (Sehene, 2005: 60. Emphasis added).

What the reader gets here is an insider view, i.e., a view of someone who should rather praise the revolution. Instead, he gave it a ridiculous turn and made *most Hutu* not its beneficiaries but its victims. Father Stanislas thought he was lucky for having chosen celibacy because, if he had chosen to get married and have children, he would have been unable to preach to them hatred against the Tutsi, including their own grandmother (*Ibid.*). The novel's intention here, with this historical context, is obviously to push the reader to the conclusion that most Hutu hated the Tutsi at the time of the genocide and that it was not their fault, since they were just victims of the 'social revolution' that had taken place some 35 years earlier.

To put the Hutu killing into perspective, Rurangwa's (2006) novel also spends some time telling the reader about the 1959 revolution and the decades that preceded it. Like Sehene (2005) who tells the story through Father Stanislas' thoughts, Rurangwa (2006) lets a Hutu character, Theodore Gakwavu, tell the story through a monologue. As mentioned in Section 2.2, Gakwavu, *The small rabbit*, was a former Physics university professor who became mad after witnessing the brutal killing of a Tutsi family that was hiding in his home (Rurangwa, 2006: 135-136). Thus in his madness in a Brussels pub, Gakwavu told his invisible interlocutor about the late 1950s and the thinking that prevailed at the time:

> …All started when they told us that you, the Tutsi, were not Africans, Black but rather Jews or White who came to colonise the Hutu of the Bantu race, the true niggers. You understand, Philibert [The Tutsi friend assassinated with his family in his home], your ancestors invaded the country of my ancestors, whom they ultimately subjected for centuries,…You're White, you're Jewish. You're laughing but that's the truth because Monseigneur Classe, Canon Louis de Lacger and Monseigneur Perraudin said it (*Ibid.*: 138. Brackets added).

This background is meant to prepare the ground for the revolution. Monseigneur Perraudin, an important figure in the late 1950s, is given a decisive role because, besides promoting the idea that the Tutsi were foreigners as the previous quote suggests, he also 'created Kayibanda. Kayibanda was the liberator of the Hutu people from the feudal yoke of the Tutsi. Kayibanda the revolutionary' (*Ibid.*). This context is provided in such a way that the reader cannot help but detect the absurdity and ridiculousness of the revolution. Can a divisive figure be a liberator? Can a revolution result in exclusion? To reinforce this idea, the monologue proceeds thus:

> I know that you, the Tutsi, call him a bloodthirsty killer because he perpetrated pogroms against you and forced a great number into exile. But for us he is a revolutionary, a hero, a messiah like Perraudin and Logiest told us (*Ibid.*: 138-139).

The 11 pages that Rurangwa's (2006: 136-147) novel dedicates to this monologue says a lot about the historical context it wants to convey to the reader. The 'mad professor' approach is comparable to the 'dreamer' technique used in many other novels, (e.g., Twagilimana, 1996: 11-15; Niwese, 2001: 52-56; Ndwaniye, 2006:

192-193; Rurangwa, 2006: 123; Mbabazi, 2007: 287; Gatore, 2008: 83-84), as both allow characters to dive into their subconscious. Usually, what comes straight from the subconscious is immune to any external corruption and is likely to be more convincing than what is consciously controlled. So the mad professor was involuntarily throwing out what came straight from his subconscious in a raw but 'authentic' fashion.

To conclude, the analysis in this section shows that Tutsi-authored novels provide the genocide with historical contexts that are in line with the official, dominant narrative. The cases I analysed invited the reader to understand the genocide as a culmination of a long process which started in the late 19th century, when the first Europeans came to Rwanda to colonise it. These Europeans, who included missionaries, ended the harmony that existed amongst Rwandans and started dividing them. They devised an ideology according to which the Tutsi were not Rwandans. This ideology guided the Hutu leaders who toppled the monarchy in what they wrongly called a revolution. The same ideology prevailed until the genocide. This is literally the version of the past that the RPF-dominated regime promotes, which means that my hypothesis holds perfectly.

6.2. Historical Background in Hutu-Authored Novels

In this section I take my analysis further to test the following hypothesis: Hutu-authored novels are likely to use the context that portrays pre-colonial Rwanda as one marked by Hutu subjugation by the Tutsi, colonial Rwanda as a step towards their emancipation, and pre-1994 Rwanda as a peaceful one. This section does not include Gatore's (2008) novel which, as mentioned earlier, conceals almost all cues linking it to Rwanda and, *ipso facto*, to its past that is long gone. It does not discuss Niwese's (2001) novel either because, despite its strong focus on the war aspect and the RPF's trigger-happy attitude (see Section 5.2), it does not ground it in any historical context. Finally, I do not discuss Bahufite's (2016) novel, because the sole background it provides is limited to the 1990 to 1994 period.

Even though Ndwaniye's (2006) *La promesse faite à ma soeur* adopts a very cautious approach that accommodates all the *storms* and *tragedies* (see Section 5.3), it nonetheless implicitly but extensively presents the 1960s and the 1970s as a rather calm and peaceful period, whereby ethnicity does not seem to play any significant role. It can even be argued that the historical context that the novel provides does not pave the way to the *storms* and *tragedies* of the 1990s. Jean Seneza was born in 1963 (Ndwaniye, 2006: 5), i.e., one year after independence, in the Kibuye region that the novel later describes as having witnessed genocide and other tragedies. This is the period that was marked by repeated attacks by the Tutsi rebels who were close to the toppled monarchy. Having a Tutsi mother, it would have been logical for Jean to at least mention those attacks, some of which took place a short distance from his place of birth. It would also have made sense to discuss how the attacks affected his family. Instead, the focus is on a peaceful childhood near a Protestant mission and its hospital that made him dream of becoming a laboratory technician in the future (*Ibid.*: 13-14). The novel does not mention ethnicity in those days as being a problem, but rather as a social given like any other given:

> At our close neighbours' home the situation was the same. A child could unexpectedly appear in their compound and join in our games without any initial introduction, as if we'd known each other for a long period. We guessed he was a nephew, a cousin, or a grand-child...In fact, we didn't know, and we didn't care. It was neither his height nor the length of his nose or the width of his nostrils that drew our attention. He was a member of our neighbours' family and that was the most important. He was our comrade (*Ibid.*: 32).

This quote summarises on its own the historical context that Ndwaniye's (2006) novel wants the reader to proceed with. Reading between the lines of this quote tells the reader that being Tutsi [long nose] or Hutu [large nostrils] was not an issue in the 1960s and 1970s. Hutu children and Tutsi children enjoyed playing together. Even at school, Jean did not mention one single instance of anti-Tutsi ideology being taught in class (*Ibid.*: 34 & 39-40). This picture is in contrast with the one that other novels about the 1960s and 1970s usually paint. Very often, the novels inspired by the official narrative take advantage of school or classroom scenes of the 1960s – 1970s to stress the idea that pupils were taught to distinguish between the Tutsi and the Hutu and to keep in mind that the formers' rights were limited (e.g., Diop, 2000: 56-58; Sehene, 2005: 35-36; Mukasonga, 2012: 36-37 & 113). So when the reader follows Jean after his return from Europe in 2003, questions arose as to why those *storms* and *tragedies* took place. Unlike most other novels, the genocide and other tragedies in the 1990s fall from nowhere and intrigue the reader. This approach might be interpreted as an invitation to the readers to find a context for themselves about the genocide and other tragedies. It is also in line with the other aspects discussed in previous chapters, where it has appeared that the novel did not attribute features of beauty or ugliness to any ethnicity, amongst other things.

In contrast with Ndwaniye's cautious approach, Mbabazi's (2007) *Sheridan* extensively dives into Rwanda's past in order to let the reader understand the happenings of the 1990s in light of the process that led to, or facilitated, them. The novel suggests that what happened in Rwanda between 1990 and 1994 should be understood in the historical context of the late 1950s. At that time, the Belgian colonial administration urged the King to democratise the political system and to address the Hutu's legitimate grievances, but the King and his entourage refused to do so. His entourage even wrote a petition 'worthy of the great dragon of the Ku Klux Klan', in which they asserted 'hard and aloud, that the Hutu had always been their slaves' and, because of that, could never claim any share in power (Mbabazi, 2007: 32-33). In other words, it all started when the Tutsi refused to share power with the Hutu (*Ibid.*: 130). The grievances of 'the Hutu cultivators without any land to cultivate' (*Ibid.*: 32) were compiled in the 1957 *Manifeste des Bahutu* [Hutu Manifesto], which was nothing but 'a timid replica of the Universal Declaration of Human Rights' (*ibid.*).

Until here, one sees exactly from which part of memory the novel is drawing its historical context. The coloniser was not as bad as the official narrative and the Tutsi-authored novels suggest. The coloniser pleaded for democracy and the emancipation of the Hutu. More interesting are the comparisons that follow. The Ku Klux Klan-like royal entourage excluded any possibility to share power with those born as slaves to the Tutsi, whereas the Hutu's grievances are equated with the Universal Declaration of Human Rights. Unlike the context provided in Tutsi-authored novels, where the 1959 revolution is despised and ridiculed (e.g., Twagilimana, 1999: 94-95; Rusimbi, 1999: 144; Sehene, 2005: 60; Rurangwa, 2006: 138; Rusimbi, 2007: 22-23; Mukasonga, 2012: 27-29 & 31 – 32), that same revolution is presented as an heroic, historic event that achieved exactly what the French Revolution achieved in 1789 (Mbabazi, 2007: 33).

The Hutu leaders who emerged from this context as revolutionaries faced repeated attacks from Tutsi monarchists in the 1960s. The Tutsi rebels were killing Hutu leaders who had dared to abolish the monarchy. The aim was to *re-conquer* power, but the 'republican Rwandan army' managed to push back the rebels *in extremis* (*Ibid.*: 93). It is with this background – the Tutsi refusing to share power and attempting to recover power by force – in the back of the mind that the reader is confronted with the war and the genocide of the 1990s. The 1990 to 1994 war, which is the novel's focus, is simply a stage in the power-recovery efforts that started in the early 1960s:

> After many years of struggle, exiled Tutsi aristocrats had managed to accomplish an unbelievable achievement: becoming the core of the Ugandan army which, with its MIG jets and about a hundred T-55 and T-54 heavy tanks, was the most powerful army in the sub-region. Two-thirds of the 30,000 Ugandan soldiers were Rwandans.
>
> In October 1990, convinced about their readiness to *re-conquer* the land and power of their ancestors, twenty-five years after their last lamentably unsuccessful attempts, and sure about their power and organisation, they launched an unprecedented offensive against the Hutu power (*Ibid.*: 33-34. Emphasis added).

Thus, as the novel invites the reader to conclude, 'after more than 25 years of civil peace', the Tutsi RPF rebels attacked Rwanda 'to take back their due' (*Ibid.*: 37). At the time that they did this, the Hutu army was completely overwhelmed, because 'the two presidents [Kayibanda and Habyarimana] had invested all resources in economic development, completely forgetting about the defence or the war…' (*Ibid.*: 37. Brackets added).

This second part of the historical context – the first one being the refusal to share power and the early attempts to recover it – contains two interesting aspects. The first one is that all those years of Hutu rule, there was civil peace and economic development, which in some ways joins Ndwaniye's (2006) point. However, the exiled Tutsi had other plans, as their sole concern was to recover their due. The second one is the description of their firing power: They dominated the most powerful regional army. This aspect becomes important when combined with the obvious willingness to exterminate all the Hutu associated with the fall of the monarchy. For instance, when Colonel Karekezi is described as a son of one of the authors of the above-mentioned *Ku Klux Klan*-like petition and as someone who grew up in nostalgia and cultivated visceral hatred against all Hutu (Mbabazi, 2007: 160), one is invited to immediately draw conclusions about what he is expected to do with the above-mentioned firepower.

The foregoing has looked into ways in which two of the five Hutu authored novels have provided an historical context to the genocide. Both Ndwaniye (2006) and Mbabazi (2007) converge in portraying a peaceful, harmonious Rwanda a few decades before the war and genocide. However, Ndwaniye (2006) did not venture further than the birth of his main character in 1963. He did not touch upon the political and military aspects of that period either. Unlike him, Mbabazi (2007) extensively dived into the past, portraying the Tutsi elite of the late 1950s as responsible for all the chaos of the early 1960s and of the 1990s. They refused to share power with the Hutu, pushing the latter to take power after a revolutionary movement. That movement resulted in peace and economic development that were going to be destroyed by Tutsi rebels who claimed power as their due.

6.3. Historical Background in Fest'Africa Project Novels

Until here, the Fest'Africa project novels have been described as presenting a narrative very close to the one in Tutsi-authored novels and thus, to the official narrative. Two main reasons can be put forward to explain this closeness. Firstly, the Tutsi novelists are very close to the RPF regime, as most of them are former refugees for whom the RPF victory opened the door back to Rwanda. The government that resulted from the RPF victory is the same that co-sponsored the Fest'Africa project and tightly supervised it. From this perspective, it is not surprising that the narratives of the two categories of authors are very close to one another. The second reason is that the project involved Jean-Marie Vianney Rurangwa, the same person who authored one of the novels [Rurangwa (2006)] I am analysing in this book. Also, as Waberi's (2000: 9) acknowledgement shows, Benjamin Sehene, another author whose novel [Sehene, (2005)] I am analysing, is thanked for his contribution to the project. It is also worth noting that Monénembo (2000) dedicated his novel to Jean Mukimbiri, a former propagandist journalist at the RPF-run Radio Muhabura between 1990 and 1994. I am providing this background to pave the way for my hypothesis, which is that the Fest'Africa project novelists used the historical background that is in line with the official narrative, i.e., one that praises pre-colonial Rwanda whilst blaming the colonisers and one that blackens the two Hutu Republics.

Diop (2000) included a very interesting note in the acknowledgements in which he informed that 'numerous available works and documents helped him better approach victims' testimonies and, sometimes, those of the killers'. This note suggests that some research was done into the historical context of the genocide and, based on that context, the novelist could give meaning to the accounts of the victims and the killers. Diop's (2000) historical context does not venture further than the late 1950s, when the Hutu revolution took place, causing the flight of thousands of Tutsi. Instead of using the narrator, Diop lets the killers and their sympathisers provide that background themselves. When Faustin Gasana, a senior Interahamwe militiaman, visited his old anti-Tutsi extremist father named Casimir Gatabazi, both of them discussed the best techniques to finish off the Tutsi. The old man evoked his memories of the late 1950s to the early 1960s so that his son could learn from the mistakes he and his friends had made:

> Well, it was in Gitarama, where we, the Hutu, were the strongest. As our people were busy plundering and raping, a four-year-old child and his parents were waiting for a car to flee to the Mutara region. Suddenly, our people realised that this *Inyenzi* family was hurriedly boarding the car. They ran [after the car]. It was too late. That's how those stupid men allowed, some thirty-seven years ago, the boy who heads the guerrilla today, to escape (Diop, 2000: 28. Brackets added).

Gatabazi's account is telling the reader exactly that a mini-genocide was being experimented at that time, which coincides with the official story. Moreover, this context does not say why the Hutu had revolted at this particular moment. According to Gasana, the old man's account was the first thing that the Interahamwe recruits learned about when they started their training. The old man perhaps knew that his story was known, but he wanted to ensure that his son would not make a similar mistake. For him, the problem was that 'our men' focused on drinking and plundering rather than on 'their work' (*Ibid.*: 29). However, despite all his pieces of advice, Gatabazi did not seem to believe in any success by 'our men', as his final remark to his son shows: 'Do whatever you please, but since 1959, we make the same errors' (*Ibid.*). With this remark, the old wise Hutu evaluated more than three decades of Hutu-dominated regimes and labelled them as ones marked by failure to completely eliminate the main threat to their power.

Diop's (2000) novel also spends some time telling the reader about the early 1970s, when President Kayibanda organised pogroms against the Tutsi. This time, the readers visit this episode through the eyes of the main character, Cornélius, a Hutu born from a Tutsi mother. One day in early 1973, two men came to Cornélius' primary school and asked the teacher to send out all of the Tutsi pupils. Seeing his friends, Stanley and Jessica, leave the classroom, Cornélius told the teacher that he had forgotten to call his name. He thought that if his friends were Tutsi, he was a Tutsi, too. The two men laughed but understood Cornélius' attitude because he was born from a bad Hutu, one who had married a Tutsi (Diop, 2000: 56-57). That night, the two Tutsi classmates came to hide at Cornélius' home, but had to go into hiding when the Hutu attackers armed with machetes and torches came to look for them. From their hideout, they saw how houses were being torched or flattened. They could hear the attackers say that 'all Tutsi must leave the country' (*Ibid.*: 58). The three of them left Rwanda for Burundi and only came back to Rwanda after the RPF's victory more than 20 years later. Described this way, the early 1970s become another mini-genocide that was paving the way for the final, large-scale genocide in 1994, which is exactly the version that the official narrative promotes.

In the same vein, Ilboudo's (2000) *Murekatete* portrays the late 1950s as the first genocidal experiment against the Tutsi. Unlike Diop's (2000) novel that covered two historical periods, Ilboudo's (2000) focuses on the late 1950s as the most decisive historical context that helps to understand the 1994 genocide. The reader is provided with this context through Venant's heart-breaking experience. Venant, as Section 5.4 has shown, is the RPF soldier who rescued Murekatete and carried her on his back to the hospital before marrying her after the victory. Venant was born during the 1959 anti-monarchy revolution. He never had a chance to know his mother, because the latter was dismembered a few weeks after his birth by a former suitor, who wanted to avenge himself. The killer left Venant with his tied-up father, promising to come back and kill the latter (Ilboudo, 2000: 20). The father, who was amongst 'the survivors of that first genocide' (*Ibid.*), decided to leave the country for good after dropping Venant at an orphanage in Nyanza. Venant was looking for him in Uganda when he enlisted in the RPF and came back to Rwanda as a liberator.

The bridge between the late 1950s and the 1990s is clearly established here. Through Venant's story, the reader imagines thousands of other Tutsi rebels' stories, all grounded in the 'first genocide' that took place in 1959. With this context in mind, one is surprised that Venant is not seeking revenge, like Colonel Karekezi in Mbabazi's (2007) novel. Even though none of the Tutsi-authored novels used the term 'first genocide' in relation to the 1959 events, there are obvious similarities in the historical context provided by Ilboudo's novel and those other novels that discussed the 1959 happenings.

Amongst the three Fest'Africa project novels that I am analysing here, Monénembo's (2000) *L'aîné des orphelins* is the one that dedicated the least amount of space to the historical context. Most of the novel is about Faustin's street life after the RPF rebels' victory. The genocide in Nyamata and his flight to Byumba are secondary to his struggle to survive in the streets of Kigali together with other street children. However, the novel does sporadically and indirectly offer brief references to the past. For instance, when child right activist Claudine Karemera was chatting with Faustin, she mentioned her refugee background in Uganda:

> Uganda, of course! That's where she was born, she once told me [Faustin]. During the first bloodshed, in 1959, her parents had fled to that country walking through the bush. Her mother, pregnant of her, had given birth at the border, two months before her due date (Monénembo, 2000: 31. Brackets added).

Even though no further comments are provided, this short comment brings to mind Venant's birth (Ilboudo, 2000), which also took place during the 1959 *first* bloodshed/genocide. The use of *first* in both novels suggests that 1959 was just the beginning and that the worse was still to come.

Monénembo's (2000) novel also slightly touches upon the early 1970s but, just as in the previous case, does not elaborate. This time, the past is evoked in a conversation between a Brazilian nun and Faustin's father, a few days before the final attack of the Nyamata church. Everybody in Nyamata was worried that the Interahamwe would launch the assault at any time, but the nun was convinced that this would not happen, because

> The killings always stopped at Kanzenze commune; they never crossed the bridge [on the Nyabarongo river], even in 1972. We've never had that in this place! At the convent we prayed all the night. The Belgian priests have celebrated a mass. Nothing will happen, you will see! (*Ibid.*: 76. Brackets added).

Here, the novel does not portray the early 1970s as visually and elaborately as Diop's (2000) novel did. Nonetheless, the way that this historical period is mentioned is highly revealing. It suggests that on many occasions the Tutsi had been attacked and killed in the past. The only thing is that these killings stopped on the other side of the river. The nun's conviction was based on nothing more but the past. She did not deny that any massacre would take place, but rather that Nyamata would be spared, just like two decades before. Thus, even if Monénembo does not elaborate upon historical events, his framing of those events places his novel amongst those that convey the dominant narrative.

As it appears from the foregoing, the three Fest'Africa novels under scrutiny confirm my hypothesis that they all embraced the narrative sponsored and promoted by the RPF dominated regime. None of them evokes pre-colonial Rwanda or colonial Rwanda, but all of them touch upon the 1959 events and define them as a decisive episode for one to place the mid-1990s into perspective. One novel labels those events as 'the first genocide', whereas another considers them as 'the first bloodshed', which implies not only that nothing had happened before, but also that other genocides or bloodsheds were to follow. The early 1970s also seem to occupy a central place in the historical context that the three novels offer. That historical period is presented to the reader as the second experimentation of genocide violence against the Tutsi. In the end, the RPF liberators in two of the novels emerge as products of a history marked by multi-stage genocide.

6.4. Summary and Discussion

The underlying idea in this chapter was that the historical context for events featured in a novel indicates more or less the memory narrative that the novel promotes. For the sake of structure, I separately analysed the historical contexts in Tutsi-authored novels, Hutu-authored novels, and Fest'Africa project novels. It has appeared that all Tutsi-authored novels provide historical contexts that consolidate the official narrative about the historical process that led to the war and the genocide of the 1990s. These novels invite the reader to view the two major events of the 1990s as stages in the process that started in the late 19th century with the arrival of European colonisers and missionaries in Rwanda. The latter divided Rwandans and opposed the Hutu to the Tutsi, ending with the massacre of the Tutsi in 1959 and the flight of many. Considered from this historical perspective, the 1990 to 1994 war is presented as a liberation struggle to end genocidal violence that had been going on for more than three decades.

Unlike the Tutsi-authored novels, two of the five Hutu authored novels grounded the 1990 to 1994 events in a historical context that contradicts the officially promoted narrative. In one novel, the 1960s and 1970s are clearly portrayed as a period of peaceful and harmonious coexistence amongst the Hutu and the Tutsi. In this novel, the genocide not only emerges as a sudden, non-premeditated event, but also as part of many other tragedies that took place in the 1990s. In another novel, the late 1950s play a central role in understanding the 1990 to 1994 war and genocide. The Tutsi aristocracy is blamed for refusing to share power with the Hutu, whose grievances were akin to the Universal Declaration of Human Rights.

With the support of the colonial administration, they organised a revolution similar to the 1789 French Revolution. Considered from this historical perspective, the 1990 to 1994 war emerges as the Tutsi aristocrats' ultimate attempt to reconquer their due and to avenge themselves.

Finally, as could be expected, the three Fest'Africa project novels analysed in this chapter followed, to a great extent, a similar approach as the Tutsi-authored novels. The year 1959 serves as the most important historical milestone to keep in mind whilst reading the novels. The events of that year are not called a revolution, but rather 'the first genocide' or 'the first bloodshed', from which the future RPF freedom fighters and genocide stoppers emerged. The early 1970s also appear to be crucial, as the novels suggest that another genocide was experimented. This historical context, which is in line with the one promoted by the RPF-dominated government, paves the way for an understanding in which the war and the genocide are seen as one, with the latter justifying the former rather than the other way around.

One point that deserves some discussion and even further research is the impact that these novels have on the general understanding of the 1990 to 1994 period, especially the historical process that led to the war and the genocide. The analyses conducted in this chapter show that most novelists, both Rwandans and non-Rwandans, converge in espousing the dominant narrative that links the 1994 genocide to more than three decades of injustices and genocidal violence, of which the Tutsi were victims. All the events from the 1950s through to the 1970s are historical ones and their descriptions do not even mention that there are conflicting interpretations about them. The consequence, in my view, is that these novels provide confirmation to the already widely circulated narrative, one that suggests that it all started when the colonisers came to Rwanda and divided Rwandans until the moment they organised massive massacres in 1959, which they wrongly called a Revolution. The resulting Hutu republics did nothing but continue the colonial divisive policies against the Tutsi, which culminated in the 1994 genocide. This, as one Hutu-authored novel has shown, is one version, another one being that the Tutsi elite refused to share power in the 1950s and, when toppled from power, continued attempting to recover it until they successfully managed to do so in 1994. In doing so, they exposed the Tutsi in Rwanda to a genocide.

People might think that the role or the task of the novelists is not to educate about the past, because the novel creates its own world and, as a consequence, its own past. I would not espouse this view especially when discussing novels that are deeply grounded in real events and display close resemblance to the real world. Whether they want it or not, these novelists do influence the understanding of the present in the light of the past and vice-versa. One can imagine a person reading some of these novels around 2009, when the popular *Gacaca* system had reached its climax. Of course, all would depend on which novel he or she would read first. If he or she began with Mbabazi's (2007) *Sheridan* or Niwese's (2001) *Celui qui sut vaincre*, then chances are that the *Gacaca* system would appear as an unjust, unfair mechanism put in place to annihilate and subject the Hutu psychologically by forcing them to collectively take on the guilt of the 1994 genocide. If one began with Rurangwa's (2006) *Au sortir de l'enfer* or Gatore's (2008) *Le passé devant soi*, or Monénembo's (2000) *L'aîné des orphelins*, one would find the *Gacaca* system justified. The same holds true for the current *Ndi Umunyarwanda* [I am Rwandan] campaign, which pushes the Hutu to collectively apologise [to prove their Rwandanness], whereas nothing is being asked from the Tutsi or the Twa to prove their Rwandanness.

The difficulty on the part of the novelists might be the internal discussion they have with themselves when trying to select a historical background for their fictionalised events. It would be incorrect to claim that all the novelists analysed in this book ignore that the 1959 events are perceived as a genocide by some Rwandans, and as a Revolution by other Rwandans. It would equally be inappropriate to imagine that these novelists ignore that some Rwandans know that the RPF was responsible for hundreds of thousands of victims amongst the Hutu, whereas other Rwandans prefer to solely remember the RPF's victory. They certainly knew that not all Hutu are collectively responsible for the genocide and that not all Tutsi were innocent. They knew all this, but they had to make choices. In this respect, Morrison (1984: 388) suggested that a novelist should not necessarily aim to reveal already established literary or historical realities upon which both the novelist and the readers agree. This means that a novelist should not be constrained by any official narrative or law in his or her creative efforts. As Morrison argued, 'If my work is to be functional to the group (to the village, as it were) then it must bear witness and identify that which is useful from the past and that which ought to be discarded' (*Ibid*: 309). Since memory is intrinsically selective depending on who is remembering, when and where they are doing so, it follows that the novelists have to decide about which details from the past they deem useful and discard the rest. In other words, it is impossible and counterproductive to try and solve the difficulties relating to selectiveness and exclusiveness, because they are intimately related to both the memory and the creative processes. The only way is to let everyone freely and creatively remember the past that they find relevant to them.

Chapter 7

Conclusions

This book started with the question of whether there was anything one could learn from novels about memory processes in Rwanda. As I write these concluding remarks, I hope to have convinced the reader that the novels of genocide are much more than mere entertainment pieces. I hope to have demonstrated that they reflect many above-the-surface and beneath-the-surface realities of post-1994 Rwanda. I have argued that contrary to non-fiction works that need evidence and have to follow field-specific constraints, novels offer unequalled freedom to turn historical events into fiction using imagination and creativity. In this closing chapter, I would like to reflect upon general remarks and to suggest a way forward.

7.1. Three Lines

One important conclusion that flows from the analyses in this book is that the same conflicting approaches to memory observed in real Rwanda are equally reflected in the different fictional Rwandas sketched by the 11 novels of genocide. At the end, one sees two straight lines and one zigzagging line that connect identity construction discussed in Chapter One and the historical contexts discussed in Chapter Six. The first line starts with Tutsi characters being constructed around cherished values and other positive attributes. It then proceeds with the same characters receiving positively connoted and value-loaded names, before continuing with their description as not only being inherently beautiful and handsome, but also as being naturally intelligent and smart. It ends with a strong emphasis on the genocide against the Tutsi and a historical context that supports that genocide. This line coincides with the dominant narrative supported by the Tutsi-dominated regime in power since 1994. It casts the Tutsi in a positive way and the Hutu as representing the opposites of the above-mentioned qualities. This line transpires and dominates all six Tutsi-authored novels and those that resulted from the 1998 Fest'Africa project.

The second line does the reverse and starts with Hutu characters who are constructed in a positive way, who have positively connoted and value loaded names, who are more or less beautiful or handsome, who can intelligently reason and achieve extraordinary things and who operate in a historical logic of the Tutsi nostalgic who needed a war to annihilate the Hutu and recover power. This line, more or less, clearly emerges from two Hutu-authored novels and is the absolute opposite of the official narrative of the memories of the 1990s.

The third line can be said to be navigating between the two extremes, with a lot of zigzags that make it coincide or intersect with either line at some point. This line begins with an identity that looks blurry, proceeds with names that either follow the Tutsi pattern or the Hutu pattern, moves to an external appearance that mixes beauty, handsomeness and ugliness, stresses characters with some intelligence mixed with stupidity and who are caught up in a war and a genocide that they do not clearly understand.

7.2. The Traps

One could wonder here: So what? Why does all this matter? This volume, like the previous, adopts the 'Memory Traps' approach that consists of spotting out eventual traps and downsides that might stem from memory processes. Each of the previous chapters in this volume contains a few traps, all of which are rooted in memory. Chapter One warns against the temptation to embrace the suggestion that most novels make, namely that the Hutu are wicked, nasty people, whereas the Tutsi are innocent and always in the role of the victim. Chapter Two draws the attention of those who understand the subtleties of Rwandan names, that character names follow certain generalisable patterns and that those patterns have ethnic implications. Chapters Three and Four sound the alarm so that the reader does not fall into the trap of associating Tutsiness with beauty, handsomeness and intelligence or Hutuness with ugliness and stupidity. As for Chapters Five and Six, they invite the reader to not lose sight of the key memory characteristics, namely its fragmentary nature and its multiplicity.

Most of the 11 novels of genocide, each in its own way, have portrayed the ethnic Other in a way that makes the author's Self comfortable. In other words, each novel has offered a subjective perspective on the memories of the 1990s. Perhaps the most dangerous trap is that most of the novels offer similar perspectives, in accordance with the first line discussed above, which might push one to lose sight of the memory principles that the remembered always hides the forgotten, that the selected implies the non-selected, and that the promoted supposes the non-promoted. The danger of definitively dividing Rwandans into the beautiful/handsome ones, who are also intelligent and smart, and who never have ill-intentions on the one hand and, the ugly, stupid ones who hate the Other and kill him at the first chance they get, on the other hand, appears more important if one considers the inspiration that these novels would give 20, 50 or even 100 years from now. Most of them, especially those promoting the official narrative, will have acquired the status of classics. Once canonised, the narratives of these novels will turn into truths that are taken for granted that permeate [history] education and signal to generations to come what is important to consider from the past (Wineburg, 2001: 113). This discussion joins Rigney's (2012: 13) notion of *monumentality* of literary works where she argued, amongst other things, that these works create stable 'canonical points of reference' by 'calibrating collectively held values'. As the analyses in this book have shown, values such as intelligence and smartness and positive attributes such as beauty seem to have been calibrated in association with one ethnicity in an almost systematic way. The monumentalising of stereotypes, i.e., values and their opposites and other attributes, is reinforced by what Rigney (*ibid.*) called the *mobility* of literary works, i.e., their capability to migrate to other media. Further research could investigate the migration of the stereotypes and other character attributes into film productions, music or theatrical representations, amongst other forms of arts.

7.3. Missing Ethics?

Unlike journalism and other fields and subfields of communication, novel writing does not have an explicit code of ethics that establishes the lines that the authors should not cross. A journalist or marketing or advertising professional who would engage in ethnic or group stereotyping would face sanctions either from peers or from justice. However, a novelist doing exactly the same does not face any penalty, simply because all contents of the novel are believed to be thought up, invented and therefore disconnected from any real group or ethnicity. In a society marked by ethnic tensions like Rwanda, it should be the responsibility of authors to avoid stigmatising any ethnic group under the cover of fiction. If the Rwanda they portray in their novels is the Rwanda that was colonised by the Belgians, the Rwanda that went through turmoil in the late 1950s, the Rwanda that had Kayibanda and Habyarimana as presidents, the Rwanda that has Kigali as its capital, the Rwanda that has the Hutu, Tutsi and Twa, the Rwanda that went through a war waged by Tutsi rebels, the Rwanda that witnessed a genocide in 1994 and in short, the Rwanda that looks so closely like the real Rwanda, then it follows suit that what happens in the fictional Rwanda is likely to influence what happens in real Rwanda.

I do not need to remind anyone of a recent shooting in a movie theatre in the United States, especially when the survivors who were interviewed converged in saying that they had first considered the shootings to be part of the movie. It is only when they saw blood streaming and heard people screaming that they realised that something terrible, which they were used to seeing in movies, was really happening at that moment. As Lamarque (2007: 117) reminded, 'familiar characters and plots are assimilated into a wider cultural consciousness and help define national stereotypes and norms of behaviour'. If the 11 novels of genocide were to be judged in the light of this observation, one would wonder whether it is an ideal and desirable situation to have the ethnic stereotypes and norms of behaviour conveyed in the novels assimilated in the wider cultural consciousness in Rwanda.

References

Auerbach, Jonathan & Castronovo, Russ (2013) 'Introduction: Thirteen Proposals About Propaganda', in Auerbach, Jonathan & Castronovo, Russ (Eds.) *The Oxford Handbook of Propaganda Studies* (Oxford: Oxford University Press), pp.1-16

Bahufite, Liliane U. (2016) *Une vie qui n'est pas mienne* (Lille: Editions Sources du Nil)

Bal, Mieke ([1985] 1997) *Narratology: Introduction to the Theory of Narrative* (Toronto: University of Toronto Press). Second Edition

Barthes, Roland (1968) 'L'effet de réel', in *Communications,* 11, pp. 84-89

Barthes, Roland (1973) *Le plaisir du texte* (Paris: Editions du Seuil)

Booth, Wayne ([1961] 1983) *The Rhetoric of Fiction* (Chicago: The University of Chicago Press). Second Edition

Brockmeier, Jens (2002) 'Remembering and Forgetting: Narrative as Cultural Memory', in *Culture & Psychology*, 8(1), pp. 15-43

Buitenhuis, Peter (1976) 'Writers at War: Propaganda and Fiction in the Great War', in *University of Toronto Quarterly*, 45, 4, Summer, pp. 277-294

Chatman, Seymour (1990) *Coming to Terms: The Rhetoric of Narrative in Fiction and Film* (Ithaca: Cornell University Press)

Chrétien, Jean-Pierre (2007) 'RTLM Propaganda: The Democratic Alibi', in Thompson, Allan (Ed.) *The Media and the Rwanda Genocide* (Ann Arbor: Pluto Press), pp. 55-61

Chrétien, Jean-Pierre (Ed.), Dupaquier, Jean-François, Kabanda, Marcel & Ngarambe, Joseph (1995) *Rwanda: Les médias du génocide* (Paris: Karthala)

Corneille (2016) *Là où le soleil disparaît* (Paris: XO Editions)

Coupez, André & Kamanzi, Thomas (1962) *Récits historiques Rwanda* (Tervuren: Musée Royal de l'Afrique Centrale)

Courtemanche, Gil ([2000] 2003) *Un dimanche à la piscine à Kigali* (Paris: Editions Denoël)

Dauge-Roth, Alexandre (2010) *Writing and Filming the Genocide of the Tutsi in Rwanda: Dismembering and Remembering Traumatic History* (Lanham: Lexington Books)

Derrida, Jacques (2003) *Genèses, généalogies, genres et le génie* (Paris: Editions Galilée)

Des Forges, Alison (2007) 'Call to Genocide: Radio in Rwanda, 1994', in Thompson, Allan (Ed.) *The Media and the Rwanda Genocide* (Ann Arbor: Pluto Press), pp. 41-54

De Villiers (2000) *SAS: Enquête sur un genocide* (Paris: Malko Productions)

Diop, Boubacar Boris (2000) *Murambi: le livre des ossements* (Paris: Stock)

Docherty, Thomas (1983) *Reading (Absent) Character: Towards a Theory of Characterization* (Oxford: Clarendon Press)

Du Bois, W.E.B. (1926, Octobre) 'Criteria of Negro Art', in *The Crisis*, 32, pp. 290-297 http://www.webdubois.org/dbCriteriaNArt.html

Dushimirimana, Thierry (2006) *A Love Letter to My Country* [Short film]

Eco, Umberto (1990) *The Limits of Interpretation* (Bloomington: Indiana University Press)

Eco, Umberto (2011) *Confessions of a Young Novelist* (Cambridge: Harvard University Press)

Ellul, Jacques (1972) *Propaganda: The Formation of Men's Attitudes* (New York: Alfred A. Knopf)

Emerson, Ralph Waldo ([1906] 1942) 'Art', in Emerson, Ralph Waldo, *Essays* (London: EJ.M. Dent & Sons Lts), pp. 192-203

Erll, Astrid & Rigney, Ann (2006) 'Literature and the production of cultural memory: Introduction', in *European Journal of English Studies*, 10, 2, pp. 111-115, DOI: 10.1080/13825570600753394

Faye, Gaël (2016) *Petit Pays* (Paris: Editions Grasset & Fasquelle)

Fèbvre, Lucien & Martin, Henri-Jean ([1958] 1984) *The Coming of the Book: The Impact of Printing 1450-1800* (London: Verso)

Fishelov, David (1990) 'Types of Character, Characteristics of Types', in Knapp, John V. (Ed.) *Literary Character* (Lanham: University Press of America), pp. 74-91

Forster, E.M. ([1927] 1974) *Aspects of the Novel and related writings* (London: Edward Arnold)

Foulkes, P.A. (1983) *Literature and Propaganda* (London: Methuen)

Freeman, Mark (1992) 'Self as Narrative: The Place of Life History in Studying the Life Span', in Brinthaupt, Thomas & Lipka, Richard (Eds.) *The Self: Definitional and methodological Issues* (New York: State University of New York Press), pp. 15-43

Frère, Marie-Soleil (2005) 'Etre journaliste avant, pendant et après le génocide', in Frère, Marie-Soleil (Ed.) *Afrique Centrale: Medias et conflits. Vecteurs de guerre ou acteur de paix* (Bruxelles: Editions GRIP), pp.: 141-178

Fujii, Lee Ann (2004) 'Transforming the moral landscape: the diffusion o a genocidal norm in Rwanda', in *Journal of Genocide Research*, 6, 1, March, pp. 99-114

Gatore, Gilbert (2008) *Le passé devant soit* (Paris: Editions Phébus)

Genette, Gérard (1968) 'Vraisemblance et motivation', in *Communications*, 11, pp. 5-21. DOI : 10.3406/comm.1968.1154

Genette, Gérard (1983) *Nouveau discours du récit* (Paris: Seuil)

Genette, Gérard (1991) *Fiction et diction* (Paris: Seuil)

Gourevitch, Philip (1999*) "We Wish to Inform You That Tomorrow We Will be Killed with our Families"* (New York: Picador)

Gusdorf, Georges (1991) *Auto-bio-graphie. Lignes de vie 2* (Paris: Editions Odile Jacob)

Hagengimana, Philbert (2016, 24th August) 'Imyigishirize y'Amategeko muri Kaminuza y'u Rwanda igiye kuvugururwa', in *Igihe.com*. http://www.igihe.com/amakuru/u-rwanda/article/imyigishirize-y-amategeko-muri-kaminuza-y-u-rwanda-igiye-kuvugururwa

Halbwachs, Maurice ([1925] 1992) 'The Social Frameworks of Memory', in Coser, A. Lewis (Ed.) *Halbwachs, Maurice On Collective Memory: The Heritage of Sociology* (Chicago: The University of Chicago Press), pp. 35-189

Harvey, J.W. (1965) *Character and the Novel* (London: Chatto & Windus)

Hitchcott, Nicki (2012) 'Benjamin Sehene vs Father Wenceslas Munyeshyaka: the fictional trial of a genocide priest', in *Journal of African Cultural Studies*, 24, 1, pp. 21-34

Hitchcott, Nicki (2013) 'Between Remembering and Forgetting: (In)Visible Rwanda in Gilbert Gatore's *Le Passé devant soi*', in *Research in African Literatures*, 44, 2, Summer, pp. 76-90

Hochman, Baruch (1985) *Character in Literature* (Ithaca: Cornell University Press)

Hofstede, Geert (2001) *Culture's Consequences: Comparing Values, Behaviors, Institutions, and Organizations Across Nations* (London: Sage). Second Edition

Hron, Madeleine (2009) '*Itsembabwoko* "à la française"? – Rwanda, Fiction and the Franco-African Imaginary', in *Forum for Modern Language Studies*, 45, 2 doi:10.1093/fmls/cqp008

Hutto, Daniel (2007) 'Narrative and Understanding Persons', in Hutto, Daniel (Ed.) *Narrative and Understanding Persons* (Cambridge: Cambridge University Press), pp. 1-15

Ilboudo, Monique (2000) *Murekatete* (Bamako: Le figuier)

Irwin-Zarecka, Iwona (1994) *Frames of Remembrance: The Dynamics of Collective Memory* (New Brunswick: Transaction Publishers)

Jackson, Léonard (2000) *Literature, psychoanalysis and the New Science of Mind* (Harlow: Person Education)

Jowett, Garth S. & O'Donnell, Victoria (2012) *Propaganda and Persuasion* (Los Angeles: Sage). Fifth Edition

Kagame, Alexis (1951) *La poésie dynastique au Rwanda* (Brussels: IRSAC)

Kagame, Alexis (1952) *Le code des institutions politiques du Rwanda précolonial* (Brussels: Institut Royal Colonial Belge)

Kagame, Alexis (1959) *La notion de génération appliquée à la généalogie dynastique et à l'histoire du Rwanda des Xe -XIe siècles à nos jours* (Brussels: I.R.S.A.C.)

Kagame, Paul (2013, 30th June) Youth Connekt dialogue – Rwandan Youth Meet President Kagame – Kigali, 30th June 2013 [Speech]. https://www.youtube.com/watch?v=pI2GhnIHbKs

Kirschke, Linda (1996) 'Broadcasting Genocide: Censorship, Propaganda & State-Sponsored Violence in Rwanda 1990-1994', in *Article 19*

Lachmann, Renate (2008) 'Mnemonic and Intertextual Aspects of Literature', in Erll, Astrid & Nünning, Angsar (Eds.) *Media and Cultural Memory* (Berlin: Walter de Gruyter), pp. 301-310

Lamarque, Peter (2007) 'On the Distance between Literary Narratives and Real-Life Narratives', in Hutto, Daniel (Ed.) *Narrative and Understanding Persons* (Cambridge: Cambridge University Press), pp. 117-132

Lamarque, Peter (2009) *The Philosophy of Literature* (Malden: Blackwell Publishing)

Landsberg, Alison (2004) *Prosthetic Memory: The Transformation of American Remembrance in the Age of Mass Culture* (New York: Columbia University Press)

Lévy, Pierre (1998) *Becoming Virtual: Reality in the Digital Age* (New York: Plenum Press)

Levy, Ronald B. (1972) *Self-Revelation Through Relationships* (Englewood Cliffs: Prentice-Hall)

Longman, Timothy & Rutagengwa, Théoneste (2004) 'memory, identity, and community in Rwanda', in Stover, Eric & Weinstein, Havery (Eds.) *My Neigbor, My Enemy: Justice and Community in the Aftermath of Mass Atrocity* (Cambridge: Cambridge University Press), pp. 162-182

Lowenthal, David (1985) *The Past is a Foreign Country* (Cambridge: Cambridge University Press)

MacIver, Robert ([1948] 1970) 'The Distorting Mirrors', in *On Community, Society and Power: Selected Writings* (Chicago: The University of Chicago Press), pp. 197-208.

Mazauric, Catherine (2007) 'Les mensonges de la mémoire: La part du lecteur dans *Le cavalier et son ombre* de Boubacar Boris Diop et *L'aîné des orphelins* de Tierno Monénembo', in Halen, Pierre & Walter, Jacques (Ed.) *Les langages de la mémoire: littérature, médias et génocide au Rwanda* (Metz : Centre de recherches "Écritures", Université Paul Verlaine), pp. 341-355

Mbabazi, Aimé Yann (2007) *Sheridan* (Waterloo House)

Mead, George H. (1913, 3rd July) 'The Social Self', in *The Journal of Philosophy, Psychology and Scientific Methods*, 10, 14, pp. 374-380

Mead, Gerald (1990) 'The Representation of Fictional Character', in Knapp, John V. (Ed.), *Literary Character* (Lanham: University Press of America), pp. 92-104

Mironko, Charles (2007) 'The Effect of RTLM's Rhetoric of Ethnic Hatred in Rural Rwanda', in Thompson, Allan (Ed.) *The Media and the Rwanda Genocide* (Ann Arbor: Pluto Press), pp. 125-135

Misztal, Barbara (2003) *Theories of Social Remembering* (Philadelphia: Open University Press)

Monénembo, Tierno (2000) *L'aîné des orphelins* (Paris: Editions du Seuil)

Morrison, Toni (1984) 'Memory, Creation, and Writing', in *Thought*, 59, 235, December, pp. 385-390

Morrison, Toni (1995) 'The Site of Memory', in Zinsser, William (Ed.) *Inventing the Truth: The Art and Craft of Memoir* (New York: Houghton Mifflin). Second Edition, pp. 83-102

Mukasonga, Scholastique (2006) *Inyenzi ou les Cafards* (Paris: Gallimard)

Mukasonga, Scholastique (2008) *La femme aux pieds nus* (Paris: Gallimard)

Mukasonga, Scholastique (2012) *Notre-Dame du Nil* (Paris: Gallimard)

Mulihano, Benedigito ([1980] 2005) *Ibirari by' insigamigani*, Vol. 1 (Butare: Ingoro y' Umurage w'u Rwanda [Rwanda National Museum]). Third Edition

Ndwaniye, Joseph (2006) *La promesse faite à ma soeur* (Bruxelles: Les Impressions Nouvelles)

Neumann, Birgit (2008) 'The Literary Representation of Memory', in Erll, Astrid & Nünning, Angsar (Eds.) *Media and Cultural Memory* (Berlin: Walter de Gruyter), pp. 333-343

Niwese, Maurice (2001) *Celui qui sut vaincre* (Paris: L'Harmattan)

Nora, Pierre (1984) 'Entre Mémoire et Histoire: La problématique des lieux', in Nora, Pierre (Ed.) *Les lieux de mémoire I- La République* (Paris: Editions Gallimard), pp. XV-XLII

Nyirubugara, Olivier (2013) *Complexities and Dangers of Remembering and Forgetting in Rwanda* (Leiden: Sidestone)

Pauwels, R. P. M. (1958) *Imana et le culte des Mânes au Rwanda* (Brussels: Académie Royales des Sciences Coloniales)

Piaget, Jean [1969] 1971) *Science of Education and Psychology of the Child* (London: Longman)

Pieterse, Jan Nederveen (1992) *White on Black: Images of Africa and Blacks in Western Popular Culture* (New Haven: Yale University Press)

Prendergast, Maria Teresa & Prendergast, Thomas A. (2013) 'The invention of propaganda: A critical commentary on and translation of *Inscrutabili Divinae Providentiae Arcano*', in Auerbach, Jonathan & Castronovo, Russ (Eds.) *The Oxford Handbook of Propaganda Studies* (Oxford: Oxford University Press), pp. 19-27

Republic of Rwanda (2008) 'Law n°18/2008 of 23/07/2008 Relating to the Punishment of the Crime of Genocide Ideology', in *Official Gazette of the Republic of Rwanda*, Year 47 n° 19, 1 October. http://www.eurac-network.org/web/uploads/documents/20090924_11845.pdf

Riffaterre, Michael (1990) *Fictional Truth* (Baltimore: The Johns Hopkins University Press)

Rigney, Ann (2012) *The Afterlives of Walter Scott: Memory on the Move* (Oxford: Oxford University Press)

Romeo, Nick (2014, 17th June) 'Is Literature "the Most Important Weapon of Propaganda"?', in *The Atlantic*. http://www.theatlantic.com/entertainment/archive/2014/06/why-the-cia-distributed-pocket-size-copies-of-doctor-zhivago-in-the-soviet-union/371369/

Rosello, Mireille (1998) *Declining the Stereotype: Ethnicity and Representation in French Cultures* (Hanover: University Press of New England)

Rothberg, Michael (2006a) 'Against Zero-Sum Logic: A Response to Walter Benn Michaels', in *American Literary History*, 18, 2, pp. 303-311. Doi: 10.1093/alh/ajj018

Rothberg, Michael (2006b) 'Between Auschwitz and Algeria: Multidirectional Memory and the Counterpublic Witness' in *Critical Inquiry*, 33, 1, Autumn, pp. 158-184. http://www.jstor.org/stable/10.1086/509750

Rothberg, Michael (2009) *Multidirectional Memory: Remembering the Holocaust in the Age of Decolonization* (Stanford: Stanford University Press)

Rothberg, Michael (2011) 'From Gaza to Warsaw: Mapping Multidirectional Memory', in *Criticism*, 53-4, Fall, pp. 523-548. DOI: 10.1353/crt.2011.0032

Rurangwa, Jean-Marie Vianney (2006) *Au sortir de l'enfer* (Paris: L'Harmattan)

Rusimbi, John (1999) *By the Time She Returned: A Refugee's Tale* (London: Janus Publishing Company Ltd)

Rusimbi, John (2007) *The Hyena's Wedding: The Untold Horrors of Genocide* (London: Janus Publishing Company Ltd)

Schmid, Wolf (2010) *Narratology: An Introduction* (Berlin: De Gruyter)

Sehene, Benjamin (2005) *Le feu sous la soutane: Un prêtre au coeur du génocide rwandais. Roman* (Paris: L' Esprit frappeur)

Semujanga, Josias (1998) *Récits fondateurs du drame rwandais: Discours social, ideologies et stéréotypes* (Paris: L'Harmattan)

Semujanga, Josias (1998) *Le génocide, sujet de fiction? Analyse des récits du massacre des Tutsi dans la literature africaine* (Quebec: Editions Nota Bene)

Smith, Pierre (1975) *Le récit populaire au Rwanda* (Paris: Armand Colin)

Sorabji, Richard (2006) *Self: Ancient and Modern Insights about Individuality, Life, and Death* (Chicago: University of Chicago Press)

Soulié, Marguerite (1980) 'Littérature populaire et propagande de la Réforme', in *Bulletin de l'Association d'étude sur l'humanisme, la réforme et la renaissance*, n°11. Actes du deuxieme colloque de Goutelas sur la littérature populaire aux XVème et XVIème siècles, 21-23 Septembre 1979. pp. 167-174

Stebbing, Susan, ([1939] 1952) *Thinking to Some Purpose* (London: The Whitefriars Press)

Steveker, Lena (2009) *Identity and Cultural Memory in the Fiction of A.S. Byatt: Knitting the Net of Culture* (New York: Palgrave MacMillan)

Straus, Scott (2007) 'What Is the Relationship between Hate Radio and Violence? Rethinking Rwanda's "Radio Machete"', in *Politics & Society, 35, 4*, pp. 609-637

Taylor, Charles (1989) *Sources of the Self: The Making of the Modern Identity* (Cambridge: Harvard University Press)

Twagilimana, Aimable (1996) *Manifold Annihilation* (New York: Rivercross Publishing, Inc.)

Vansina, Jan (1971) 'Once upon a Time: Oral Traditions as History in Africa', in *Daedalus*, 100, 2, pp. 442-468

Vansina, Jan (2000) 'Historical Tales (Ibiteekerezo) and the History of Rwanda', in *History in Africa*, 27, pp. 375-414

Waberi, Abdourahman (2000) *Moisson de crânes* (Monaco: Editions du Serpent à Plumes)

Wineburg, Sam (2001) *Historical Thinking and Other Unnatural Acts: Charting the Future of Teaching the Past* (Philadephia: Temple University Press)

Yanagizawa-Drott, David (2013) 'Propaganda vs. Education: A Case Study of Hate Radio in Rwanda', in Auerbach, Jonathan & Castronovo, Russ (Eds.) *The Oxford Handbook of Propaganda Studies* (Oxford: Oxford University Press), pp. 378-394